Action Orient:

OK with Less [

FAST PACED

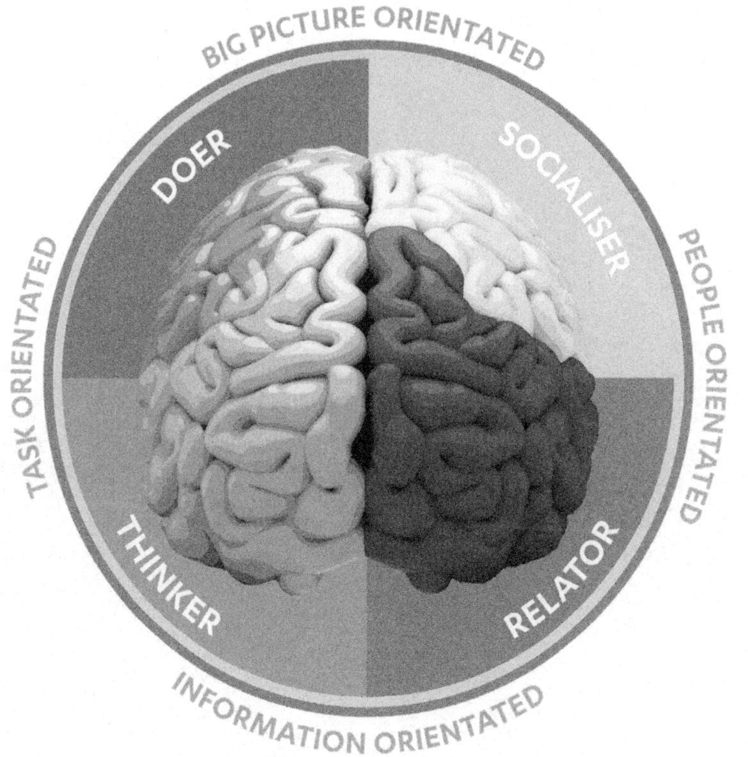

BIG PICTURE ORIENTATED

DOER

SOCIALISER

TASK ORIENTATED

PEOPLE ORIENTATED

THINKER

RELATOR

INFORMATION ORIENTATED

Information Orientated

Likes More Detail

STEADY PACED

ENDORSEMENTS

'Personalities Remixed is more than a book—it's a wake-up call to anyone still stuck in reactive living. The E-Colours system strips away judgment and replaces it with self-awareness, real communication, and intentional leadership. This is the blueprint for creating teams, relationships, and lives that actually work.'

— Mike Radoor,
International Best-Selling Author of
Above Average, Coach and Serial Entrepreneur

'What I love most about Personalities Remixed is how human it feels. The authors aren't preaching—they're sharing experiences, tools, and insight with humility and purpose. You can tell this isn't just a corporate product—it's a movement born from real passion and a genuine desire to make a difference. If you're serious about self-awareness and improving how you work with others, this book is a must-read!'

— George Jerjian,
Creator of the DARE Method and author of
DARE to Discover Your Purpose: Retire, Refire, and Rewire

'Personalities Remixed is a powerful guide to self-awareness, communication, and connection. The E-Colours framework brings clarity and compassion to every relationship—personal and professional. A must-read for anyone who values growth and authentic collaboration.'

— Dr. Peggy McColl,
New York Times Bestselling Author

'Personalities Remixed is a personality framework that invites you into a process of real self-discovery. Before we can truly connect with or lead others, we need to understand ourselves first. This book offers a clear, thoughtful guide to using their tool in a way that feels both accessible and meaningful.'

— Christine O'Shaughnessy,
Award Winning and Best-Selling Author of
Mindful Presence in Leadership

We are all surrounded by potential—our own, and that of the people around us. Personalities Remixed gives us the tools to recognize it, nurture it, and bring it to life. Whether you're an entrepreneur, educator, coach, or executive, this book is your guide to turning intention into impact through deeper understanding and better connection.

— Judy O'Beirn,
President and CEO of Hasmark Publishing

PERSONALITIES
REMIXED

Lewis Senior, Mark Wilkinson and Paul Grant

Published by
Hasmark Publishing International
www.hasmarkpublishing.com

Copyright © 2025 Equilibria Services Pte Ltd.

First Edition

All rights reserved.
Equilibria refers to the Equilibria Group of companies consisting of Equilibria Holdings, Equilibria Services Pte Ltd and Equilibria Services Limited, with the IP referenced in this book and content of the book owned by Equilibria. This book in no way allows for transfer nor sharing of this IP ownership.

No part of this book may be reproduced or transmitted in any form or by any means, electronic or mechanical, including photocopying, recording or by any information storage and retrieval system, without written permission from Equilibria Services Pte Ltd, except for the inclusion of brief quotations in a review.

Disclaimer
This book is designed to provide information and motivation to our readers. It is sold with the understanding that the publisher and the authors are not engaged to render any type of psychological, legal, or any other kind of professional advice. The content of each article is the sole expression and opinion of its authors, and not necessarily that of the publisher. No warranties or guarantees are expressed or implied by the publisher's choice to include any of the content in this volume. Neither the publisher nor the individual authors shall be liable for any physical, psychological, emotional, financial, or commercial damages, including, but not limited to, special, incidental, consequential or other damages. Our views and rights are the same: You are responsible for your own choices, actions, and results.

Permission should be addressed in writing to Paul Grant at paul.grant@equilibria.com.

Editor: Brad Green brad@hasmarkpublishing.com
Cover Design: Anne Karklins anne@hasmarkpublishing.com
Interior Layout: Amit Dey amit@hasmarkpublishing.com

ISBN 13: 978-1-77482-363-7
ISBN 10: 1-77482-363-2

DEDICATION

'It is not our differences that divide us. It is our inability to recognise, accept, and celebrate those differences.'

– **Audre Lorde (1934–1992)**, renowned American writer, poet, feminist, womanist, librarian, and civil rights activist

To all those who understand, or seek to understand, the richness of personality diversity and recognise its immense power in helping everyone achieve their life's goals. May this book inspire you to embrace and celebrate the unique strengths within yourself and others.

To those who have participated – over 1.4 million Personality Diversity Indicator questionnaires taken so far – we appreciate how your engagement has greatly supported the E-Colours & Personal Intervention process. We thank you for being part of this journey.

To our esteemed clients, customers, coaches, and practitioners, and to all who have supported the idea and growth of Equilibria – your unwavering trust and encouragement have been the cornerstone of our work. This book is a tribute to your inspiration, your challenges, and your aspirations. We are deeply grateful for the privilege of serving you and growing alongside you. Your stories, feedback, and loyalty have helped shape this book, and we dedicate it to you with heartfelt appreciation.

To Dagfinn Tromborg – In loving memory. Your invaluable contributions helped lay the foundation of Equilibria, but it is your friendship we will cherish forever. We remain deeply grateful for both.

To all the support staff who have helped along the way, we will always be thankful for your efforts.

The world is filled with many wonderful aspects that inspire awe, appreciation, and dedication – areas where we, as human beings, have helped to influence or preserve great achievements. Here are a few we should never forget. Viewed through our own personality filters, we do not all think or act the same way. Appreciating these differences can help make us all better people:

Natural Beauty: From majestic mountains to serene oceans, the natural landscapes of our planet offer breathtaking views and diverse ecosystems. As human beings, we are called to preserve such beauty.

Biodiversity: The incredible variety of life, from tiny insects to giant whales, reflects the complexity and wonder of the natural world. We are here to help protect this diversity.

Human Creativity: Art, music, literature, and technology reflect the limitless creativity and ingenuity of the human spirit. It is our responsibility to continue nurturing that growth.

Cultural Diversity: The rich tapestry of cultures, languages, traditions, and customs around the world speaks to the uniqueness and shared humanity of people. We must not only protect this heritage but deepen our understanding of it and support its flourishing.

Scientific Discoveries: Advances in science and technology continue to expand our understanding of the universe and improve our quality of life. We cannot stand still. This book is dedicated to those who advance our understanding of science and technology.

Acts of Kindness: Everyday gestures of compassion and generosity – large and small – reveal the goodness in people. As it was once said, it is better to give than to take. This book is dedicated to those givers.

Resilience and Growth: The ability of individuals and communities to overcome challenges and emerge stronger is a powerful testament to the human spirit. We dedicate this book to those who make a difference in the lives of others.

Love and Connection: Relationships with family, friends, and communities bring deep meaning and joy to life. Personality diversity is about appreciating the differences we all bring, and this book is a dedication to those who have chosen to do just that.

Exploration and Adventure: The thrill of discovering new places, ideas, and experiences adds richness and wonder to life.

The Universe: The vastness and mystery of the cosmos inspire reflection, curiosity, and a sense of our place in something greater.

These and many other aspects make the world a truly awe-inspiring place. *Personalities Remixed* is dedicated to helping people recognise and appreciate these wonders through a deeper understanding of personality diversity, and to supporting every individual in realising their full potential.

ACKNOWLEDGEMENTS

'If I have seen further, it is by standing on the shoulders of giants.'

– **Isaac Newton (1642–1727)**, English mathematician, physicist, astronomer, and author widely recognised as one of the most influential scientists of all time

Writing *Personalities Remixed* has been a truly collaborative endeavour between Lewis Senior, Mark Wilkinson, and Paul Grant. Each has contributed their own unique thoughts and experiences to the project, united by a shared hope that you, the reader, will not only understand but also value the benefits of Equilibria's personality diversity technology, expressed through the E-Colours. Together, they have worked to ensure this book serves both as a guide and a source of inspiration for embracing personality diversity across many areas of life.

They extend heartfelt thanks to Laura Senior and David Senior for their invaluable contributions. Their expertise, thoughtful feedback, and generosity in sharing their knowledge have been instrumental in shaping the ideas and principles presented here. Their support has been a cornerstone of this project, and we are deeply grateful for their consistent dedication. Thanks also go to Emma Wilkinson, whose ideas have influenced several aspects of this work.

To everyone who has participated in the Personality Diversity Indicator (PDI) over the years, they owe their deepest gratitude. Your engagement, reflections, and feedback have been central to their efforts, offering perspectives that have significantly shaped not just this book but also the continued evolution of our strategies and initiatives. Your involvement has deepened their understanding and strengthened their ability to serve diverse audiences around the world.

They also wish to offer special thanks to every customer who has engaged with them over the years – whether through meaningful conversations, constructive critique, or creative suggestions. Your input has been essential to the development of this book, guiding its direction and enriching its content. This work belongs as much to you as to them, and they are honoured to have had the opportunity to learn from and collaborate with you.

Particular appreciation is due to Paul Grant for his exceptional contribution to the development and execution of this book. His tireless work in drafting, revising, and perfecting each chapter has been crucial to ensuring the clarity, cohesion, and overall quality of the final result. His creativity and perseverance have been indispensable, and the book is significantly stronger because of his efforts.

We would also like to acknowledge the outstanding support of the Equilibria IT, materials, and finance teams. They play a vital role in all of our efforts and often don't receive the recognition they truly deserve.

Finally, we want to thank the many individuals who have supported and inspired them throughout this journey. From family members and colleagues to mentors and friends, your encouragement and belief in this project have sustained us at every stage of its development.

Personalities Remixed stands as a testament to the power of collaboration, the value of shared ideas, and the profound importance of diversity in all its forms. To everyone who has contributed in any way to this work, we are truly grateful. Your influence is felt on every page, and this book would not exist without you. Thank you.

CONTENT

'We all should know that diversity makes for a rich tapestry, and we must understand that all the threads of the tapestry are equal in value no matter their colour.'

– **Maya Angelou**, poet

Preface xvii
Foreword xix
Introduction xxxiii
Chapter 1: Are We Really Surrounded by Idiots? 1
Chapter 2: The Evolution of Personality Diversity 13
Chapter 3: Equilibria & Mark Wilkinson 37
Chapter 4: The Importance of Equilibria's Ethics 65
Chapter 5: Strengths & Potential Limiters 89
Chapter 6: Green Tendencies – The Thinker 117
Chapter 7: Yellow Tendencies – The Socialiser 137
Chapter 8: Red Tendencies – The Doer 155
Chapter 9: Blue Tendencies – The Relator 173
Chapter 10: Managing Your Tendencies – Personal Intervention 191

Chapter 11: Understanding and Applying
Psychological Safety Using the E-Colours &
Personal Intervention 221

Chapter 12: Practical Applications of the E-Colours &
Personal Intervention 237

    The Wells Model 240

    Intentional Communication. 243

    How Can I Get Hurt? 248

    Intentional Leadership Behaviours 255

    How to Delegate to Me 260

    If You Want Me to Listen 264

    When Working with Me 266

    Effective Form of Recognition 271

    Conflict Resolution 276

    Doubt & Resistance......................... 284

    Premium Reports........................... 294

    Alignment Reports.......................... 295

    Essential Leadership Cycle 298

    Intentional Leadership 306

    Advanced Error Reduction in Organisations (AERO). . 308

Chapter 13: E-Colours for Education................. 317

Chapter 14: Real Time Legacy..................... 403

Chapter 15: Developing Yourself 421

About the Authors 433

PREFACE

'The ability to connect with people who are different from ourselves is a superpower. It's the key to understanding and embracing diversity.'

— **Simon Sinek**, renowned author and motivational speaker best known for his work on leadership and organisational culture

The journey of writing *Personalities Remixed* began in 2004 when Equilibria first encountered the fascinating world of personality diversity in the workplace. Their professional experience and personal curiosity led them to explore the topic more deeply, uncovering ideas they felt compelled to share with a broader audience.

This book aims to offer a clear and practical understanding of how personality diversity can be harnessed to create more effective and harmonious interactions. Through extensive research and real-world examples, we will explore the many dimensions of personality and their influence on self-awareness, team dynamics, and organisational success.

We would also like to express our gratitude to our families and friends for their unwavering support and encouragement throughout this journey. Your belief in us has been a constant source of motivation.

Just a heads-up – in *Personalities Remixed*, some contributors may have used different spellings in their forewords, stories, and personal reflections. This simply reflects the country they're from and how they naturally write.

Lastly, we hope this book serves as a valuable resource for professionals, educators, young adults, children – and indeed anyone interested in understanding and embracing personality diversity. Thank you for joining us on this journey.

Sincerely,
Lewis Senior
Mark Wilkinson
Paul Grant
Laura Senior Garcia
David Senior Garcia
Emma Wilkinson
And all at Equilibria

FOREWORDS

'Books allow you to fully explore a topic and immerse yourself in a deeper way than most media today. I'm looking forward to shifting more of my media diet towards reading books.'

– **Mark Zuckerberg**, co-founder of Facebook

Introduction

A heartfelt thank you to each of you who generously contributed a foreword to *Personalities Remixed*. Your words bring unique perspectives, setting the stage for what this book is all about - understanding ourselves and others more deeply. Your contributions have added depth and richness to this work, and we're sincerely grateful.

Mark Nelson (Red/Green) – Vice Chairman, Chevron

Equilibria has been helping people realize their potential for decades. If you are interested in testing your knowledge about yourself; learning more about how you impact others; and how you can be better, *Personalities Remixed* is an easy, impactful read. Lewis Senior and the Equilibria team are driven to help and connect people, and this book demonstrates just that.

My personal experience with Equilibria began while leading an organization that spanned Europe, Africa, the Middle East, and Asia. With these geographies, there were many historic cultural differences that created a lack of understanding between different employee groups at a time where progress was required. Application of E-Colors created a common dialogue across the enterprise that enabled improvement in relationships, leadership, and business performance.

I was raised with the 'Golden Rule' in mind, which is about treating people the way you yourself would want to be treated. This is not a bad foundation, but incomplete. This book and the tools it provides focus on the 'Platinum Rule' of treating people the way they want to be treated. In the simplest terms, this work helps you understand yourself; understand others; and meet people in the 'middle' for better outcomes and experiences.

As an individual whose E-Colors are Red/Green and who has been in the working world for nearly four decades, I often reflect on what things I would have liked to accelerate in my career and I have come up with the following items I would have liked to happen sooner:

- Learn more about myself sooner
- Confirm my purpose
- Understand that it is not about me; it is about enabling everyone else

Lewis' words will help with all of these. Enjoy!

* * *

Joni Baird (Yellow/Red) – Business and Community Leader

Equilibria's E-Colors personality system has profoundly impacted my life and the lives of many others. Gaining an understanding of my own E-Colors has brought clarity, greater self-awareness, and the ability to foster stronger relationships – both professionally and personally. It has been a privilege to collaborate with Lewis Senior, Laura Senior, and David Senior – leaders who have committed themselves to helping people maximise their potential through self-awareness and effective communication.

As a Yellow/Red, I thrive on interaction, enthusiasm, and action. My natural Yellow tendencies make me an engager and motivator, while my Red brings drive and determination. At times, my 'Red' side has served me well, particularly in high-stakes, high-pressure environments. Early in my career as an investigator for a Sheriff's department, I was the first woman in that role, and it demanded a strong presence. My 'Red' helped me stand my ground, prove my worth among colleagues, and ensure that those I encountered knew I meant business.

Years later, transitioning into the corporate world, I had to adapt my approach. The high-intensity drive that once defined me needed to be balanced by my Yellow's collaborative spirit and my Blue's ability to nurture and care. I also came to appreciate the importance of incorporating Green – bringing thoughtful planning and strategic execution into the mix. The beauty of the E-Colors system is that it provides a roadmap for understanding oneself and making intentional adjustments. We all have blind spots, but the awareness that E-Colors brings allows us to recalibrate and realign with our strengths.

In my role as a Public Affairs and Community Engagement professional for a major corporation, E-Colors became more than a personal development tool – it became a framework for leadership, teamwork, and organizational success. Becoming an E-Colors trainer allowed me to introduce the methodology to a wide range of organizations and communities. The results spoke for themselves: enhanced communication, stronger collaboration, and a shared understanding that promoted both success and fulfilment. Seeing these transformations reaffirmed what we all seek – fulfilment, connection, and purpose.

Real-World Impact

The reach of E-Colors spans sectors from non-profits to sports, education, and corporate leadership. Here are just a few compelling examples where I've seen its impact first-hand.

Non-profits: Dress for Success

Dress for Success, an organization dedicated to helping women achieve economic independence, embraced E-Colors training for both staff and clients. The results were immediate and meaningful. Team members developed a deeper understanding of how to collaborate more effectively, while clients reported feeling more confident in their new workplaces. Many women shared how E-Colors became a lasting tool, helping them build stronger relationships both on and off the job.

Sports: Super Bowl 51 Host Committee

One of the most exciting applications of E-Colors was in the world of sports. I had the opportunity to introduce Lewis Senior to Sallie Sargent, CEO of the Super Bowl 51 Host

Committee – Green/Red. That introduction led to more than 10,000 volunteers and staff receiving E-Colors training. The outcome? Unprecedented teamwork and synergy. PR expert Helen Vollmer – Yellow/Red – played a key role in amplifying the message, ensuring that even more people were reached through the power of self-awareness and effective collaboration.

Education: Southwest Schools

Perhaps the most transformative experience was seeing E-Colors implemented in an educational setting. Janelle James – Red/Green – Superintendent of Southwest Schools, fully embraced the methodology. With support from Dave Payne – Red/Yellow – a senior executive at an Energy Company and passionate advocate for E-Colors, we launched an initiative to integrate E-Colors into the school system.

The results were remarkable. Students were selected as E-Colors Champions and became leaders within their school communities. One young man, previously struggling both academically and socially, found renewed purpose through E-Colors. Once at risk of not graduating, he not only finished school with honours but went on to study engineering and eventually joined an Energy Company as an engineer – a testament to the power of mentorship and self-awareness.

Another student, inspired by her E-Colors journey, earned a degree in accounting and now serves as a school finance director. Beyond academic success, E-Colors helped one young girl mend strained family relationships, showing that its principles extend far beyond the workplace.

To celebrate the students' achievements, Equilibria and Lewis Senior presented computers to the E-Colors Champions – a gesture that reflected the heart of what E-Colors represents: empowering individuals to realise their full potential.

A Call to Action

Throughout my career, I've worked with many senior leaders – sometimes without them even realising I was tapping into their 'Blue' tendencies: empathy, mentorship, and social responsibility. Once that switch is activated, the ripple effect can be extraordinary. When people truly grasp the value of understanding themselves and others, they become catalysts for positive change, within their organisations and beyond.

To those beginning their Equilibria journey, buckle up! You're about to experience one of the most powerful and rewarding transformations of your life. E-Colors is more than a personality assessment – it's a blueprint for success, fulfilment, and meaningful impact. By embracing self-awareness and intentional communication, you will unlock your greatest potential and uplift those around you.

Wishing you joy, success, and a journey full of growth and discovery!

* * *

David Payne (Red/Yellow) – Retired Vice President, Energy Company USA

In 2006, I received the greatest honour of my life when I was asked to lead an energy company's global drilling and completions organisation. I moved from Bangkok to Houston and embarked on a journey I had never imagined. As I was settling in, I met Lewis Senior, who was in the early stages of his journey with Equilibria. He spoke with enormous passion about the work his team was doing for an energy company in Nigeria and the broader potential within the energy sector.

That meeting began a partnership that lasted until I retired – and still continues today. I was personally unprepared for the enormity of the position I had assumed and, during those early years, had to grow into the role. Equilibria was also growing and learning, and we helped each other considerably during that time. As you can imagine, not everything worked as envisioned, but we learned from our mistakes and kept moving forward.

The E-Colors have had a big impact on both my career and my life. We were able to use them to make our operations safer, saving lives and reducing injuries. And while we initially focused on using the E-Colors as a safety tool, we learned they could be used in a broad range of applications.

We used the E-Colors to more effectively create communication tools that connected with all personality styles.

We used the E-Colors to develop leadership skills in both new and very experienced leaders. I saw poor leaders become great leaders as they learned more about themselves by understanding their personal strengths and limiters.

I saw the E-Colors used in education to help children learn about themselves and others – with remarkable results. Bullying was nearly eliminated. Kids who were struggling found themselves and grew into amazing adults.

I saw people improve their marriages and relationships with their children by learning about different personalities and how they interact.

I even saw the E-Colors used to communicate with horses, helping a collegiate equestrian team win a national championship.

This book is a great starting point for anyone wanting to learn more about the E-Colors and begin their own journey. It can also serve as a refresher for those who have already been on that journey for some time.

Regardless of where you are on your path, the journey never truly ends – there is always something new to learn, fresh insight into personality styles, and new ways to apply these ideas.

My life was changed for the better by learning about myself and others through the lens of the E-Colors, and I am confident that anyone reading this book will have similar experiences.

*   *   *

Sarah Abi Saab (Green/Yellow)

I've been part of Equilibria since the third grade. I didn't know it then, but being pulled out of Mrs. Chavoya's class once a week would turn out to be one of the most important things to ever happen to me. It felt like we were gone for about an hour each time – just me and a group of friends, learning things that didn't seem all that serious at first… until they did.

One of the first major moments I remember was taking the PDI, Equilibria's personality self-assessment. Even at such a young age, I could tell how accurate it was. Seeing my strengths written out was encouraging, but it was the list of 'potential limiters' that stuck with me. I didn't even know what that phrase meant at first, but it hit me hard once I understood. I felt exposed – almost defensive.

It's one thing to know your flaws in the back of your mind; it's another thing entirely to see them printed out in front of you. And yet, that discomfort sparked something in me. I wasn't just confronted – I was challenged. And I wanted to grow. It made me realize that any tendency could be either a strength or a weakness, depending on how I used it. That simple truth – that 'what it is, is what we make of it' – became a kind of compass for me.

Equilibria didn't just help me understand who I was; it helped me understand who I could become. As a kid, I often overcompensated for my insecurities by being loud. I didn't feel confident in myself, so I constantly measured success by how I performed compared to others. If I had a higher grade or a better score, I thought that meant I was doing okay. But Equilibria gave me something more valuable than external validation: it gave me the space and the tools to reflect.

To pause. To respond instead of reacting. That changed everything. Equilibria didn't fix me – because I wasn't broken – but it helped me understand myself, who I was, and who I was becoming. I started to grow closer to my friends, my sisters, and myself. I realized that it's not about being the best in the room; it's about being the best version of myself.

This program taught me how to be intentional with my actions, how to understand my emotions, and how to treat myself and others with more kindness and patience. Without a doubt, I still use what I learned every single day. And I live better because of it.

Note: Sarah began her E-Colors journey in third grade and now (in 2025) is about to begin university.

* * *

Sallie Sargent (Green/Red) – President & CEO, Houston Host Committee for Super Bowl LI

In 2014, I was introduced to Lewis Senior in Houston by a mutual friend who was deeply engaged in Lewis' work for Chevron. A charming, soft-spoken and delightful Brit who spoke fluent Spanish and continually traveled the globe, Lewis was the epitome of an international businessman with a very distinct exception – he has a great big heart overflowing with love for all humankind.

From my initial encounter with the E-Colors concept of personality diversity, taught by Lewis and the team at Equilibria, I quickly realized this was more than a self-awareness tool – it was a lens through which entire organizations, teams, and communities could transform the way they communicate, collaborate, and connect. This seemed to be precisely what I needed as the head of the Super Bowl Host Committee to coalesce 10,000 volunteers selected to be the faces of Houston and deliver the highest level of hospitality to over a million people that would descend upon our city for Super Bowl LI in 2017.

The challenge was to deliver the E-Colors personality indicator and train this massive number of volunteers, succinctly and effectively, within an extremely compressed amount of time. First, Lewis introduced the program to the executive team of the Houston Super Bowl Host Committee who immediately understood how using this personality indicator as the underpinning to train a massive volunteer corps would create an army of superb ambassadors or, as they were aptly named, the Super Hosts. Next, the team at Equilibria created an online curriculum so the volunteers could get through the learning on their own schedules, mostly in the evenings after their day of work. Once we received all 10,000 confirmations of completion, we were ready to meet in person.

With the help and support of the City of Houston, we staged our volunteer assembly at the Toyota Center for a full day of learning, knowledge exchange, and camaraderie – all facilitated by Equilibria. It gave the volunteers a chance to meet their teammates already armed with the same foundational information of understanding how to make everyone's Super Bowl experience an enjoyable and truly special event.

The result was beyond anything we could have imagined. The volunteer corps delivered excellent customer service over 10 days of activities, continuing to show up when scheduled with eagerness and excitement right out of a movie script. What we didn't know at the time is that we were actually creating a legacy – one of the key pillars of Equilibria's teachings. The long-lasting effect and afterglow for 10,000 Houstonians still comes up in random conversations today, nearly 10 years later. They all cite their experience as a Super Host and E-Colors program as one of the highlights of their lives. A career highlight for me and for which I am extremely proud. That's the impact we've seen. And that's the potential this book holds for you.

This book, *Personalities Remixed*, is a landmark. It distils decades of fieldwork, innovation, and human connection into a format that is as engaging as it is transformative. Lewis and his co-authors have created something special: a guide not just to understanding others, but to unlocking potential – in ourselves and those around us.

What sets this approach apart is its fundamental belief that every personality has value. By embracing our diversity, rather than flattening it, we make better decisions, build stronger cultures, and foster more inclusive environments.

As you turn the pages ahead, I encourage you to reflect not only on the perspectives you will gain, but also on the possibilities they open. Imagine a world where teams don't merely tolerate difference but thrive because of it. Where leaders are as fluent in emotional intelligence as they are in strategy and where authenticity is a strength, not a liability.

That's the world envisioned in these pages. And if this book finds its way into enough hands – and hearts – it just might become our shared reality.

Great communication isn't a soft skill. It is the foundation of success for all business and personal relationships and should be viewed for what it is: a strategic advantage. In a world where not everyone thinks and acts the same, recognizing and embracing our personality diversity isn't just important, it's essential.

Personalities Remixed represents the next chapter in that journey.

I am honored to contribute to this important work and excited for what it will unlock in the lives of readers around the world. If we enable great communication, we empower people to achieve great things they never imagined were possible – together.

*   *   *

Marie-Louise Chandler (Blue/Yellow) – UK Safety Director, QinetiQ

In the fast-paced world of modern leadership, the ability to understand ourselves, and those around us, is no longer optional; it's essential. Effective communication, team cohesion, and a culture of mutual respect are key ingredients to success – and yet, these are so often the very areas that prove most challenging. That's where *Personalities Remixed* makes its mark.

Lewis Senior, Paul Grant, and Mark Wilkinson – the team behind Equilibria – have an exceptional ability to take complex behavioural dynamics and distil them into something practical, relatable, and immediately impactful. Through their work with E-Colours, Lewis, Paul, and Mark equip teams with a shared language that fosters deeper awareness of tendencies, strengths, and potential limiters – not just as individuals but as cohesive, high-performing units.

I had the pleasure of experiencing E-Colours sessions with my own team, and the results have been transformational. The sessions are engaging, insightful, and, above all, useful. My team came away with a heightened awareness of how we interact, where we excel, and where we might need support, coaching, or training. We now have a common language that helps us communicate more effectively and work more safely and collaboratively.

Personalities Remixed is more than a book – it's a practical guide to unlocking the full potential of your people. If you're looking to elevate your leadership and team performance, look no further. This is a must-read.

Thank you, Mark, Lewis, Paul, and the entire Equilibria team for your outstanding work. You're making a real difference.

INTRODUCTION

'Diversity is not a reason to fight;
it is an opportunity to grow.'

– **John C. Maxwell**, a well-known leadership expert, speaker, and author who has written extensively on leadership, personal development, and team dynamics

The Big Rocks Story

A professor once stood before his class, holding a large, empty jar. He began by placing several big rocks into the jar, filling it to the brim. He asked the students if the jar was full, and they agreed it was.

Next, the professor added a container of pebbles, shaking the jar so the smaller stones filled the gaps between the big rocks. He asked again if the jar was full, and the students nodded in agreement.

Then he poured in sand, which filtered into the spaces between the pebbles. Once more, he asked if the jar was full, and the students affirmed it was.

Finally, the professor took a pitcher of water and poured it into the jar, filling the last remaining gaps.

He explained that the jar represents life. The big rocks symbolise the most vital priorities and values, like family, health, and personal growth. The pebbles stand for secondary but still important responsibilities, such as work and social obligations. The sand represents minor, everyday tasks and trivial concerns.

The key takeaway is that if you fill your jar with sand first – focusing on the small, unimportant tasks – you won't have room for the big rocks, the truly important parts of your life. But if you prioritise the big rocks first, then add the pebbles, sand, and water, you can fit everything in without sacrificing what really matters.

This story serves as a reminder to focus on life's most meaningful priorities first. By doing so, you ensure there's space for what truly counts while still making room for life's smaller details.

The Urgency of Addressing Safety in the Oil & Gas Industry – Lewis Senior

From 1974 to 1996, I climbed the ranks in the oilfield, starting as a roustabout and eventually becoming an Offshore Installation Manager. I worked in several countries around the world, driven by a deep commitment to fostering a generative work environment where everyone on board could thrive. Time and again, I was sent to the most challenging operations, and the rigs under my leadership came to be known as the 'university of safety' – a reputation that caught the attention of senior management. In recognition of these efforts, I was appointed

Health, Safety and Environmental Manager in 1996, a role I held until 2002.

During that time, I was responsible for safety across Transocean, one of the world's largest international drilling contractors. The company underwent three major mergers and acquisitions, each one shifting the culture I had worked so hard to shape. But the greatest challenge wasn't corporate restructuring; it was facing the stark reality of multiple fatalities on our rigs. Every life lost was more than a statistic.

Behind each tragedy was a family, a circle of friends, and an entire community forever changed by an accident that should never have occurred. We had safety rules, programmes, and processes in place, yet they failed to account for the human element – the fact that the people expected to implement these measures were, above all else, individuals shaped by their own personalities. This wasn't just a Transocean issue. It was an industry-wide challenge that demanded a new way of thinking about safety, leadership, and human behaviour.

I had a moment of profound realisation that would forever alter the trajectory of my life. I could no longer continue the same actions that failed to halt this relentless cycle of personal tragedy. These were not just statistics. They were people – colleagues, friends, family members – affected by a system not built to protect them as individuals.

I call these challenges the industry's 'big rocks' – enormous, looming issues that felt immovable. But to me, they weren't insurmountable; they were a call to action. I refused to accept the status quo. Something had to change, and I was determined to be part of that change. The weight of this responsibility sat heavily on my shoulders, but it also sparked a fire within me, a relentless drive to find solutions, challenge conventions, and help build a safer future for every person in our industry.

At the time, I had no roadmap for what lay ahead. The idea of launching a company – one that would revolutionise safety practices – was both thrilling and daunting. My mind raced with questions: What exactly would we offer? How could we make a genuine impact? How would we build trust in an industry that had long tolerated unacceptable risks? Who would walk this journey with me? The more I reflected, the clearer it became that this mission was far bigger than me alone.

That's when fate stepped in, and I found myself in conversation with two outstanding individuals – Dagfinn Tromborg and John Lake. We had all worked together in the Health, Safety, and Environment department at Transocean, and both men were not only highly respected but also deeply passionate about safety. Dagfinn's extensive experience as a Senior Toolpusher and Offshore Installation Manager, combined with John's remarkable depth of knowledge, made them ideal partners. I knew that together, we could build something with lasting impact.

As Transocean was in the process of acquiring Reading & Bates, I met with Dagfinn and John in Bilbao, Spain. Over lunch, I shared my vision – a bold departure from the traditional corporate safety model and a leap toward something new. To my surprise and delight, they didn't hesitate. They recognised the urgency, the need, the opportunity. They believed in the mission as deeply as I did. In that moment, we made a pact to take action.

A few months later, we gathered at Dagfinn's farm to strategise. It was there, in an atmosphere of trust and shared commitment, that our journey truly began. We had the safety expertise, the coaching background, and the unwavering will to make a difference – but we were missing one final piece: a sharp, business-minded leader to help steer the ship. The question loomed: who could complete our team?

As John and I left the farm and headed toward the airport, he turned to me and asked, 'Who do you think could complete our team?'

Without hesitation, I said, 'Paul Grant.'

Paul was a brilliant strategist, a marketing expert with an exceptional ability to navigate business challenges. I had worked with him during the Transocean–Sedco Forex merger and knew his talents would be crucial. Days later, while coaching Ricardo Rosa, Transocean's former CFO, in Vietnam, I reconnected with Paul and shared our vision. His eyes lit up. He saw what we saw – an opportunity to create lasting change. And with that, our team was complete.

Together, we brought our strengths to the table – my boots-on-the-ground experience spanning over 30 years, Dagfinn and John's operational depth, and Paul's business acumen. It was an electrifying mix, and we were ready to take on the world. But let's be clear: this wasn't simply about building a company. It was about something greater – a mission to reshape an industry that had too long accepted unnecessary risk. We weren't just starting a business. We were starting a movement.

Safety isn't just a corporate objective. It's not a tick box or a statistic to improve. It's about human lives, the people who put on their boots each morning and head into high-risk environments to keep the world running. It's about their families, who expect them to return home safely. It's about challenging the mindset that 'accidents happen' and demonstrating that preventable incidents should never be tolerated as an inevitable cost of doing business.

Every year, countless lives are affected by workplace accidents – lives that could be saved with the right systems, the right awareness, and the right leadership. For too long, organisations have tolerated a level of risk that should be unthinkable. That's why we acted. That's why we set out to change the conversation. And that's why the work continues.

In the pages ahead, I'll share the lessons we've learned, the obstacles we've encountered, and the breakthroughs that helped turn our mission into reality. But above all, I hope to spark something in you, the reader, the leader, the doer, the change-maker. The urgency of safety isn't just a workplace challenge; it's a personal commitment, a moral responsibility, and a shared duty.

This isn't just about what we've done. It's about what all of us must do – because the cost of inaction is simply too high. The time for change isn't tomorrow. It's now.

Paul Grant's Perspective

During a challenging week at the Renaissance Hotel in Ho Chi Minh City, Vietnam, in early 2004, Paul Grant found himself seeking solace and a glimmer of hope. The recent release of a colleague under what he perceived as unjust circumstances weighed heavily on his mind. However, fate intervened when he unexpectedly crossed paths with Lewis Senior, a familiar face from their time working together in the Houston office. Lewis had always possessed a unique ability to bring positivity to any situation, and in that moment, he became a beacon of light in Paul's darkened world.

As they rekindled their friendship, Lewis sensed the turmoil within Paul. With an empathetic smile, he initiated a conversation that would forever alter the course of his life. 'We're starting a coaching company,' Lewis announced, his words carrying a sense of purpose and excitement. 'Are you interested?'. Paul's initial instinct might have been to brush off the opportunity, but fate had brought them together at just the right moment.

Ever since Dean Masters, another friend and business partner of Paul's, had sparked something in him – urging him to pursue new ventures and explore exciting opportunities – Paul had been contemplating his next step. Should he stay with Transocean and climb the management ladder, look elsewhere, or strike out on his own with new partners? As Lewis spoke, it felt as though he had poured fuel onto that internal fire. The timing couldn't have been more impeccable.

Uncertainty mingled with curiosity as he considered Lewis's idea. Was this the sign he had been waiting for? Could this coaching company be the catalyst to help him find purpose and reach his full potential? As doubts lingered, Lewis exuded quiet confidence and belief in what they could accomplish together.

The world seemed to hold its breath as Paul weighed the decision. The weight of his past experiences and the significance of the present moment converged, opening the door to new possibilities. With a renewed sense of courage, he finally replied, 'Yes, Lewis, I am very interested.'

Little did he know that single choice would set him on a journey of inspiration, empowerment, and the pursuit of meaningful goals. Together, they would go on to build a legacy that reached far beyond corporate walls and into a more purposeful future.

Thus, Equilibria was born. With a shared commitment to transforming industry practices and improving safety outcomes, we began a journey to build a company capable of addressing the root causes of safety issues and delivering lasting change in the Oil & Gas sector. The vision of *PEOPLE FIRST* and the purpose of *REALISING POTENTIAL* were established.

Equilibria initially represented not just a business idea but a deeper commitment to reshaping industry norms and ensuring safer, more effective working environments. At the time, we couldn't have imagined how far the impact would spread. The principles and tools we developed have since resonated across multiple industries, from healthcare and education to sports, construction, law enforcement, manufacturing, hospitality, and more. Through these applications, Equilibria has touched countless individuals, teams, and organisations around the world, advancing the understanding and management of personality diversity in all kinds of settings.

Why Use E-Colours & Personal Intervention?

At Equilibria, we specialise in enhancing personal, professional, and organisational performance by helping people understand, embrace, and apply personality diversity. Using our proprietary tools – including the Personality Diversity Indicator (PDI), E-Colours, and Personal Intervention – we equip individuals, teams, companies, sectors, and schools around the world to achieve exceptional results by creating self-awareness, strengthening leadership, and building high-performance team dynamics.

What is Personality Diversity?

Personality diversity refers to the range of personality styles and tendencies that exist within any group or organisation. It reflects the different ways people think, feel, and behave, which can strongly influence team dynamics, decision-making, and everyday interactions. Embracing personality diversity means recognising and valuing these differences to foster better collaboration, creativity, and effectiveness.

Key Aspects of Personality Diversity

1. **Understand Personality Styles**

   Personality Frameworks: Tools like the E-Colours help identify and categorise different personality styles. Equilibria refers to personality styles rather than 'types' to avoid the rigidity of 'typing' people and placing them into fixed personality boxes.

   Individual Differences: Each person has a unique percentage combination of tendencies such as doer, relator, socialiser, and thinker.

   The E-Colours concept, developed by Equilibria, was designed to be a memorable and impactful system. It was created with the vision of building an ethical and modern community that simplifies the understanding and application of personality diversity. The aim was to provide a practical tool that anyone could use in their daily life to foster greater awareness and collaboration.

2. **Impact Teams and Organisations**

   Team Dynamics: Diverse personalities can lead to more creative solutions and a broader range of perspectives. However, they can also present challenges in communication and collaboration.

   Leadership and Management: Understanding personality diversity helps leaders tailor their approach to meet the needs of different team members, creating a more inclusive and supportive environment.

3. **Enhance Communication and Collaboration**

   Tailoring Interactions: Recognising personality differences can improve how people relate to and work with each other, resulting in more effective communication and fewer conflicts. E-Colours essentially offers a fast track to intentional communication and achieving positive, successful results.

   Harnessing Strengths & Potential Limiters: By recognising the strengths and potential limiters, often referred to as weaknesses by others of different personality styles, individuals can better manage their natural tendencies to collaborate more effectively and achieve greater success. We use the term 'potential limiters' instead of 'weaknesses' because these tendencies can be addressed and transformed through conscious effort and choice.

4. **Promote Inclusivity and Innovation**

   Valuing Differences: Embracing personality diversity ensures that all perspectives are acknowledged, which can lead to more innovative solutions and comprehensive problem-solving.

Creating an Inclusive and Psychologically Safe Environment: Acknowledging and respecting different personality tendencies helps foster a positive, creative, and generative workplace culture.

5. **Promote Personal and Professional Growth**

    Self-Awareness: Understanding one's own personality tendencies, and those of others, can lead to greater self-awareness and personal growth.

    Professional Development: Leveraging personality diversity enables individuals and teams to develop skills that enhance performance, teamwork, and job satisfaction.

Applications of Personality Diversity

Self-awareness: Understanding your personality tendencies as the first step to unlocking many opportunities.

Family & Friends: Understanding others to create an environment that is more social, effective, organised, and harmonious.

Workplace: Improving team collaboration, enhancing leadership effectiveness, and choosing to embrace a positive work culture.

Education: Tailoring teaching methods to suit different learning and personality styles. We have introduced E-Colours and personality diversity to children as young as seven. We've also introduced the concept of Personal Intervention to children from the age of nine. Both showed remarkable results. See Chapter 13 – E-Colours for Education.

Healthcare: Enhancing patient care by understanding diverse communication needs and preferences.

Sports: Building cohesive teams by leveraging varied personality tendencies for optimal performance.

Hospitality: Better understanding your customers' needs and interacting with them more effectively.

All Customer-facing Industries: Treating the customer in the way they need to be treated and creating a successful and harmonious environment for everyone involved.

By recognising and valuing personality diversity, individuals and organisations can build more dynamic, effective, and successful environments.

The E-Colours

The E-Colours concept, developed by Equilibria, was designed to provide a simple yet powerful method for understanding and applying personality diversity. The aim was to introduce a clear, memorable, and easily usable system that could be applied in day-to-day interactions. Initially created to help prevent workplace accidents and incidents, the simplicity, usability, and practical applications of the E-Colours quickly extended its impact to a wide range of areas and contexts.

As you explore E-Colours in this book and through Equilibria's broader work, it's important to understand that the styles reflect tendencies, not fixed traits. This distinction is key: we all exhibit elements of all four E-Colours. For example, even someone who primarily identifies with Blue (Relator) and Yellow (Socialiser) will still display tendencies associated with Red (Doer) and Green (Thinker), albeit usually to a lesser degree.

Here's an overview of the E-Colours concept.

Purpose and Development

Simplification: E-Colours simplifies the complex topic of personality diversity by categorising individuals into distinct colour-coded personality styles. This makes it easier for users to quickly understand and apply the concepts in a wide range of contexts.

Practical Application: The system is designed to be easily integrated into everyday interactions, team dynamics, and organisational practices. By providing clear, actionable ideas, E-Colours supports better communication, collaboration, and understanding.

Core Elements

Colour Categories: E-Colours uses a set of primary colour codes to represent different personality styles. Each colour corresponds to a unique set of tendencies and preferences, making it easier to identify and remember various personality tendencies.

- **Red** – Doer
- **Green** – Thinker
- **Yellow** – Socialiser
- **Blue** – Relator

Practical Tools and Applications: The E-Colours approach includes tools and resources that help individuals and teams apply the concept effectively. This includes 1-2-1 coaching, awareness and leadership workshops, assessments, and guides to support understanding and the use of personality diversity and personal intervention.

Memorability: The use of colour codes and visual elements makes the concept more engaging and easier to remember, helping individuals and teams recall and apply it with confidence.

E-Colours Applications

Team Building: E-Colours helps teams understand each other's personality styles, improving communication and collaboration.

Leadership: Leaders can use E-Colours to tailor their management style to suit the diverse needs of their team and communicate more effectively.

Personal Development: Individuals gain thoughts into their own tendencies and learn how to interact more effectively with others.

Conflict Resolution: Understanding personality styles helps manage conflict more constructively, leading to more harmonious relationships.

Safety, Risk Awareness, Risk Management: E-Colours has led to breakthroughs in workplace safety by addressing key questions: How can I get hurt? What makes it difficult to follow procedures? What makes it difficult to speak up or stop a job?

Error Traps: E-Colours helps people recognise how they may set error traps for themselves and others based on their own and others' personality tendencies.

Business Development: Understanding how others think enhances effectiveness when offering products and services.

> **Realising Potential:** Using E-Colours as the foundation for a coaching programme offers a fast track to helping others grow and succeed.

E-Colours Impact

> **Deepened Understanding:** E-Colours provides a structured way to understand personality diversity, making it easier to navigate interpersonal relationships.
>
> **Enhanced Communication:** The system promotes improved communication by encouraging people to recognise and value different personality tendencies.
>
> **Boosted Effectiveness:** Applying E-Colours helps teams and organisations improve their performance and productivity.
>
> **Safer Work Environment:** By encouraging the right questions, E-Colours raises awareness and significantly improves safety conversations and performance.

* * *

A Real-Life Big Rocks Story – Lewis Senior

As you read earlier in this introduction about the 'big rocks' concept, I wanted to share a real-life experience of replicating this exercise during a workshop on an offshore oil rig. Given the limited resources available, I improvised by borrowing various sizes of nuts from the rig store and using a bucket instead of a glass jar. The participants were seated in a horseshoe formation grouped according to their E-Colours.

Immediately to my right were individuals whose predominant E-Colours were Yellow/Blue. As I poured the nuts into the bucket, one nut caught the rim and began to fall towards the floor. Out of the corner of my eye, I saw an engineer leap from his chair, catch the nut mid-air, hand it back to me, and return to his seat, calmly placing the nut in the bucket.

When the session concluded, I asked the engineer to stay behind, as I wanted to share an observation – one I had noticed before in individuals with a strong Yellow/Blue personality combination. I said, 'I noticed how instinctively you jumped up to help when the nut started to fall. Are you aware that such an action could potentially get you killed?'

His response remains vividly etched in my memory, even though this happened over 15 years ago. He replied, 'Lewis, if I lost my life saving another, then so be it. It would have been worth it.'

This moment served as a powerful reminder of how deeply our personality tendencies can shape our natural reactions and thought processes. His instinct to help, driven by innate empathy and care for others, demonstrated the strong influence of personality on behaviour, even in high-risk environments. It's a striking example of how understanding personality dynamics can not only strengthen teamwork but also help us manage our instincts in critical situations.

*   *   *

In summary, the simple yet effective E-Colours concept, developed by Equilibria, fosters understanding of personality diversity through a memorable, colour-coded system. This approach makes it easier to apply personality tendencies in practical ways, improving communication, collaboration, and overall effectiveness across a wide range of industries and situations. E-Colours has also become a coping tool for many, offering support for mental wellbeing and continued personal development.

Knowing your E-Colours helps you embrace who you are, while recognising that others may share similar tendencies, and many will differ. At the same time, it teaches you how to communicate with people in ways they will understand and appreciate.

You can discover your E-Colours for FREE now at www.equilibria.com/PDI-home

CHAPTER 1

ARE WE REALLY SURROUNDED BY IDIOTS?

'Everybody is a genius. But if you judge a fish by its ability to climb a tree, it will live its whole life believing that it is stupid.'

– **Albert Einstein (1879–1955)**, German-born theoretical physicist widely recognised as one of the most influential minds of the 20th century

In a world increasingly divided by opposing opinions, it's not uncommon to hear people express frustration by labelling others as 'idiots' – a sentiment you might find familiar! This reaction often arises when individuals encounter perspectives and behaviours so different from their own that they feel bewildered or exasperated. Yet, the idea of a single, universal standard for intelligence or rationality oversimplifies the complexity of human interactions and is fundamentally misleading.

With *Personalities Remixed*, our mission is to empower individuals, families, teams, and organisations to harness their strengths and address their potential limiters by exploring personality diversity through the E-Colours framework. This book aims to examine whether the perceived lack of intelligence in others stems from genuine shortcomings or from differences in personality and cognitive styles. By understanding how these diversities influence our viewpoints and relationships, we can enrich our own lives, create better connections with those around us, and help build a world that thrives on collaboration and mutual understanding. Through this lens, we'll examine the true nature of disagreement and the misconceptions behind any perceived 'idiocy'.

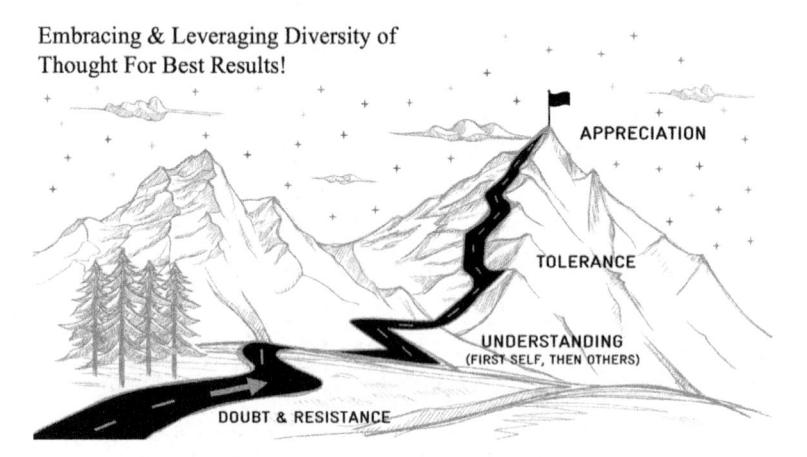

Figure 1 – The Pathway to Appreciation
Copyright © 2025 Equilibria Services Pte Ltd. All rights reserved.

When people are introduced to a new concept, it's typical to progress through a series of milestones before reaching full acceptance and appreciation. An early experience with the E-Colours is no different. It's completely natural for some to begin their journey with doubt and resistance. If you've purchased this book, there's a good chance you're ready to make your own journey up that mountain, and we welcome you, no matter where your base camp may be.

The Concept of Intelligence

To address the idea of being surrounded by 'idiots,' we must first unpack the concept of intelligence. Traditionally, intelligence has been measured through IQ tests and academic achievement, but these metrics capture only a fraction of human cognitive abilities. American psychologist Howard Gardner's theory of multiple intelligences, for example, identifies various forms of intelligence that describe the different ways people learn and process information, including linguistic, logical-mathematical, spatial, musical, and interpersonal. This broader perspective suggests that intelligence is not a monolithic tendency but a spectrum of diverse abilities and talents.

This raises the question: can different personality styles perceive people's intelligence differently, based on their own personality style – Red (Doer), Yellow (Socialiser), Green (Thinker), and Blue (Relator)?

Personality Diversity

Personality diversity plays a crucial role in shaping how we perceive and interact with others. The E-Colours framework, developed by Equilibria, offers a model for understanding individual differences in behaviour and communication styles. This system categorises people into four primary personality styles: Red (Doer), Yellow (Socialiser), Green (Thinker), and Blue (Relator). Each style reflects distinct tendencies and preferences that influence how individuals engage with the world.

Understanding these E-Colours can provide valuable ways into how we perceive intelligence and how different personality styles shape our views on what constitutes intelligent behaviour. Here's a brief overview of what we mean.

Reds (Doers): Individuals with a Red personality style are characterised by assertiveness, decisiveness, and a goal-oriented mindset. They tend to prioritise results and efficiency and are typically direct and confident in their interactions.

Yellows (Socialisers): Yellow personalities are known for enthusiasm, creativity, and sociability. They are often charismatic and enjoy engaging with others, bringing energy and innovation to their environments. Yellows value relationships and are generally optimistic.

Blues (Relators): People with a Blue personality style are recognised for their patience, empathy, and reliability. They are supportive, prefer stability and harmony, and are often good listeners who value loyalty and consistency in their relationships.

Greens (Thinkers): Green personalities are analytical, detail-oriented, and methodical. They prioritise accuracy and careful planning and are often seen as thorough and conscientious. Greens value structure and are typically more reserved in their interactions.

Personality Styles and Perceptions of Intelligence

The E-Colours framework helps us understand how different personality styles view intelligence – and how these perspectives influence their interactions with others.

Red Personalities and Intelligence: Reds (Doers) often associate intelligence with achievement and decisive action. They may view intelligence in terms of practical problem-solving skills and the ability to make quick, effective decisions. As a result, they often prioritise assertiveness and results as key indicators of intelligence.

Yellow Personalities and Intelligence: Yellows (Socialisers) may view intelligence through the lens of creativity and interpersonal skills. They appreciate innovative thinking and the capacity to inspire and motivate others. For Yellows, intelligence often shows up as social influence, enthusiasm, and a knack for generating new ideas.

Blue Personalities and Intelligence: Blues (Relators) tend to perceive intelligence in terms of emotional understanding and the ability to maintain harmony. They value interpersonal skills and the ability to empathise with others. For Blues, emotional intelligence, patience, and supportive behaviour are key signs of being smart.

Green Personalities and Intelligence: Greens (Thinkers) generally view intelligence as analytical and methodical thinking. They value thoroughness, accuracy, and attention to detail. For Greens, intelligence is reflected in the ability to process complex information, make sound decisions, and maintain high standards.

Personality diversity can lead to a wide range of behaviours and viewpoints, some of which may be perceived as 'idiotic' by people with contrasting styles. For example, a person with high conscientiousness might view someone with a more spontaneous approach as careless or irresponsible, while the spontaneous individual might view the structured person as overly rigid or uptight.

Moreover, cognitive biases – such as the Dunning–Kruger effect, a phenomenon where individuals with low ability in a task overestimate their competence – can further fuel misunderstandings. People who lack expertise may express flawed or overconfident views, which others might dismiss as foolish.

Implications for Understanding Intelligence

The E-Colours framework shows that perceptions of intelligence vary according to personality style, with each style valuing different qualities that shape how intelligence is interpreted.

This diversity illustrates that intelligence cannot be universally defined, as each personality style offers a unique lens through which to view cognitive and emotional abilities.

Communication and Interaction: Recognising different perspectives on intelligence can enhance communication and collaboration by deepening appreciation for each other's strengths.

Conflict Resolution: Acknowledging personality-driven views on intelligence can help ease conflict. For example, Reds may focus on results, while Blues may prioritise empathy. Understanding these differences promotes mutual respect and shared understanding.

Educational and Professional Settings: Awareness of personality styles allows intelligence to be nurtured and recognised in more personalised ways – supporting learning, performance, and productivity by leveraging individual strengths.

Cultural and Social Context

Cultural and social contexts also shape how we perceive intelligence and foolishness. Norms and values vary widely, and what is considered wise or intelligent in one culture may be viewed quite differently in another. For instance, direct confrontation may be valued as honesty in one setting but seen as rude or inappropriate in another.

Social groups can also reinforce their own norms and beliefs, creating echo chambers where dissenting opinions are dismissed or ridiculed. This often leads to the belief that those outside one's circle are less informed or rational.

The Role of Empathy and Understanding

To bridge the gap between differing perspectives, we must actively cultivate empathy and understanding. Recognising how personality diversity shapes our views can help us approach disagreement with more tolerance, and even appreciation. Rather than labelling others as 'idiots,' we can choose to see the value in diverse perspectives, leading to more constructive dialogues and collaborations.

Educational efforts that promote emotional intelligence and cognitive flexibility can help us appreciate the viewpoints of others. By understanding that others may approach problems from different angles due to their personality tendencies and cognitive styles, we foster a more respectful and inclusive environment.

The Platinum Rule

Equilibria adopted the Platinum Rule as a foundational principle within the E-Colours & Personal Intervention models. Often referenced during coaching sessions, the Platinum Rule provides an important contrast to the Golden Rule. While the Golden Rule suggests treating others as you would like to be treated, the Platinum Rule emphasises treating others as they would like to be treated.

This shift promotes empathy and understanding by focusing on individual preferences and needs – rather than assuming everyone shares your perspective. In relationships and intentional leadership, the Platinum Rule improves communication, strengthens mutual respect, and leads to more effective connections.

By applying the Platinum Rule, we move beyond a limited view of intelligence and begin to value the rich diversity of personalities and cognitive styles that shape how we experience the world.

The Catastrophic Consequences of Unchecked E-Colours – Lewis Senior

One of the earliest and hardest lessons I learned about personality, and how it influences behaviour, came shortly after I became the Health and Safety Manager for Transocean.

One afternoon, I received a call asking me to travel to Mobile, Alabama. A close friend, someone I'd worked with for years, had been involved in a catastrophic accident. When I arrived at the hospital, the reality hit me hard. There he was in intensive care, the crown of his head removed, recovering from a traumatic brain injury. His life had changed in an instant.

My friend had a Yellow/Blue personality style – naturally optimistic, warm, and always eager to help. But on that day, his willingness to lend a hand collided tragically with the behaviour of a colleague whose E-Colours were Red/Green – independent, fast-paced, task-focused, and always ready to move on to the next job. Their individual tendencies, unmanaged and unrecognised in a high-risk setting, led to an accident that could have been prevented had both understood how their personalities shaped their choices.

The incident happened during routine maintenance on a rig docked nearby. My Yellow/Blue friend, walking along the dock, saw the other man finishing an inspection of one of the lifeboats. Without hesitation, he climbed up to assist at the motor winch, intending to wind up the boat the final few inches by hand. Meanwhile, the Red/Green colleague, unaware that anyone was up there, pressed the raise button to secure the lifeboat into position. In that moment, the winch handle whipped around, striking my friend's head with brutal force. His hard hat was smashed in half. His skull was split open. The injury led to a life-altering injury that continues to affect him and his family today.

A couple of years later, when we began building Equilibria, we introduced the E-Colours and posed the question: *How could I get hurt?* As we gathered data, we compiled common answers from people with different personality combinations – including Yellow/Blue and Red/Green – highlighting how unchecked tendencies can create risk.

When I shared these ideas with my friend's Red/Green colleague, he was stunned. His response stuck with me: 'Did you write these answers for us?' He recognised instantly that his own unmoderated Red/Green drive to act quickly and independently had collided with my friend's helpful Yellow/Blue nature, setting the stage for a devastating outcome.

That moment became a vivid, painful reminder of how real and irreversible the consequences can be when we're unaware of our personality-driven behaviour.

As we said earlier, the idea that we're 'surrounded by idiots' is a narrow way of interpreting intelligence. It fails to account for the richness of personality diversity and the cognitive styles that shape how we perceive, process, and respond to information. Understanding this can help mitigate frustrations that arise from differing viewpoints. By embracing this diversity and creating an environment of psychological safety, we can improve beyond superficial judgements and engage in more meaningful, constructive, and productive exchanges.

Ultimately, valuing the complexity of others is key to creating a more harmonious and enlightened society. We don't all think or act the same way, and that's fine. The key is recognising and appreciating these differences in every interaction.

E-Colours isn't just a tool for individual development. It's a transformative resource for humanity. As many clients have said, E-Colours is the universal key to communication.

We don't believe we're surrounded by idiots – we believe we're surrounded by potential.

Matthew's Story

> *I was sceptical at first, but my initial Equilibria training session on E-Colours changed everything. It taught me how different people communicate and receive information, which has profoundly influenced my career and team management as an HSE Director.*
>
> – *Matthew Taylor* (Yellow/Blue)
> – HSE Director, Meta-Transform, UK

Martin's Story

> *The E-Colours course is the best course we have done. The approach and looking at safety differently was exactly what we were after. This course has given our team an amazing tool to understand not only our own strengths and potential limiters but also our wider team. One question asked that opened everyone's mind was: How could I get hurt? I cannot recommend this course highly enough for people who want to make tomorrow safer than it is today.*
>
> – *Martin Brogan* (Blue/Green or Blue/Red)
> – HSE Director, Dulsco Dubai

Fenu's Story

I thought it was all just grey matter, but now I see the Colours!

– *Fenu Sasi Rehana* (Red/Yellow)
– QHSE Manager, Dulsco Dubai

* * *

Remix Opportunities

- Discover your own E-Colours at www.equilibria.com.
- Purchase your own Premium Report ($49.99 / approx. £41).
- Begin your own self-awareness journey.
- Book a Premium Report Debrief Session with Lewis Senior or Mark Wilkinson.

CHAPTER 2

THE EVOLUTION OF PERSONALITY DIVERSITY

'Everything that irritates us about others can lead us to an understanding of ourselves.'

– **Carl Jung (1875–1961)**, Swiss psychiatrist and psychoanalyst who founded analytical psychology

This quote reflects Jung's deep understanding of the complexity of human personality and the interconnectedness of individual differences. By recognising our reactions to others, we gain a deeper awareness of our own personality tendencies and behaviours, highlighting the diversity that exists both within and between individuals.

Equilibria is Born – Lewis Senior

Equilibria was born out of a shared vision and a collective dream. On 4th April 2004 – a date none of us would ever forget, 04/04/04 – we embarked on this remarkable journey together. That day, Dagfinn Tromborg, John Lake, Paul Grant, and I gathered in John's barn, nestled in the peaceful countryside of southern England. It was in those humble surroundings that we laid the foundation of Equilibria. We crafted our vision: *REALISING POTENTIAL*, and defined our purpose: *PEOPLE FIRST*. Together, we mapped out the paths we would walk to bring this vision to life.

With the pillars of our enterprise established, we made the bold decision to leave the security of our roles at Transocean and embrace the uncertainty of a new venture. It was a leap into the unknown but also a leap towards untapped potential and limitless possibility. This book explores the transformative journey that followed, one fuelled by daring dreams and a steadfast commitment to our purpose.

At the heart of Equilibria's creation was a pressing issue: people were getting hurt in the offshore energy industry, and much of it stemmed from how individuals thought, interacted – or failed to interact – with one another. Personality diversity was a significant factor. I often said, 'If we can predict it, we can manage it,' and that became a guiding principle for us. This mindset led to the foundation of the E-Colours.

We wanted to create a tool that was both impactful and memorable, and colours felt like the obvious choice. Inspired by the ancient Chinese concept of four personality elements – Earth, Wind, Fire, and Water – we developed the E-Colours. The E-Colours is a Personality Diversity Indicator unlike any other. While it uses a quadrant matrix like many existing tools, ours stands apart because it integrates a brain model, linking the quadrants to left-brain and right-brain thinking patterns. To make it more accessible, we associated each personality style with one of four primary colours: Red, Yellow, Green, and Blue.

Our approach is based on the idea that we all possess all four personality styles to varying degrees, but most of us have a natural predominance of two. By understanding the order in which our styles present themselves, especially the dominant two, we gain understanding of ourselves and those around us. That awareness has the power to transform not only how we interact but how we grow and thrive, both personally and professionally.

Earth (Green – Thinker): Delves into the roots of issues, with strengths in analysis, accuracy, and logical thinking.

Wind (Yellow – Socialiser): Easily engages with others, bringing enthusiasm, talkativeness, and a high level of interaction.

Fire (Red – Doer): Quick to act, decisive, and independently driven – though sometimes impatient with others.

Water (Blue – Relator): Supports everyone around them like the ocean supports fish – calm, agreeable, and dependable.

Basic E-Colour Concept

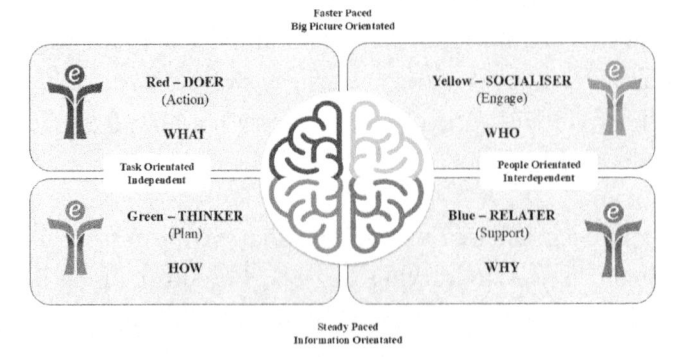

Faster Paced
Big Picture Orientated

Red – DOER (Action) **WHAT**	**Yellow – SOCIALISER** (Engage) **WHO**
Task Orientated / Independent	People Orientated / Interdependent
Green – THINKER (Plan) **HOW**	**Blue – RELATER** (Support) **WHY**

Steady Paced
Information Orientated

The Doer – The part of your personality that helps you to take action and get things done.

The Socialiser – The part of your personality that helps you interact and engage with others.

The Thinker – The part of your personality that helps you plan and analyse information.

The Relator – The part of your personality that helps you empathise with and support others.

Figure 2 – The Brain Model
Copyright © 2025 Equilibria Services Pte Ltd. All rights reserved.

Celebrating the Mosaic of Humanity

The history of personality diversity is a rich tapestry woven from threads of ancient philosophy, religious doctrine, scientific inquiry, and cultural evolution. From the earliest recognition of individual differences in prehistoric communities to the sophisticated theories and tools we use today, understanding and celebrating personality diversity has always been a continuing journey – and one that will undoubtedly continue to evolve in the decades ahead.

For those who enjoy more detailed context, the rest of this chapter offers an exploration of the history and evolution of personality diversity. Please read on.

Beginnings and Early Recognition

Long before the dawn of recorded history, when humans lived in small nomadic groups and painted their stories on cave walls, there was already an awareness of the differences between individuals. Around communal fires, some would tell captivating tales of gods and monsters, others would lead hunts with courage and strategy, while still others would heal and nurture. These informal roles reflected an early understanding of personality diversity.

In the fertile crescent of Mesopotamia, as civilisation began to take root, the Sumerians, Akkadians, and later the Babylonians, made observations about human behaviour. They often attributed these differences to divine influence, believing the gods played a role in a warrior's bravery or a sage's wisdom. The *Epic of Gilgamesh*, one of the world's earliest literary works, reflects this ancient perspective, portraying its hero's multifaceted personality: brave yet flawed, strong yet vulnerable.

Ancient Philosophical Foundations

The ancient Egyptians, through their detailed records, provide a glimpse into the personalities of rulers and deities alike. Pharaohs were shown to possess a range of qualities: some fierce and unrelenting like Sekhmet, others wise and just like Thoth. These portrayals underscored a belief that leadership and character were deeply intertwined.

In ancient Greece, philosophical inquiry into personality gained momentum. Socrates, through his method of probing questions, sought to understand human virtue. Plato, his student, introduced the concept of the tripartite soul in *The Republic*, proposing that human behaviour is governed by reason, spirit, and appetite. Aristotle expanded on these ideas, categorising virtues and vices and exploring how different balances among them shaped individual character.

The Middle Ages and the Role of Faith

Following the fall of the Roman Empire, European thought became heavily influenced by religious interpretations of human nature. During the Middle Ages, personality was often understood through the lens of Christian virtues and vices. Saints were revered for qualities like humility, piety, and compassion, while sinners were condemned for pride, greed, and wrath. The seven deadly sins and their corresponding virtues offered a system for evaluating moral character.

In the Islamic world, scholars such as Al-Farabi and Avicenna built upon the Greek philosophical tradition while integrating Islamic theology. They examined the faculties of the soul and the ethical implications of personal tendencies, emphasising the balance between reason and passion.

The Renaissance and the Flourishing of Individualism

The Renaissance heralded a renewed interest in the individual, sparking a renewed focus on the uniqueness of the human spirit. The arts and sciences flourished, driven by a spirit of inquiry and humanism. Leonardo da Vinci, driven by insatiable curiosity and talent across disciplines, embodied the ideal of the Renaissance man. His notebooks reveal a mind constantly exploring the interplay between observation and imagination.

Michelangelo, in contrast, expressed his inner depth through introspective, emotionally charged works. His sculptures and paintings, marked by their emotional depth and physical realism, reflect his inner struggles and relentless pursuit of perfection. These artists and their contemporaries showcased the diversity of human creativity and the varying temperaments that fuelled the Renaissance.

The Enlightenment and the Birth of Psychology

The Enlightenment introduced a more scientific approach to understanding human nature. Philosophers such as John Locke and Jean-Jacques Rousseau debated whether personality was shaped primarily by nature or nurture. Locke's theory of the mind as a *tabula rasa* suggested that experience played a vital role in shaping character, while Rousseau emphasised the inherent goodness of humans, believing it was society that corrupted them.

In the 19th century, the emerging field of psychology began to systematise the study of personality. Wilhelm Wundt, widely regarded as the father of experimental psychology, established the first psychology laboratory in 1879. His work centred on introspection and the structure of the mind, laying a foundation for future exploration of personality.

The Psychoanalytic Revolution

Sigmund Freud's psychoanalytic theory radically changed how personality was understood. He proposed that unconscious desires and internal conflicts, often rooted in early childhood experiences, played a major role in shaping behaviour and personality. His structural model of the psyche, comprising the id, ego, and superego, provided a framework for interpreting the complex interplay between instinct, reality, and morality.

Carl Jung, originally a close collaborator of Freud, later expanded on these ideas and introduced the concepts of archetypes and the collective unconscious. He argued that certain personality patterns were universal and embedded in the human psyche across cultures. Jung's work on introversion and extraversion also laid the groundwork for many modern personality assessments.

The E-Colours framework, however, does not categorise individuals as either introverts or extroverts, as these traits do not consistently align with E-Colours tendencies. For example, Lewis Senior and Mark Wilkinson both have Yellow/Red tendencies, yet while Lewis describes himself as an introvert at times, Mark is unmistakably an extrovert.

Behaviourism and Humanism

The early 20th century saw the rise of behaviourism, which focused on observable behaviour rather than internal mental states. Psychologists such as John Watson and B.F. Skinner stressed the influence of environmental factors and reinforcement in shaping behaviour. Skinner's operant conditioning experiments demonstrated how actions could be modified through rewards and punishments, highlighting the impact of external stimuli on personality development.

In contrast, the humanistic approach, championed by figures like Abraham Maslow and Carl Rogers, emphasised personal growth, autonomy, and self-actualisation. Maslow's hierarchy of needs proposed that individuals are motivated by a progression of needs, culminating in the desire to realise one's full potential. Rogers' client-centred therapy highlighted the role of empathy and unconditional positive regard in fostering personal development.

The Rise of Personality Assessments

The mid-20th century saw the development of various personality assessments aimed at quantifying and categorising individual differences. The Myers–Briggs Type Indicator (MBTI), based on Jung's theories, grouped individuals into 16 personality styles based on preferences in perception and decision-making. While widely used, the MBTI has faced criticism from scientists and psychologists for its lack of empirical support and reliability. Notably, Briggs and Myers began developing their indicator during World War II, believing personality preferences would help women entering the industrial workforce identify the wartime jobs they were most comfortable with and suited to.

Equilibria's ethics clearly state that the E-Colours should not be used for hiring, firing, promotions, job assignment, or task selection.

The Big Five personality traits, also known as the Five-Factor Model (FFM), emerged as a more robust and empirically supported framework. The Big Five: Openness to Experience, Conscientiousness, Extraversion, Agreeableness, and Neuroticism, provided a comprehensive and scientifically grounded approach to understanding personality. Extensive research across cultures and contexts has validated the Big Five as a reliable tool for measuring personality tendencies.

We recognise there are several other tools available to help people identify their personality 'styles,' and we fully respect each of them. However, we remain true to our vision of *REALISING POTENTIAL* and our core value of *PEOPLE FIRST*, with a strong commitment to continually improving our offerings.

Personality Diversity in the Workplace

As societies industrialised and workplaces evolved, understanding personality diversity became increasingly important for organisational success. Early 20th-century industrialists like Frederick Taylor aimed to maximise efficiency by aligning workers with roles suited to their skills and temperament. This approach laid the foundation for the future of organisational psychology and human resource management.

In the late 20th century, companies began to recognise the value of personality diversity in fostering innovation and adaptability. Teams composed of individuals with complementary strengths were found to be more effective at solving complex problems and driving creativity. The idea of 'cultural fit' emerged, highlighting the importance of aligning individual values and personality with organisational culture.

The Digital Age and Global Perspectives

The advent of the internet and social media in the 21st century has transformed how personality diversity is understood and expressed. Digital platforms provide unprecedented opportunities for individuals to share their perspectives and connect with like-minded people around the world. This interconnectedness has created a broader appreciation for cultural and personality diversity, challenging traditional stereotypes and promoting inclusivity.

Personality psychology has also evolved to include more cross-cultural perspectives. Research has explored how cultural contexts shape the expression and perception of personality styles. For example, individualistic cultures such as the United States may prioritise extraversion and assertiveness, while collectivist cultures like Japan may value harmony and agreeableness. Understanding these nuances is essential for fostering effective communication and collaboration in a globalised world.

Biological and Genetic Research

Advances in genetics and neuroscience have deepened our understanding of the biological basis of personality. Twin studies have shown that genetic factors account for roughly 40-60% of individual personality differences. Specific genes have been linked to traits such as impulsivity, aggression, and novelty-seeking, though these relationships are complex and shaped by environmental factors as well.

Neuroscience has also shed light on how brain structure and function relate to personality tendencies. For instance, studies suggest that extraversion is linked to increased activity in brain regions associated with reward processing, while neuroticism is associated with heightened sensitivity to negative stimuli. These findings highlight the dynamic interaction between biology and life experience in shaping personality.

The Future of Personality Diversity

As the study of personality diversity continues to evolve, several emerging trends and challenges are shaping its future. One key development is the growing interest in positive psychology, which emphasises strengths, wellbeing, and optimal functioning. Positive psychology interventions aim to enhance both individual and collective wellbeing by promoting qualities such as resilience, gratitude, and empathy.

Another area of growing interest is the impact of technology on personality. As artificial intelligence and machine learning become more embedded in daily life, researchers are exploring how these tools can be used to assess and enhance personality tendencies. For example, AI-driven platforms can deliver personalised feedback and recommendations for personal growth, while virtual reality environments can simulate social interactions to help improve emotional intelligence and interpersonal skills.

Ethical considerations also remain central to the study of personality diversity. Ensuring fair and respectful treatment of individuals, safeguarding privacy, and avoiding misuse of personality assessments are all critical concerns. As the field continues to evolve, maintaining high ethical standards and promoting inclusivity will be essential to advancing our understanding of personality diversity and its impact on society. These very concerns led Equilibria to develop the E-Colours Ethics – see Chapter 4.

Relating Theory to Practicality in Personality Diversity

Connecting theoretical ideas to practical examples is essential for fully understanding and leveraging personality diversity.

Based on what we know and what scholars have documented about Michelangelo's work, let's explore how his personality style may have influenced his extraordinary achievements in the Sistine Chapel.

Michelangelo's creation of the Sistine Chapel ceiling and *The Last Judgment* fresco is a vivid reflection of his thinking, analytical, and detail-oriented personality style. His approach to these monumental works highlights his ability to plan meticulously, analyse deeply, and execute with precision. Here's how those tendencies came to life in his work:

Meticulous Planning and Conceptualisation: Michelangelo's thinking and analytical skills were evident in the extensive planning that went into the Sistine Chapel ceiling.

Complex Compositions: The ceiling features a series of intricate compositions, including nine central panels depicting scenes from the Book of Genesis, framed by figures of prophets and sibyls, along with other decorative elements. This required careful planning to maintain both coherence and balance in the overall visual narrative.

Preliminary Sketches: Michelangelo produced numerous preparatory sketches and studies for individual figures and scenes. These drafts reflect his analytical process in capturing human anatomy, experimenting with poses, and refining details to ensure accuracy.

Anatomical Precision and Detail: Michelangelo's detailed personality style is perhaps most evident in his masterful depiction of the human body.

Anatomical Studies: He was known for his thorough anatomical studies, including dissections, to understand muscle structure and movement. This deep knowledge enabled him to portray the human form with striking accuracy and dynamism.

Intricate Details: Each figure, from Adam and Eve to the various prophets and sibyls, is rendered with meticulous attention to detail. The precise depiction of muscles, veins, and skin texture showcases Michelangelo's dedication to realism and his detail-oriented nature.

Innovative Techniques and Problem Solving: Michelangelo's analytical mindset led him to develop creative solutions to the technical challenges of fresco painting.

Scaffolding Design: He designed his own scaffolding system, allowing him to paint the ceiling while lying on his back. This inventive solution reflected his practical problem-solving skills and his grasp of the physical demands of the project.

Fresco Technique: Fresco painting demands quick execution on wet plaster. Michelangelo mastered this medium, maintaining vibrant colours and sharp details despite time constraints. His methodical thinking helped him adapt and refine his technique to meet the challenge.

Symbolic and Theological Depth: Michelangelo's thinking style also emerged in the symbolic and theological richness of his work.

Theological Themes: The ceiling's iconography is rich in theological symbolism. Michelangelo's analytical mind enabled him to interweave themes of creation, fall, and redemption into a cohesive story that aligns with Catholic doctrine.

Symbolic Elements: Scenes such as the separation of light from darkness, the creation of Adam, and the Deluge are visually stunning and rich in meaning. His ability to incorporate symbolic depth demonstrates intellectual rigour and spiritual thoughts.

Attention to Proportion and Perspective: Michelangelo's attention to spatial accuracy showcases his analytical and detail-oriented personality.

Foreshortening: He employed foreshortening – a technique used to create depth on a flat surface – which required precise visual calculations to ensure the figures appeared realistically three-dimensional from the chapel floor.

Scale and Proportion: Michelangelo carefully scaled the figures so they appeared proportionate when viewed from below. His foresight and understanding of visual perception reflect his analytical and detail-oriented approach.

Emotional Expression and Psychological Thoughts: Michelangelo's analytical tendencies also extended to his portrayal of human emotion and psychological nuance.

Expressive Figures: The ceiling's figures are not only anatomically correct but also emotionally rich. Michelangelo's deep study of human emotion is evident in the varied expressions – from the calm of the Creator to the torment of the condemned in *The Last Judgment*.

Narrative Clarity: Despite the visual complexity of the ceiling, Michelangelo maintained narrative clarity, directing the viewer's eye with deliberate use of lighting, composition, and focal points to ensure that the central themes and emotions were conveyed effectively.

As you read through this description of Michelangelo's work, which personality tendencies and style come shining through?

Michelangelo's work on the Sistine Chapel ceiling is a testament to his thinking, analytical, and detailed personality style. His tendencies – reflected in his meticulous planning, anatomical expertise, technical innovation, symbolic depth, proportional accuracy, and emotional expressiveness – all reflect his extraordinary ability to blend intellectual rigor with artistic genius. The time taken to complete the work was of little concern to him; social interaction was limited, and collaboration was not a priority. He focused entirely on the task at hand. Through these innate tendencies, Michelangelo created masterpieces that continue to inspire admiration centuries later.

From the book *The Platinum Rule* by Tony Alessandra PhD and Michael J. O'Connor PhD, descriptions of each possible personality style of Michelangelo, with E-Colours interpretations added, offer a fun and thoughtful way for us all to reflect on the many dimensions of personality.

Relator (Blue): If Michelangelo had been a Relator (Blue), he would first listen carefully to the Vatican officials, asking in detail what they wanted from the mural, and what kind of relationship they envisioned with him before, during, and after the project. Then, he'd gather a loyal team, making sure they had the right brushes, paints, and enthusiasm.

After drawing up a precise, step-by-step plan, he'd ask the team to work collaboratively, using consistent colours, and even standardised brushstrokes. Once underway, he'd ensure that everyone persevered until every smile was in place on every angel.

Would the ceiling be a masterpiece for the ages? Some critics might say it lacked flair, but others would admire it for being done earnestly, methodically, and thoroughly. And the team members themselves would say it was the most fulfilling experience of their lives.

Thinker (Green): If Michelangelo had been a Thinker (Green), he would have taken the project with utmost seriousness, expecting to be judged on the precision of his details. He'd painstakingly plan the intricate design, right down to the perfect tint on each angel's wings. He would also make sure every scene could stand alone – just in case he fell ill, or the Pope, for some reason, decided to cancel the project.

Then he'd begin painting, mostly on his own. He wouldn't mind spending four years lying on his back, 70 feet in the air. The hardship would be worth it, knowing the final result would be nothing short of perfect.

Would it be a masterpiece? Quite possibly – at least, that's what a Thinker would aspire to. He wouldn't expect the job to be fun, but he'd like to believe that his work might one day be hailed as a marvel of skill, taste, and self-determination.

Doer (Red): If Michelangelo had been a Doer (Red), here's how he would probably have approached painting the frescoes on the ceiling of Rome's famous Sistine Chapel:

- Make a quick sketch.
- Tell the Vatican to back off.

- Hire a crew to erect the scaffolding.
- Delegate the painting to half a dozen artists, each giving him a daily progress report detailing how many square feet were being covered.
- Review their work and add his own final touches.

This would give him control yet still free him up to take on bigger challenges – such as, say, St. Peter's Basilica.

Socialiser (Yellow): If Michelangelo had been a Socialiser (Yellow), he'd talk about countless ideas but have no single plan. He'd start in one corner and simply wing it, painting whatever struck his fancy as he chatted merrily with whoever happened to be nearby.

His work would show flair and style. He'd enjoy himself and likely make new friends as he paused to tell stories and show off freshly completed sections. When it was all done, he'd throw a huge kick-off celebration and sell postcards of the finished ceiling.

Would the painting be a masterpiece? Perhaps in the conception, if not the execution. But either way, the Vatican would still be talking about what a great guy Michelangelo was!

Bridging Theory to Reality: Harnessing Personality Diversity with E-Colours

Understanding and applying theoretical knowledge to real-life scenarios is crucial for effectively leveraging personality diversity. The E-Colours system provides a practical framework that enables individuals to recognise and utilise their unique strengths across a variety of contexts and settings.

Let's look at some everyday interactions where E-Colours makes a real difference.

Workplace Collaboration: Picture a tech project team composed of members with diverse E-Colours. Jane, a Red/Yellow (Socialising Doer), leads with energy and motivation, though she occasionally overlooks details. Mike, a Green/Blue (Relating Thinker), complements Jane with meticulous planning and empathy, ensuring thorough execution and constructive conflict resolution. By understanding their E-Colours, Jane and Mike balance each other's strengths, building an effective and harmonious team dynamic.

Family Dynamics: At home, Sarah, a Blue/Green (Thinking Relator), values harmony and thoughtful dialogue, while Tom, a Red/Yellow (Socialising Doer), favours quick decisions. Through E-Colours, Sarah appreciates Tom's decisiveness and clarity, while Tom comes to value Sarah's thoughtful ideas. Adjusting their communication styles allows them to strengthen their relationship and make more balanced decisions together.

Education: Teachers like Mrs. Lee, a Yellow/Blue (Relating Socialiser), rely on their enthusiasm to engage students, but may lack structure. By consciously managing her tendencies and planning ahead, Mrs. Lee develops a curriculum that accommodates diverse learning needs, creating a more effective and inclusive classroom.

Healthcare: Dr. Patel, a Blue/Red (Doer Relator), excels at diagnostics, but struggles to build rapport with patients. By observing Dr. Johnson, a Yellow/Green (Thinking Socialiser), who naturally connects with people, Dr. Patel adjusts her approach to build trust and improve satisfaction, enhancing both patient outcomes and reducing legal risks.

Sports Teams: Coaches like Martin, a Red (Doer), focus on results and high performance, but may unintentionally demotivate players. Assistant Coach Rivera, a Blue (Relator), creates a supportive atmosphere, valuing each player's contributions and boosting morale and performance, thereby curating a winning team dynamic.

These examples highlight how applying the E-Colours framework turns theory into practical strategies, using either primary or primary/secondary E-Colours. By embracing personality diversity, individuals and teams enhance communication, collaboration, and performance in both personal and professional environments. The clarity and accessibility of E-Colours make it an invaluable tool for navigating human interaction, promoting inclusivity, and achieving shared goals.

In everyday settings, the power of personality diversity becomes unmistakable. This approach enriches individual understanding and nurtures environments where diversity thrives, driving success across all areas of life. The scientific research behind Equilibria's personality theory, which we will expand on later in the book, sets it apart and deepens its value for understanding human potential.

To thrive in a diverse world, we must embrace and value all people. Happiness, health, and prosperity are the birthrights of every individual. E-Colours empowers us to understand our own strengths and potential limiters, as well as those of others.

This self-awareness leads to greater happiness and contributes to a more harmonious world.

The Dash in Between – A Story from Lewis Senior

Over the years, I've had the privilege of working with people across many cultures and industries. A common thread in my work has been learning how to relate to people based on their personalities, a concept that crystallised for me in a vivid way during an assignment in India many years ago.

I had been asked to coach a rig manager for a drilling contractor, a man whose commitment to his work had raised concerns among his supervisors. They feared he was verging on burnout, so focused on his responsibilities that he seemed to leave little room for anything else. Described as an 'early riser', his workdays were reportedly endless, and he rarely took time off. Given his strong-willed, self-reliant Red/Green personality tendencies, it wasn't surprising that he often took everything upon himself – even tasks that easily could have been delegated.

I flew to Mumbai, and my first step was to confirm what I had been told. I arrived at his office early, at 4 a.m., only to find him already at his desk. He was deep into paperwork, preparing helicopter manifests for the upcoming week. Typically, this task would fall to a technical assistant, but he had chosen to handle it himself.

When I asked him about it, he simply said, 'I prefer to do it myself.' His independence and focus were impressive, but I wondered if he recognised the toll it might be taking. Throughout the week, I observed him – always the first to arrive, always the last to leave, and showing little interest in anything beyond his work. On Friday evening, however, I received a surprising invitation: he asked if I would like to spend the weekend with him and his family.

That Saturday, I met his wonderful family – a beautiful wife and two bright children, whom he clearly cherished. I could tell that they, too, only saw him in the rare free moments he could spare. I began to realise that although he was kind-hearted and proud of his family, he was so immersed in his work that he hadn't left enough room for them in his daily life.

The following Monday, we flew out to his rig, where his priorities became even more apparent. As we toured the site, he focused almost exclusively on the equipment, taking detailed notes on things like the state of handrails. His interactions with the crew, the very reason I had been brought in to coach him, were minimal. By midweek, it was clear that he was more driven to perfect every operational detail than to engage with people. So, I decided to try a different approach.

On our way back to Mumbai, I asked his driver to take us somewhere unexpected. We arrived at one of the city's largest cemeteries, a peaceful place where rows upon rows of gravestones stretched out before us. We entered in silence, surrounded by markers of lives once lived. Standing there, I asked him, 'What do you see?'

At first, he looked around and, with a small laugh, replied, 'Is it the housekeeping?'

I smiled and pointed out that we were looking at the lives represented here, each marked by two dates: a birthdate and a death date. I explained that while we can't control the dates at either end, we can control what we do with the small dash between them. The dash – that single mark – represented everything these people had done, achieved, and become.

In that quiet cemetery, something shifted in him. He stood still for a long moment, taking in the lesson. His legacy, I suggested, would not be defined solely by his meticulous work but also by the time he shared with others and the impact he had on the people closest to him.

That conversation took place over 25 years ago, and remarkably, he recently reached out to me as he prepared for retirement. He shared that the memory of our visit to the cemetery had stayed with him throughout his career, helping him find a better balance between his professional responsibilities and his life beyond work.

So now I ask you, dear reader: not dissimilar to the story we shared in the introduction of this book, with the anecdote about the 'Big Rocks' – what are you doing with your dash in between? See Chapter 14 – Real Time Legacy.

Claire's Story

Working in the profession of health and safety for many years, along with leading teams, regularly drives me to look for new opportunities to improve communication and develop how we interact and understand cultures and personalities.

E-Colours is a fantastic development tool that can help individuals and teams better understand their strengths but more importantly, in my opinion, understand that we are all wired differently and what style of communication works well for one person may have the opposite effect on another. E-Colours has helped our team recognise our own tendencies and those of others, helping us to build connections and recognise that we are all unique and sometimes require different interactions to achieve the best outcome.

– *Claire Binns* (Green/Red)
– HSSEQ Director, Venterra Group

*   *   *

Remix Opportunities

- Continue exploring the history of Personality Diversity, along with Equilibria's scientific research and validation of the theory.
- Reflect on your own journey and consider how you intend to use your 'dash in between'.
- Deepen your understanding of your E-Colours percentages in each area, as well as those of your partner, family members, and colleagues.

CHAPTER 3

EQUILIBRIA & MARK WILKINSON

'We do not always think and act in the same way, and that's ok; every personality style brings value to the table.'

– **Lewis Senior**, Co-Founder Equilibria

Lewis Senior, Mark Wilkinson, and Paul Grant are co-authors of this book. Key figures in the Equilibria story also include Laura Senior Garcia and David Senior Garcia. All of us have played pivotal roles in Equilibria's development and growth over the years. Understanding each of our reasons for joining Equilibria is essential for understanding the full scope of this journey.

Meeting Lewis Senior – A Story from Mark Wilkinson

In 2013, as I waited in the bustling Terminal 3 at Heathrow Airport, I had no idea I was about to meet someone who would completely change my life. My heart was already set on working in high-risk environments. I wanted to help and make a difference. From what little I had learned about the E-Colours,

I felt deeply drawn to the impact I understood the tool was already making in these settings. But as I stood there that day, it still felt like a distant dream.

Then I saw the man I was there to meet, Lewis Senior. I'd heard about his groundbreaking work, his book *At The End Of The Day*, his dedication, and his unmistakable passion for helping others.

He wore his bold and unmistakable signature Yellow/Red wristband. He radiated purpose: a vibrant yellow representing optimism, and a solid red suggesting strength and resilience. It felt like I was witnessing the embodiment of the qualities I hoped to develop in both my personal and professional life.

With my Yellow/Blue tendencies at the time, I introduced myself a little nervously. To my surprise, he greeted me warmly, as though he already sensed we were connected by a shared mission. He listened attentively as I described my aspirations and explained why I wanted to work with Equilibria and E-Colours. His responses were rich with stories from his own path – a journey shaped by global work in high-risk environments and the unwavering desire to uplift and help those around him, ultimately keeping them safe and getting them back to their families.

He spoke about the importance of appreciating Personality Diversity and E-Colours in high-risk work, the ability to communicate beyond words, to create positive dialogue in dangerous spaces, and to inspire high-pressure teams to keep improving. Yet more than the ideas themselves, it was his dedication that struck me most. His passion for helping others wasn't just professional, it was personal. He believed that everyone could become a beacon of positive change if they learned to harness their true strengths through the E-Colours, and he challenged me to consider how my own work could amplify that mission.

By the end of our conversation, I felt changed. Meeting Lewis had reignited my sense of purpose, showing me that my dream wasn't only possible, it was necessary. I left Heathrow that day with a fire I hadn't felt before, ready to walk a path where risk met purpose, and where E-Colours became a language of hope and resilience. That meeting wasn't just a chance encounter – it was a defining moment, setting me on the journey I continue today, thanks to one unforgettable meeting with Lewis Senior.

Meeting Mark Wilkinson: A Story from Lewis Senior

Mark Wilkinson's journey with Equilibria is a testament to the power of resilience, optimism, and a shared vision for growth. I first met Mark in 2013 at Heathrow Airport, where his vibrant, positive energy left an immediate impression. Although Equilibria wasn't in a position to offer him a role at the time, his presence stayed with me – a clear sign of the lasting impression he leaves on those he meets.

Mark's enthusiasm and openness to possibility resonated deeply, and about a year later, we reconnected over lunch. That conversation was filled with a mutual hope of future collaboration. The timing still wasn't right, but the seed of partnership had been planted.

Over the years, Mark and I stayed in touch through thoughtful exchanges and genuine care. I remember reaching out with encouragement when he faced challenges like his knee surgeries. These moments underscored Mark's tenacity and reaffirmed our commitment to staying connected.

The turning point came in early 2021 when I had the privilege of reading a draft of *Life Remixed*. I was moved by its message, and over the course of that weekend, I felt inspired to contribute by writing the foreword. That collaboration brought us closer and reignited conversations about working together, even as the world faced the disruption of COVID-19.

Mark's influence on Equilibria, and his passion for expanding the reach of the E-Colours, are unmistakable. His warmth, determination, and ability to connect deeply with others make him an extraordinary asset. Together, we're exploring new ways to share the E-Colours with a wider audience, making a positive difference in countless lives.

Mark Wilkinson isn't just part of Equilibria – he embodies its spirit of growth, connection, and balance. It's a privilege to collaborate with someone who continually inspires, motivates, and challenges us to dream bigger.

As I write about Mark, I can't help but smile because there's another part to the story: his partnership with his wonderful wife, Emma, the 'Eagle Eye.' As you, the reader, will soon discover, Mark – like me – leans strongly towards Yellow/Red behaviours: outgoing, optimistic, and full of energy. Emma, by contrast, is more Green/Blue: highly organised, detail-oriented, and methodical, with a clear preference for time and space to plan.

Emma's style complements Mark's dynamic approach beautifully, and now that Mark is deeply involved with Equilibria, we are fortunate to know Emma, too. Despite the demands of her own business, Emma contributes meaningfully when she can – bringing a keen eye for detail, creativity, and a strong commitment to excellence. Her edits, input, and determination to get things just right enhance everything we do.

The balance that Mark and Emma bring – the combination of his energy and vision with her structure and precision – is truly inspiring. Together, they are a powerhouse of positivity and professionalism, embodying the synergy Equilibria aims to cultivate in all its relationships. They remind us of the magic that happens when different E-Colours unite around a shared purpose, and I am grateful to count them both as valued members of the Equilibria family.

Laura Senior Garcia, Red/Yellow – The Socialising Doer

In 2004, when Equilibria was founded, I was drawn to the opportunity to join a new venture that had the potential to make a meaningful impact on people's lives. In the year leading up to the formation of Equilibria, my father, Lewis Senior, had increasingly become a guiding presence in my life. His dedication to positively influencing others strongly shaped my decision to become involved.

With my E-Colour tendencies being Red/Yellow, Socialising Doer, the chance to contribute to positive change while connecting with others was deeply appealing. Equilibria gave me a platform to use my strengths as a natural Doer, driven by a genuine care for people through the Socialising connection. It allowed me to immerse myself in diverse cultures and environments that would be otherwise inaccessible through other industries. Some of the original founders, my early mentors, were kind individuals who invested in my growth and exemplified the human side of industrial work. Their guidance and support played a crucial role in shaping my career.

In those early years, I spent a great deal of time offshore and was incredibly grateful for the experience. As my career progressed, I had the privilege of working with leaders, creating positive change across their organisations, impacting thousands of lives. This continues to energise me to this day, as I continue to work with leaders, helping them drive transformation within their organisations.

Lewis and I also co-authored a book in 2012 called *At the End of the Day* – a must-read that later inspired Mark Wilkinson to write his own book, *Life Remixed*.

Gasping and clutching his chest on the floor of a French hotel room, Lewis Senior – my father, the workaholic – believed he had taken his final breath. *At the End of the Day* helps readers understand that unhappiness is a choice, suffering is optional, and circumstances are meaningless; it's how we choose to respond to life that makes all the difference. For anyone trying to balance family and career, it truly is an essential read.

The first time I found myself in an E-Colours session in Houston, alongside a group of other top E-Colour Reds – mostly male Oil and Gas leaders at the time – I quickly realised the power of E-Colours to help people find common ground with anyone, in any situation.

One of the additional key attractions of Equilibria has always been the accessibility of its tools, especially the E-Colours, which have the potential to benefit people of all ages and backgrounds. This holistic approach to personal and professional growth continues to resonate with me and fuels my passion for Equilibria's vision of *REALISING POTENTIAL*.

Lewis Senior – Building on Laura's comments, I want to express my gratitude for her unwavering dedication, professionalism, and relentless drive for growth. She is always seeking the best ways to serve our clients and has developed a unique skill set that has opened doors to opportunities and impact for organisations – possibilities that simply wouldn't have existed without her.

Over the years, Laura has mastered managing her Red/Yellow tendencies, and her journey has offered valuable lessons. One idea she shared with me years ago has always stuck with me: 'Always remember that my internal clock is going much faster than the one on the wall.' This observation is often echoed by others with strong Red/Yellow tendencies, crossing both cultural and geographical boundaries – it captures a universal tendency of this personality combination.

David Senior Garcia, Blue/Yellow – The Socialising Relator

My journey with Equilibria began well before its formal creation. Growing up in an environment shaped by my father's work at Transocean, I was introduced early to personality diversity and the related workshops.

My initial contributions to Equilibria – developing PowerPoints and visual aids – reflected my natural Blue (Relator) tendencies and marked the start of my path toward self-management, even as I worked through my own early challenges.

While completing my MBA studies in Brighton, I took the opportunity to intern with Equilibria in Thailand, which confirmed my aspiration to join the company. After finishing the programme, I was welcomed into Equilibria, initially exploring the coaching side of the business. It quickly became clear that coaching was my true calling – combining my passion for helping others with the personal challenge of public speaking, particularly significant for a Blue as a top colour.

Now approaching my 12th year with Equilibria at the time of writing, I hold a core leadership and management role, guided by a strong commitment to helping people uncover and reach their full potential.

Lewis Senior – Building on David's comments, I want to highlight the tremendous value he has brought to Equilibria across many roles. When we asked him to lead our relationship with Fisher Improvement Technologies, it was with the aim of building a successful partnership in the field of error reduction – linking the science of human and organisational performance with the actionable intelligence of the E-Colours. David has played a central role in making that collaboration a success.

David has also contributed significantly to the development of much of our intellectual property, including the widely used Premium Report and Alignment Reports. These resources have become core elements of Equilibria's offerings, reflecting his enduring impact on the organisation and its continued growth.

Mark Wilkinson, Yellow/Red – The Doing Socialiser

I recall my first experience with Equilibria back in 2012. As part of my commitment to personal growth and development,

I completed the excellent online Personal Diversity Indicator (PDI) assessment. I'm deeply grateful to Paul, Lewis, and the wonderful Equilibria team for creating the E-Colours programme – it showed me which areas of my personality I needed to work on in order to become a more rounded individual and, at the time, to succeed in both the workplace and, eventually, in business ownership and leadership roles.

I was wondering what to do with my life when I discovered my E-Colours. It was another light bulb moment: my first report identified my strengths and potential limiters, and I used Equilibria's coaching material to help me climb the corporate ladder to a six-figure salary within three years. All I did was focus on the areas that E-Colours highlighted for development – my potential limiters. I took the online PDI, which only took 15 minutes, and I was genuinely amazed by the results. The initial report was incredibly accurate and revealed that I had Yellow/Blue tendencies, reflecting a Relating Socialiser personality. It described me perfectly, right down to my previous 25 years in the music industry, and showed me what I could do to grow, both personally and professionally. My E-Colours percentages revealed that Green, logical thinking, was my lowest tendency, so I knew what I had to do. I focused and studied for several years, passed many exams, and gained qualifications that allowed me to advise and consult with directors at some of the UK's largest companies.

Now, I sit here happy and grateful – as a Success and E-Colours Coach, the owner of the Life Remixed coaching business as well as my HSE Consultancy Hillmont Associates, the holder of a property portfolio, a multiple best-selling author, and now the Global Director of Business Development for

Equilibria. We have a tremendous opportunity ahead – see Figure 3 below for just some of the benefits of embracing personality diversity. We want everyone to experience the value of E-Colours & Personal Intervention. Just like Coca-Cola's famous 1971 vision, *'I'd Like to Teach the World to Sing (In Perfect Harmony),'* our goal is to make this work universally recognised and embraced. Co-authoring this book is one of the many incredible opportunities I (and we) have attracted by applying the E-Colours & Personal Intervention tools. So ask yourself: what would you like to attract and achieve in your life? Then begin taking the actions that will get you there. Start today. Start now!

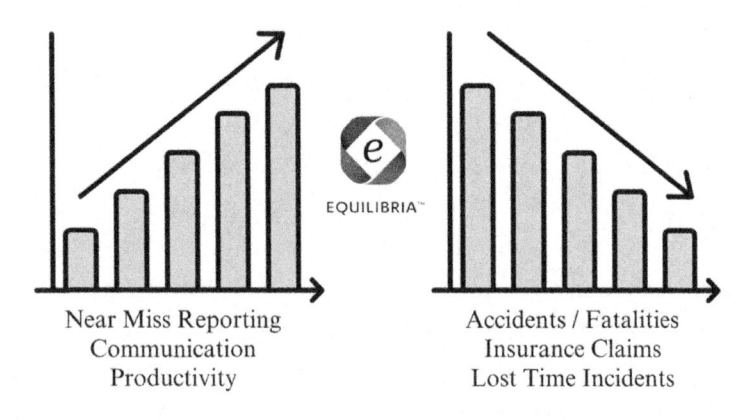

Near Miss Reporting
Communication
Productivity

Accidents / Fatalities
Insurance Claims
Lost Time Incidents

Figure 3 – The Benefits of the E-Colours & Personal Intervention
Copyright © 2025 Equilibria Services Pte Ltd. All rights reserved.

About Equilibria

When we describe Equilibria as a company, we do so in terms of what each top E-Colour tells us is most important to individuals.

Yellow (Socialisers) – Strengths: High Yellow individuals are often optimistic, enthusiastic, and skilled at engaging others. This can make them effective at diffusing tension. They usually want to know *who* is involved and often prefer to be involved themselves.

Red (Doers) – Strengths: High Red individuals are action-oriented, decisive, and goal-focused. They are typically most interested in *what* we are doing, and *when* it needs to be done.

Green (Thinkers) – Strengths: High Green individuals are analytical and objective, helping them approach life in a logical, structured way. They usually lead with *how* questions.

Blue (Relators) – Strengths: High Blue individuals are empathetic, patient, and attentive listeners. This makes them skilled at understanding different perspectives and showing compassion. Blues typically lead with *why*.

WHO We Are: Yellow (Socialiser)

Equilibria specialises in personality diversity, with over 20 years of expertise in helping people understand, embrace, and apply the diversity of thought among individuals. This approach enhances both personal and professional performance across a wide range of settings. Founded in 2004 by four visionaries from the oil and gas industry, Equilibria has since evolved into a global network – empowering coaches, E-Colour practitioners, affiliates, and licensees to deliver value to our clients and theirs.

WHAT We Do: Red (Doer)

We provide coaching that enables individuals, teams, organisations, and communities to understand and apply our proprietary Personality Diversity Indicator. This helps reduce errors, minimise risk, and improve human performance. By combining the PDI with our core tools – E-Colours & Personal Intervention – we foster heightened awareness, better communication, stronger leadership, and enhanced teamwork and safety. The process helps individuals become less reactive, more responsive, and better equipped to lead and live with conscious intent.

HOW We Do It: Green (Thinker)

Through a series of intentional engagement leadership workshops, we introduce clients to our core coaching tools and collaborate with them to create tailored, sustainable performance enhancement strategies aligned with their specific goals.

WHY We Do It: Blue (Relator)

Our vision is *REALISING POTENTIAL*, and our core value is *PEOPLE FIRST*. We are driven by a genuine desire to help people, teams, organisations, and communities achieve their full potential.

Personality vs Character

Once individuals gain a heightened sense of personal and team awareness through the E-Colours and can distinguish between personality-driven *reactions* and character-based *responses*, they can begin using the concepts of PLAY & PAUSE to shift from reaction to response mode and start to make conscious choices leading to intentional outcomes. We call this process Personal Intervention. We will explore this in more detail in Chapter 10.

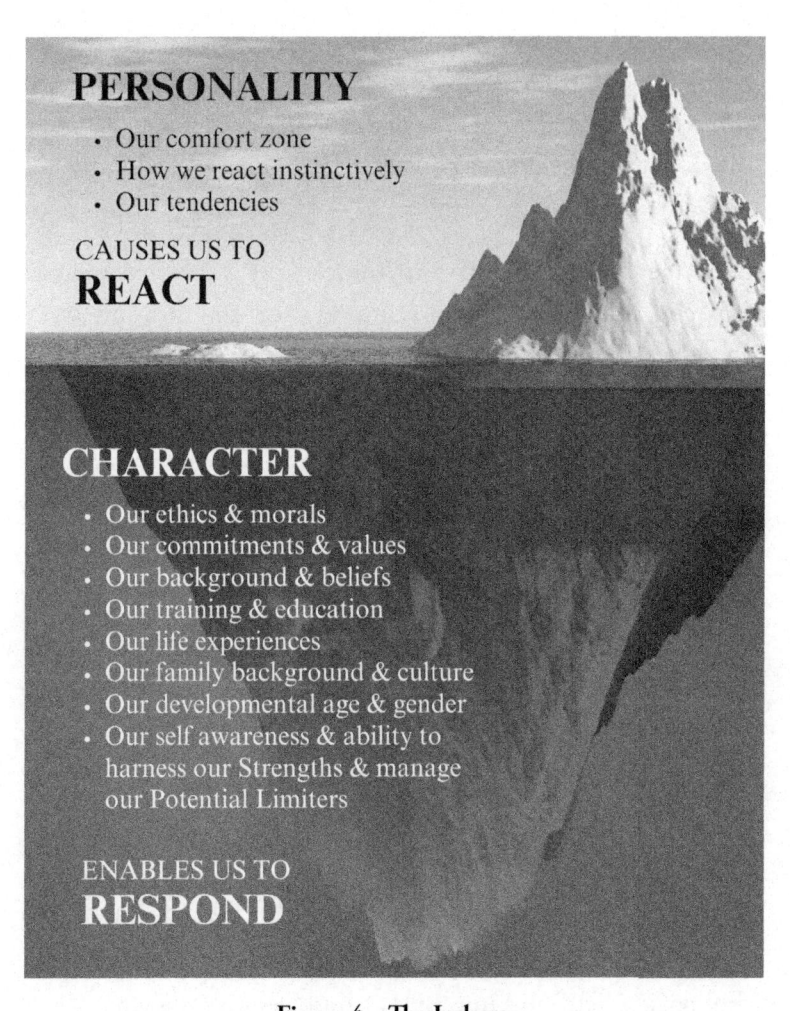

PERSONALITY
- Our comfort zone
- How we react instinctively
- Our tendencies

CAUSES US TO
REACT

CHARACTER
- Our ethics & morals
- Our commitments & values
- Our background & beliefs
- Our training & education
- Our life experiences
- Our family background & culture
- Our developmental age & gender
- Our self awareness & ability to harness our Strengths & manage our Potential Limiters

ENABLES US TO
RESPOND

Figure 4 – The Iceberg
Copyright © 2025 Equilibria Services Pte Ltd. All rights reserved.

Why Use E-Colours & Personal Intervention?

Key features and benefits include:

Simplified Understanding of Personality Styles: Utilises four distinct colours – Red, Yellow, Green, and Blue – to represent different personality tendencies (Doer, Socialiser, Thinker, and Relator), making it easier to remember and identify the strengths and potential limiters of ourselves and others.

Enhanced Communication: Improves interpersonal interactions by providing thoughts into the communication styles preferred by each of the different personality styles, fast-tracking clearer and more effective communication.

Conflict Resolution: By improving communication, E-Colours equips individuals with the tools to better understand potential sources of conflict based on personality differences, enabling more effective resolution strategies and reducing tension between people, both at home and at work.

Team Collaboration: Encourages teams to leverage diverse personality strengths and manage potential limiters, enabling more balanced and effective team dynamics, communication, and project management.

Leadership Development: Assists leaders in adapting their management styles to better suit the personality make-up of their teams, enhancing leadership effectiveness, creating psychological safety, and improving employee engagement.

Enhanced Safety and Risk Management: Improves behavioural and psychological safety by raising individual awareness of how they manage risk, aligning risk strategies with personality tendencies, and reducing the likelihood of errors and accidents through improved communication across organisations.

Cultural Integration and Inclusivity: Promotes an inclusive organisational culture that values diversity of thought and personality, contributing to a more harmonious and dynamic workplace, and supporting improved mental health.

Empowered Self-Management and Mastery: The Personal Intervention tools – learning and mastering the PAUSE & PLAY technique (explored further in Chapter 10) – empower individuals to manage their reactions intentionally. This approach promotes mindfulness and improves decision-making by encouraging response over reaction. These skills must be developed, not demanded, and the use of Equilibria's E-Colours as a coaching tool sets our approach to personality diversity apart from any other on the market.

What Do Our Clients Think? – Lewis Senior

I vividly recall that first trip to the USA with Paul Grant. Our goal was ambitious: to promote Equilibria's capabilities using nothing more than a single card outlining our offerings. Looking back, it wasn't easy, but we gave it everything we had.

That journey taught me a great deal, and I'm forever grateful for the tremendous support we received from Transocean. Once we introduced the E-Colours system, emphasising strengths, potential limiters, and the impact on safety, things started to fall into place. Work soon flowed in from Africa and the UK, and an energy company began to take notice. What began in Nigeria quickly expanded across the globe. Equilibria grew rapidly, expanding into multiple industries and building a strong client base that included companies such as Transocean, Chevron, BP, Songa, Noble, Shelf Drilling, Halliburton, Schlumberger, Baker Hughes, Houston Super Bowl, CVX Energy, Stena Drilling, Pacific Drilling, GSK, QinetiQ, Expanse Electrical, Houston Zoo, American Liberty Hotels, Siemens, Alotten Inc, Methodist Hospitals, Sodexo, Gladiator Energy, SLB, Transdev Airport Services, Emergency Medical Services, Christ Church School Singapore, and many more.

It would be remiss not to mention one of our greatest champions, someone we often called 'our number one client,' Rob Weakley, Red/Yellow. His words appear at the end of this chapter. Rob, who was Drilling Manager for Nigeria and Thailand at an energy company, was a constant source of support during those early years. He believed in what we were building, and his encouragement played a key role in our journey. From all of us at Equilibria, we owe him a debt of gratitude. He was both an inspiration and instrumental in the development and delivery of the E-Colours & Personal Intervention materials.

I must also mention Dave Payne, Red/Yellow, who was appointed Vice President of an energy company, Drilling and Completions, almost immediately after we launched Equilibria. Once he saw what we could offer his organisation, he quickly took me on as his coach and thinking partner – a relationship we maintained until his retirement over 17 years later. Dave not only encouraged us to expand our sphere of influence in his world but also strongly supported our work in schools. He truly embraced strategic business partnering, and over the years, that partnership opened the door to many opportunities to deliver world-class programmes and processes benefiting people around the globe.

When asked about our clients, I speak with genuine enthusiasm. They've been a profound source of inspiration as we've pursued our vision of *REALISING POTENTIAL* and our purpose of *PEOPLE FIRST*. Their feedback has been invaluable in guiding the creation of bespoke solutions tailored to individuals across various sectors. Our unwavering focus on improving safety in the oil and gas industry is reflected in tools such as 'How Can I Get Hurt?' We'll explore this further in Chapter 12. The collaboration and ideas shared by our clients have helped shape a deeper understanding of the many ways personality diversity can positively impact lives.

For me personally, as a Yellow/Red Doing Socialiser, this journey has always been about legacy. Helping people and staying true to my purpose have kept me grounded and motivated at every stage.

You can read more from Dave in Chapter 14 – Real Time Legacy.

The Power of Partnerships

Partnerships are instrumental in achieving success, especially when they bring together complementary strengths to tackle complex challenges. Over the past decade, our collaboration with Fisher Improvement Technologies – FIT at www.improvewithfit.com – has exemplified this potential. Together, we have seamlessly integrated Equilibria's personality diversity technology, expressed through E-Colours & Personal Intervention, into the field of human and organisational performance science. This collaboration has played a key role in enhancing workplace safety, streamlining processes to minimise human error, and driving transformative organisational change. By combining FIT's expertise in Human and Organisational Performance (HOP) with our knowledge of personality dynamics – what we call AERO, or Advanced Error Reduction in Organisations – we have developed strategies that not only improve operational efficiency but also save lives. Our shared dedication to making a positive, lasting impact on individuals and companies, both large and small, continues to thrive through this enduring partnership.

Rob's Story

> *We joined forces with Equilibria and started using the E-Colors about 10 years ago to bring to light the fact that people see and manage risk differently, and that each of us, with our personality tendencies, tends to go at risk, all different styles of risk, from a different perspective.*
>
> *– Rob Fisher* (Yellow/Blue)
> – President, Fisher Improvement Technologies, USA

With a Little Help from Our Friends

At Equilibria, one of our core attributes has always been listening actively to client feedback as they interact with our technology and using their reflections to enhance our offerings. Many of the ways E-Colours has positively impacted others are the direct result of thoughtful suggestions from engaged participants.

For example, one participant asked, 'How can I get hurt?' That simple question inspired us to explore new practical applications focused on personal safety and more informed decision-making, further demonstrating the real-world effectiveness of our tools.

Other examples of client-driven innovations include replacing terms like 'weaknesses' or 'improvement opportunities' with 'potential limiters' – a term more aligned with positive growth. During one of our early diversity and inclusion workshops, another participant suggested using 'Personality Diversity Indicator' (PDI) instead of 'test' – a recommendation we implemented immediately.

The 'Wells' analogy (see Chapter 12), which visually represents the four personality styles, also came from a client. It emerged during a Train-the-Trainer session and made the concept more relatable for many people.

Our children's version of the E-Colours materials was inspired by students who mentioned that, while the content was engaging, it was still presented in adult language. Over a single weekend, a passionate group of students, parents, and teachers collaborated to create a student-friendly edition of the E-Colours & Personal Intervention Pocketbook.

The concept of 'tactical empathy' came from a client with a military background, who highlighted its importance in high-pressure scenarios like hostage negotiations – even for those who don't naturally score high in empathy. This methodology is now part of our broader approach.

The E-Colours ethics framework was developed in collaboration with an anchor client who noticed the methodology being used in unintended ways within their organisation. A working group of clients and Equilibria coaches came together to create guidelines that ensure the responsible, ethical use of E-Colours in any setting.

To each of you, we are hugely grateful.

From Technical Expert to Trusted Leader – A Story from Lewis Senior

Four years ago, I was approached by the head of a large organisation to coach a highly intelligent and experienced subject matter expert. He was extremely well-regarded for his technical ability, but every time his name came up for promotion to a team lead role, the feedback was the same: 'He's brilliant technically, but he's not good with people.' As an intentional leadership coach, my task was to help him bridge that gap.

His E-Colours were predominantly Green/Red, meaning he was intensely focused on detail, data, and logical precision. Understanding this helped me tailor my approach – speaking in ways that matched his mindset. I could see that with the right tools and guidance, there was no reason he couldn't become a strong leader while retaining his technical strengths.

Over 18 months, we met regularly and explored how his personality, expressed through E-Colours, influenced his communication and relationships. Each session focused on helping him tailor his approach to better connect with others. These conversations often extended into his personal life, including relationships at home. Gradually, people at work began noticing a change in how he engaged with his team, and he was eventually promoted to team lead.

His performance in that role was so strong that, within another year, he was offered the opportunity to lead part of the organisation in a different country. From the outset, I had challenged him to shift from using the word 'but' to 'and' – to be recognised *not* only for his technical skills, *but also* for his people skills.

One of the most humbling moments of my career came when he called me after an interview for the new role. He told me that the HR business partner had looked him in the eye and said, 'We know your people skills are top-class. Do you have any technical ability as well?' It was a full-circle moment – proof of his transformation and a reminder of the power of intentional coaching, using the E-Colours and related tools to produce lasting, meaningful outcomes.

The E-Colours of Unity – A Story from Lewis Senior

Throughout *Personalities Remixed*, you'll see how the E-Colours framework has positively impacted various parts of society. I vividly remember being invited in 2015 to meet Sallie Sargent, CEO of the Houston Super Bowl Host Committee. Our goal was to support her newly formed team in creating a memorable Super Bowl 51 experience in 2017 – one that would benefit not just the event itself but also the city of Houston.

Sallie was no stranger to the Super Bowl. Her previous successes in securing bids for cities had made her a powerhouse in the sports world. She was determined to make Super Bowl 51 a defining part of her legacy. In our first meeting, I grasped her vision for the event, which went far beyond logistics. She wanted to foster community spirit and inclusivity, ensuring the Super Bowl resonated deeply with Houston's diverse population.

As we discussed the possibility of working together, I set two conditions: I didn't want any tickets to the game, and I wouldn't charge for my services. Sallie, whose E-Colours are predominantly Green/Red, was visibly moved by my commitment to the cause. It marked the beginning of a meaningful partnership and lasting friendship.

Over the next two years, we worked closely with the host committee, an experience that was both humbling and exhilarating. Our main focus was training over 10,000 volunteers to communicate effectively with the public and with one another using the E-Colours framework. This training helped create a cohesive and welcoming atmosphere leading up to the event.

Sallie navigated numerous discussions with the NFL, securing our place as an official partner of the host committee. This was a groundbreaking moment, as no coaching company had previously been involved in this way. Being embedded with the team gave us the opportunity to introduce our student E-Colour champions to the NFL experience. We reached out to neighbourhoods that typically had limited access to major events, creating opportunities for children aged eight and up to teach others about the power of E-Colours.

The collaboration led to extraordinary experiences. Young students – our E-Colour champions – took part in various activities, including the televised distribution of uniforms to the 10,000 volunteers. They were actively involved in the final week's festivities, contributing to an event that drew more than 1.5 million visitors to Discovery Green in downtown Houston.

As the Super Bowl approached, we witnessed the transformative impact of our work. The E-Colour champions gained access to parts of society that had once felt out of reach and, in turn, instilled pride and a stronger sense of belonging in their communities.

Years have passed since that monumental event, but I still feel a deep sense of gratitude every time someone in Houston recognises me as 'the E-Colours guy from the Super Bowl.' Their stories and reflections remind me of the impact we made and reinforce the idea that the power of unity can truly change lives.

Looking back on those years with the host committee, I'm humbled by the lives we touched and the friendships we built. The success of Super Bowl 51 was about far more than football – it was about community, connection, and the enduring legacy of the E-Colours. Our work showed that with the right tools and a shared vision, we can bridge divides and create a vibrant tapestry of experiences that honour the heart and spirit of a city.

Mark and Emma Wilkinson – A Story from Mark Wilkinson

When I first met Emma, it felt like her calm, empathetic presence filled the room before I even knew much about her. She had a natural steadiness, a quiet way of observing that seemed almost effortless. Her kindness and compassion – her Blue E-Colour – felt like the missing piece that balanced my livelier, more optimistic side.

As we got to know each other, I began to see her remarkable attention to detail, how she considered everything with precision and care, a classic Green E-Colour tendency. I used to joke that she caught every little thing I missed – Eagle-Eyed

Emma – and I loved that about her. It was like we each brought something the other didn't have. She kept me grounded and focused, while I brought energy, spontaneity, and action into her world through my Yellow/Red style.

In many ways, our personalities were opposites. But right from the beginning, we found a rhythm. That natural balance has only grown stronger over time. Now, 11 years later, it's that same complementarity that keeps us connected and fulfilled. Together, we're proof that E-Colour opposites really can make an unbeatable team.

Nuala's Story

From a young age, I have had the privilege of working with and engaging with personality diversity tools to understand myself and others, and to learn and grow to be a better version of myself. I recall with joy the first time I reviewed a profile describing me and thinking, This is amazing! I wish everyone could learn about themselves – that we are different, not difficult. What a more peaceful and fulfilled world we could live in.

What I found challenging about the earlier tools I worked with was the 'stickability' and ease of relating to others. Fast-forward to my business partner introducing me to E-Colours, and my joy in becoming a certified practitioner. Whether I use this tool at work, with my family, or with friends, it is an excellent catalyst for inspiring conversations that allow us to live intentionally. Most importantly, it is easy to understand and relate to. In a work context, this makes E-Colours a game-changer!

Understanding my tendencies as a Relating Socialiser allows me to embrace my strengths, adapt to those around me, and be conscious of how I respond.

The more we understand ourselves and others, the safer, more efficient, and better work environments are co-created!

– *Nuala Gage* (Yellow/Blue)
– E-Colours Practitioner & Leadership Coach, South Africa

Sallie's Story

Every city is different, and Houston is all about its people. We wanted to showcase and celebrate that, and we needed our front-line ambassadors to be representatives for the city. When you bring a team like this together from all kinds of backgrounds, we needed help to get everyone on the same page and to learn how to work together to become one team. By adding Equilibria's E-Colors programme to the volunteer training, it taught people how to communicate with each other and, of course, with the one million plus visitors that enjoyed the downtown activities and events pre-Super Bowl.

– *Sallie Sargent* (Green/Red)
– CEO, Houston Super Bowl Host Committee, USA

Rob's Story

By indoctrinating all our business partners – an oil and gas business – in the use of the E-Colors as a way of working together as a united team, we were able to achieve the best safety record in the corporation and the industry.

> *The added benefits resulted in business partners visiting one another's facilities and sharing ideas, business partners loaning their competitors critical equipment to keep their operations going, and the setting of new records for the reduction of well construction costs.*
>
> *In my view the E-Colors should be taught in school to kids as a way of life.*
>
> – Rob Weakley (Red/Yellow)
– Retired Drilling Manager, USA

Sana's Story

> *Happy, happy anniversary, Equilibria. I am so happy for you on this huge milestone – 20 years of helping leaders around the world to help themselves and others bring their best selves to work. You've had such an impact on me and completely changed the way I lead, and how I listen and communicate with others.*
>
> – Sana A. Manjeshwar (Yellow/Red)
– Global Ombuds Leader, USA

Mark's Story

> *Thanks to Equilibria – not only for 20 years, but also for making people better. You have made me better, and many of the people at Chevron better, which is why I appreciate you so much. As someone whose E-Colors are Red/Green, I always wanted to know about the actions you made us take in the different parts of the Chevron portfolio. But most of all, I appreciate how*

we can all learn about ourselves. Thank you for staying intentional.

— *Mark Nelson* (Red/Green)
— Vice Chairman, Chevron, USA

* * *

Remix Opportunities

- Capture early wins and positive stories from E-Colours information and training sessions.

- Embed E-Colours into your training and coaching programmes, your company inductions, and your learning and development initiatives.

CHAPTER 4

THE IMPORTANCE OF EQUILIBRIA'S ETHICS

'Ethics is knowing the difference between what you have a right to do and what is right to do. Our ability to reach unity in diversity will be the beauty and the test of our civilization.'

– **Albert Einstein (1879–1955)**, German-born theoretical physicist widely recognised as one of the most influential minds of the 20th century

The Importance of Ethics in Personality Diversity

Ethics are not a constraint – they are a compass. They don't limit us; they liberate us to bring out the best in ourselves and others.

At the heart of every breakthrough, whether within a team, a family, or an entire organisation, lies one simple truth: trust. And trust begins with ethics. As we navigate the dynamic terrain of personality diversity, we must ask not only what is possible but what is right. In a world that often moves too fast and decides too quickly, Equilibria chooses to pause – to reflect, to listen, and to build something designed to stand the test of time.

From its very inception, Equilibria was never meant to be just another personality tool. It was born from a bold vision: to empower people not to be boxed in by labels but to be uplifted through deeper understanding – of ourselves and of others. And to do so ethically. This chapter is a testament to that commitment – a declaration that understanding ourselves and one another comes with responsibility. We've observed that Personality Diversity without ethics can be dangerous – but with them, it becomes truly transformative.

Equilibria's ethics are not about restriction; they are the foundation of respect, the guideposts for growth, and the safeguards that ensure personality diversity becomes a bridge, not a barrier. As you turn these pages, we invite you to explore how a principled approach to personality diversity and self-awareness can spark collaboration, fuel innovation, and unlock the true potential within every person and every team.

When ethics lead the way, unity in diversity isn't just an ideal – it becomes reality.

In contemporary society, the importance of ethics in both workplace and social interactions cannot be overstated. As organisations and communities grow increasingly diverse, the integration of different personality styles presents both opportunities and challenges. At Equilibria, we learned that effectively leveraging personality diversity requires a strong ethical framework – one that ensures all individuals are respected, valued, and given equal opportunities to contribute. We will explore the importance of ethics when leveraging personality diversity, examining their role in promoting inclusivity, enhancing collaboration, and encouraging creativity and innovation.

Understanding Personality Diversity

When properly applied, personality diversity enhances the workplace by bringing a range of perspectives to problem-solving and decision-making. This often results in more creative and innovative outcomes, as individuals with different personality styles approach challenges in distinctive ways. However, harnessing this diversity effectively requires an ethical approach to maximize the benefits while minimising any potential conflicts and misunderstandings.

Challenges

During Equilibria's early work with the E-Colours, it became clear that personality tools could be misapplied. To avoid misuse, a set of ethical guidelines was co-created with input from both coaches and clients, ensuring the E-Colours would be used strictly for their intended purpose.

Historically, other tools, such as the Myers-Briggs Type Indicator (MBTI), developed during World War II, were used to assign individuals to roles based on personality traits. While this method may have been effective in its time, it would today be regarded as discriminatory. Despite this, similar psychometric tools are still sometimes used in recruitment processes, potentially disadvantaging some candidates.

Taking a forward-thinking and ethical stance, the founders of Equilibria chose a different route. They positioned the E-Colours as a coaching tool designed to help individuals and teams identify and manage their strengths and potential limiters. This empowering approach enables people to thrive in any role they choose, unlocking their potential and supporting both personal and professional growth.

The Ethical Imperative

Ethics, when applied to personality diversity, involves principles that promote fair and respectful treatment for everyone, regardless of their personality tendencies. It rests on the values of equality, inclusivity, respect, and integrity – all of which are vital for creating environments where diverse personalities can thrive and contribute meaningfully.

Promoting Inclusivity

Inclusivity is a key ethical principle that values the unique contributions of people with varied personality tendencies. In an inclusive environment, individuals feel free to express their authentic selves without fear of judgement or discrimination, leading to greater happiness, engagement, and overall wellbeing.

Some individuals prefer quiet, solitary environments, while others thrive in more collaborative, social settings. To support all members of a team, particularly in the post-COVID era, ethical leaders can design work environments that cater to different needs. This might include offering remote work options, creating quiet spaces, encouraging team building and awareness activities, providing coaching opportunities, and improving communication channels across the organisation.

Enhancing Collaboration

Effective collaboration is essential for any organisation, and ethics play a vital role in fostering a healthy collaborative culture.

When people feel respected and valued, they are more inclined to engage in open and honest communication, share ideas, and work collectively towards shared goals.

Ethical collaboration means deliberately seeking and valuing input from individuals with a range of personality styles. This includes creating equitable opportunities for all voices to be heard, addressing power imbalances, and avoiding unconscious bias that may favour particular tendencies. For example, during meetings, ethical leaders can ensure that all team members can contribute as they would like to, perhaps by incorporating written feedback mechanisms or rotating facilitation roles.

Encouraging Innovation

Innovation flourishes in environments where diverse perspectives and diversity of thought are not only welcomed but actively valued. Ethical leadership helps foster a culture of openness, curiosity, and continuous learning. It also creates a psychologically safe space where individuals feel empowered to take risks and share new ideas without fear of retribution. Building and sustaining this culture of safety is a core responsibility of ethical leaders. By embracing personality diversity, organisations can unlock a broader range of creative solutions and approaches from every team member.

An ethical approach to encouraging innovation includes recognising and addressing biases that may limit creativity. For example, individuals with unconventional ideas might be dismissed or overlooked in biased environments. Ethical leaders can actively challenge such bias and cultivate a culture where different perspectives are celebrated. This could involve encouraging anonymous idea submissions, employing an E-Colours

Coach to train staff to become E-Colours Practitioners, or forming cross-functional teams with varied personality styles.

Ethical Challenges in Managing Personality Diversity

While the ethical management of personality diversity brings many benefits, it also presents several challenges. These require thoughtful consideration and proactive strategies to address challenges effectively.

Bias and Stereotyping

Bias and stereotyping remain significant ethical challenges. Preconceived notions about certain personality tendencies can lead to unfair treatment and discrimination. For instance, quieter individuals may be wrongly perceived as less capable leaders, while those who are more outspoken might be seen as naturally better in social situations.

Overcoming these assumptions requires ongoing education and awareness. Ethical leaders can implement training that highlights the value of different personality tendencies and helps to challenge harmful stereotypes. In addition, organisations can adopt objective performance metrics and feedback systems to ensure individuals are evaluated on their actual contributions rather than assumptions linked to personality.

Balancing Individual Needs and Organisational Goals

Another ethical challenge lies in balancing individual needs with organisational goals. While it is important to support diverse personality tendencies, accommodations must still align with broader objectives and available resources. For instance, flexible working arrangements may benefit some employees but be harder to implement in certain roles or industries.

Ethical leaders can choose to engage in open dialogue with employees to understand their needs and explore mutually beneficial solutions. This includes transparent communication around constraints and a willingness to find creative ways to support diverse personalities. For example, a company might offer flexible hours or provide tools for remote collaboration while still meeting productivity targets.

Conflict Resolution

Conflict is inevitable in any diverse environment, and ethical conflict resolution is key to maintaining a positive, inclusive culture. Clashes stemming from personality differences can be particularly challenging, as they may reflect deep-seated preferences and behaviours.

Most of us have likely heard of, or experienced, a 'personality clash' at work, in teams, or among friends.

Ethical conflict resolution involves addressing issues promptly, fairly, and with empathy. Leaders can create safe spaces where individuals feel comfortable voicing concerns and encourage open dialogue to uncover root causes. The goal is to find solutions that honour the needs and perspectives of all personality styles involved. Mediation support and conflict resolution training can help leaders and team members alike develop the skills to navigate these situations constructively.

USA Women's Water Polo Team – A Story from Lewis Senior

In 2010, while running a leadership programme for an anchor client, one of the participants approached me during a break and said he thought his daughter could benefit from our coaching in personality diversity and intentional leadership. At the time, she was captain of a California university water polo team and a silver medallist from the 2008 Beijing Olympics. I agreed to connect with her, and over the next year, we had several conversations about her journey as both a team leader and an Olympic athlete.

Leading up to the London Olympics, she invited me to visit their training facility in California. Seeing the opportunity, I arranged for several of our student 'E-Colour Champions' from Houston, along with their school principal, to join me. These students had never travelled outside Texas, which made the visit especially memorable. Thanks to the coach's support, we held an E-Colours workshop with the team just a few weeks before the Olympics.

The session was remarkable. These elite athletes found surprising parallels between themselves and the 7 to 12-year-old students who had joined us. A standout moment came when two players, both Red/Yellow, realised their occasional friction came from shared tendencies. Their newfound understanding transformed their relationship completely – they went from just tolerating each other to high-fiving and laughing together over their common ground.

A few weeks later, the team went on to win gold in London. They sent us thank-you videos and notes, and many of them stayed together for the 2016 Rio Olympics. We were once again invited to spend time with them before that event, which ended in another gold.

While their achievements were undoubtedly the result of tireless effort and training, I like to think that our work played a small part in helping them appreciate their unique strengths and better understand each other, giving them an edge that set them apart from their competitors.

Strategies for Ethical Management of Personality Diversity

To effectively manage personality diversity, organisations can adopt ethical strategies that promote inclusivity, collaboration, and innovation. The following strategies provide a roadmap for fostering an ethical and diverse workplace.

Leadership Commitment

Ethical management of personality diversity begins with leadership commitment. Leaders must model ethical behaviour and demonstrate a genuine effort to value and leverage diverse personalities. This includes setting clear expectations, supporting inclusive policies, and holding themselves and others accountable for ethical conduct.

Intentional leaders can also prioritise their own growth and awareness by seeking training, coaching, and mentorship to deepen their understanding of personality diversity and ethical leadership. By living these values, leaders can inspire a culture of respect, inclusion, and psychological safety across the organisation.

Comprehensive Training Programmes

Training programmes are essential for raising awareness and building skills around personality diversity and ethics. Equilibria's programmes cover topics such as unconscious bias, communication, conflict resolution, and intentional leadership – all through the lens of E-Colours and personality diversity. Training and coaching must be ongoing and tailored to the needs of each organisation and its people.

In the spirit of inclusion, we recognise that some E-Colours combinations do not respond well to role-playing exercises. However, interactive workshops featuring team-building tasks, games, and real-life case studies can still help participants gain a stronger understanding of the challenges and opportunities that come with personality diversity. Providing resources such as reading materials, online courses, and access to experienced coaches also supports continuous development.

Inclusive Policies and Practices

Organisations can implement policies that promote inclusion and the ethical management of personality diversity. This includes creating flexible work arrangements, offering professional development opportunities, and establishing clear guidelines for respectful behaviour and conflict resolution. Such practices help create safe and harmonious working environments – spaces where people enjoy what they do, work effectively, and ultimately, over a period of time, deliver productivity and positive results for the company.

Regular assessments of these policies and practices are essential to ensure their effectiveness and identify areas for improvement. Gathering ongoing feedback from employees is a practical way to refine and enhance organisational approaches to personality diversity.

Diverse Teams and Collaborative Structures

Leveraging the diversity already present within teams is a practical way to drive innovation and success. Organisations can intentionally support teams in recognising and applying the full range of personality tendencies in their group, ensuring that diverse perspectives are present in decision-making processes.

Cross-functional teams, rotating leadership roles, and collaborative projects are effective ways to facilitate idea exchange and build mutual understanding across different personality styles. In addition, providing informal platforms, such as social events or team-building activities, can help deepen relationships and foster a greater sense of shared purpose.

Transparent Communication

Transparent communication is a cornerstone of ethical leadership. Organisations that create clear and open channels for communication – and ensure that every employee has access to information and an opportunity to voice their opinions and concerns – tend to enjoy increased success and lower attrition rates.

Regular updates from leadership, open forums, and feedback mechanisms all help support transparency. Ethical leaders make it a point to actively listen, address concerns with empathy, and involve employees in decisions that affect their work and wellbeing.

Starbucks – A Story from Lewis Senior

In customer-facing industries, the E-Colours can be a powerful tool. Here's a perfect example. I've always been drawn to the idea of 'Cappuccino Coaching,' a concept I explored in my writing some years ago. It's about learning leadership lessons from the act of sharing a coffee – creating spaces where real conversations happen, people feel seen, and genuine connections are made. Starbucks once embodied this idea. It wasn't just about coffee; it was about offering a moment of pause and connection in a busy world. Its true success came not only from its product or market share but also from the community it fostered.

Through my work with Equilibria, I've seen how understanding personality diversity can transform an organisation. If Starbucks were to embrace fully such a framework, it could discover new ways to connect deeply with customers and staff alike.

Interestingly, years ago, Starbucks introduced the 'Little Green Apron Book' for employees. It was a brilliant idea that seemed to reflect an understanding of the four personality styles. Each section of the book catered to a specific style: the 'Red' pages simply read 'Know Coffee'; the 'Green' pages were full of structured processes; the 'Blue' pages shared the story of coffee and its positive impact on communities; and the 'Yellow' pages were left blank, inviting creativity. It was a thoughtful approach, one that recognised the different ways people relate to information and ideas.

Starbucks has always thrived on its ability to adapt and its willingness to listen to its audience. With the support of intentional leadership, the brand could reaffirm its position as a space where every individual feels valued – not only as a customer but as a person. We would love to see their E-Colours displayed on their aprons to help engage all those individuals.

The E-Colours Ethics
Guiding Principles:

- All E-Colours combinations are valuable – no E-Colour combination is better than any other.
- Our E-Colours are not an excuse for unacceptable behaviour – realise your potential by tapping into your strengths and managing your potential limiters.

Guiding Ethics:

- Resist the temptation to guess and tell people which E-Colours we think represent their personality style. Provide individuals with the opportunity to discover their personality style for themselves through the E-Colours Personality Diversity Indicator (PDI).
- Advocate that people should never falsify answers to the E-Colours PDI survey for perceived gain.
- Insist that there should be no discrimination against any E-Colour combination, nor should someone's E-Colours be used as a reason for exclusion.
- Highlight that it is outside the ethics to imply that one E-Colour combination is superior to another.
- Inform individuals and organisations that the E-Colours were not created to determine job placement or assign roles based on someone's E-Colours.

This set of ethics around the use of personality diversity ensures that Equilibria and the E-Colours stand apart from the crowd of other personality tools available and remain true to the organisation's core values.

We do not authorise the E-Colours to be used as a profiling tool. Equilibria and the E-Colours represent a positive coaching experience for individuals and teams – designed to help them remix their lives and improve their work, relationships, and results.

Adopting An Ethical Approach

We support companies globally in a variety of ways, adapting and integrating into each organisation's processes and procedures. When asked, we recommend the following sequence as an ethical approach to introducing E-Colours and personality diversity for new starters.

1. Pass the interview.
2. Get the job.
3. Receive a company induction.
4. Receive the organisation's induction.
5. Discover your E-Colours.
6. Attend an E-Colours awareness session.
7. Share your E-Colours within your team.
8. Join your team, who are already leveraging and appreciating diversity of thought expressed through the E-Colours.

The Ethical Management of Personality Diversity

In Mark's Institute of Leadership (IoL) accredited Life Remixed Coaching and Equilibria's Intentional Leadership and Team Coaching, all incoming clients complete their E-Colours questionnaire as the first step on their journey. These sessions focus on self-awareness, reading, understanding, and discussing their E-Colours Premium Reports – including their personal strengths and potential limiters – and serve as a fast track to improved communication.

The ethical management of personality diversity is essential for creating inclusive, collaborative, and innovative environments. By promoting inclusivity, enhancing collaboration, and encouraging innovation, ethical leaders can unlock the full potential of diverse personalities. However, this requires a commitment to address ethical challenges, including bias, balancing individual needs with organisational goals, and managing conflict effectively.

Through leadership commitment, comprehensive training programmes, inclusive policies, diverse teams, and transparent communication, organisations can build a culture that values and leverages personality diversity. In doing so, they can unlock the benefits of diverse perspectives, drive organisational success, and contribute to a more equitable and inclusive society.

By adopting our ethical approach, Equilibria offers individuals, teams, and organisations the opportunity to break free from the limitations they may have unintentionally placed on themselves and others. We provide the tools and support needed to realise everyone's full potential. Our personality styles can sometimes limit our growth if we continually reinforce our natural tendencies without seeking to expand our capabilities.

For example, if you're naturally a good planner – a common tendency of a top E-Colour Green – and are consistently praised for this strength, you may repeatedly take on planning roles. While this can be beneficial, it may also prevent you from developing other skills, such as people management. Though this area may lie outside your comfort zone, not developing it could restrict your future potential. An ethical approach provides opportunities for each of us to go beyond our natural capabilities and comfort zones.

Ethics are fundamental when applying personality diversity. Equilibria's Ethics offer a framework that helps ensure people's contributions are respected and valued, nurtures a sense of belonging, and maintains a culture of continuous learning and innovation. As individuals, organisations, and communities continue to evolve, the ethical management of personality diversity will remain a key factor in achieving sustainable success and broader social harmony.

The Team That Worked Together – A Story from Mark Wilkinson

At a large energy company known for its safety standards and rigorous project deadlines, an engineering team was brought together to work on a high-risk project. The project manager, Sarah, was passionate not only about meeting deadlines but also about creating an inclusive, ethical environment that valued each team member's personality strengths and individual needs. Sarah had recently attended a training session on personality diversity using the Equilibria E-Colours and was eager to apply what she had learned with her team.

During their first meeting, Sarah introduced Equilibria and the E-Colours model, explaining how each person's unique combination and percentage of E-Colours – based on the four main colours: Yellow for socialising tendencies; Green for thinking, planning and structure; Red for doing and action; and Blue for empathy and care – could reveal valuable team strengths as well as opportunities for growth. She also emphasised the importance of respecting these differences ethically, allowing people to feel valued rather than categorised, and reinforcing the distinction between personality 'styles' and 'type'. Her aim was to ensure the model would help the team collaborate more effectively, while also protecting each member's individuality and autonomy.

As each person completed their E-Colours questionnaire, Sarah observed a wide range of personalities. Tom, an enthusiastic engineer, led with Yellow/Red tendencies and was always eager to share ideas and take quick action. Lisa, the lead safety officer, had Green/Blue tendencies and preferred thoughtful analysis and structure. Meanwhile, Juan, a project architect, had a balanced Red/Blue combination – often thoughtful but ready to act when needed.

The ethical challenges of personality diversity soon became apparent. Tom wanted to jump straight into decision-making, at times overlooking critical details. Lisa, who preferred thorough analysis, felt uncomfortable with his fast-paced approach. Juan, with his balanced nature, often found himself mediating between the two. Recognising the potential for friction, Sarah introduced the E-Colours model as a way to help team members understand and appreciate one another's perspectives.

Sarah held a team session to explore ethical guidelines for using personality awareness. Together they established a code of conduct, emphasising that the E-Colours must never be used to stereotype or limit anyone. In fact, the opposite was true – the tool was there to support individual development and help the team realise its collective potential. Sarah made it clear that everyone's unique perspective was a strength, not a label. The aim was to build trust and respect by encouraging people to contribute authentically, not to change who they were.

As the project progressed, this ethical foundation made a real difference. Tom began checking in with Lisa before making big decisions, allowing her to provide the structure and detail he sometimes overlooked. Lisa, in turn, learned to rely on Tom's action-oriented nature when speed was essential. Juan, now more aware of his Red/Blue strengths, found himself not only bridging the gap between team members but also bringing valuable perspectives that balanced thoughtfulness with decisive execution.

By the time the project was completed, the team had not only achieved its goals but had also grown more cohesive and connected. Each person felt respected for their individual strengths and appreciated for their contributions. Sarah's ethical approach to the E-Colours had transformed a potentially challenging group dynamic into a powerful example of what personality diversity, when used ethically, can achieve.

The project wasn't just a success on paper – it was a success in the experience of each team member. It fostered a positive, supportive environment where everyone felt they belonged. And it all stemmed from Sarah's commitment to using personality awareness as a tool for respect and growth.

By respecting and ethically applying the E-Colours, Sarah's team showed how understanding personality diversity can improve collaboration, enhance safety, and support meaningful personal and professional growth.

A Proactive Approach to the E-Colours Ethics

It is always encouraging when an organisation requests a customised workshop focused on one of Equilibria's technologies. Such was the case recently in the UK with QinetiQ, who asked for a working session for their team built around the E-Colours framework, with an emphasis on ethical decision-making and the influence of personality diversity. The primary goal was to align individual tendencies with team values and ethical standards. Below is an overview of the exercise components.

1. **Ethical Dilemmas Discussion**

   Participants explored ethical dilemmas related to personality diversity. Key points included:
   - How these dilemmas relate to E-Colours Ethics.
   - The influence of individual tendencies, based on E-Colours, on ethical decision-making.
   - The use of Personal Intervention – PAUSE & PLAY – to act ethically and stay aligned with team values.

2. **Group Feedback**
   - Each group shared their scenarios and ideas with the wider team.
   - Discussions highlighted:
     - Potential biases or ethical challenges revealed in the scenarios.
     - Strategies for upholding E-Colours Ethics in similar real-world situations.

3. **Ethics in Action Plan**
   - Teams were divided into three groups to co-create an actionable plan, focusing on:
     - Five commitments for applying E-Colours ethically in decision-making and behaviour.
     - A Personal Intervention Protocol to identify and respond to ethical drift.

- ○ A communication strategy to support respectful dialogue around E-Colours, reinforcing commitment without implying superiority or exclusion.

4. **Personal Reflection**
   - Participants reflected on:
     - ○ Recent situations where E-Colours Ethics could have been applied more effectively.
     - ○ Personal actions they can take to ensure their E-Colours tendencies help strengthen the team and uphold ethical integrity.

5. **Debrief**
   - Reflections centred on:
     - ○ The importance of sustaining E-Colours Ethics.
     - ○ Shifts in perspective regarding the ethical use of personality tendencies.

This workshop provided QinetiQ with practical tools and ideas to integrate E-Colours Ethics into their team dynamics, fostering both ethical integrity and respectful collaboration.

ETHICS ACTION PLAN
QINETIQ
UK Safety Team

Commitment

HONOR EVERY PERSONALITY, EMPOWER EVERY VOICE.

H onesty in self discovery

O peness in diverse personalities

N o discrimination based on E-Colours

O ne value for all E-Colour combinations

R espect for ethical use of E-Colours

Personal Intervention Protocol

Protocol steps for when we notice unethical behaviours were not agreed.

However, we are clear in our intention of setting the expectation and that everyone is responsible for upholding our agreed ethical values.

So what would that look like to each of us individually?

How would we like to call this behaviour in and coach each other through it?

Communication Strategy

- Discuss buy in.
- This is a TOOL in the tool bag.
- We are all equal to bring our strength together to make our company better.

HOW? Wear our E-Colours;
- Hard hats
- Lanyards
- Desk
- Media
- Training

Figure 5 – QinetiQ & Equilibria Ethics Action Plan
Copyright © 2025 Equilibria Services Pte Ltd. All rights reserved.

Marie-Louise's Story

> A fantastic E-Colours session that has really helped my team to become more aware of our tendencies and improve how we interact with each other. E-Colours is a simple, effective tool that can help teams build upon their strengths and identify areas where they may need support, coaching, or training as part of their development. I highly recommend E-Colours if you want to link your tendencies with safety – it's a real eye-opener. I'm really seeing the difference in the way the team interacts and how they now have a common language to speak about their tendencies and potential limiters. It was a really engaging session. Thank you. Great work!
>
> *– Marie-Louise Chandler* (Blue/Yellow)
> – Safety Director, QinetiQ UK

Anne's Story

> Twenty years ago, I was told by a trainer of another personality tool that I would never be a great leader because I did not display the tendencies of a Red (Doer). Now, through understanding the E-Colours & Personal Intervention, I've learned that anyone can be a great leader by understanding themselves and learning to manage their strengths and potential limiters.
>
> *– Anne* (Green/Yellow)
> – Leader, Digital Marketing, UK

* * *

Remix Opportunities

- Understand and apply the Equilibria Ethics.
- Set up an Ethics exercise within your own team.
- Appreciate that everyone, and every personality style, has value.

CHAPTER 5

STRENGTHS & POTENTIAL LIMITERS

'Strength lies in differences, not in similarities.'

– **Stephen Covey**, American educator, author, businessman, and keynote speaker

Stephen Covey was best known for his book *The 7 Habits of Highly Effective People.* This quote highlights how diversity in strengths and perspectives among individuals can lead to greater overall success and innovation, reinforcing the value of recognising and leveraging both strengths and potential challenges in diverse personalities.

Bob Proctor – Some Thoughts from Mark Wilkinson

Bob Proctor, a renowned philosopher and success coach who built his career inspired by Napoleon Hill's classic book *Think and Grow Rich*, often emphasised the importance of understanding one's own strengths and weaknesses during his seminars and coaching sessions. I remember thinking, 'But how am I supposed to know that?' That question was answered when I completed the online Equilibria questionnaire and received my first Yellow/Blue report. It clearly identified my strengths and, beautifully, my 'potential limiters'. I quickly realised this was a fast track to self-awareness, and it will be incredible when more people can understand and apply it.

The Importance of Strengths in Embracing Personality Diversity

Knowing your strengths is powerful. Knowing your potential limiters – and choosing to grow through them – is transformational.

Imagine being handed a personal blueprint – not to tell you who you are, but to remind you of all you can become. That's the promise of understanding your E-Colours. Within each of us lies a rich mix of strengths waiting to be activated, and tendencies that, if left unchecked, can become hidden barriers. But here's the truth: every one of us has the power to choose awareness, to transform friction into flow, and to turn limitations into launchpads.

This chapter is about more than understanding personality – it's about unlocking potential. It's a reminder that what makes you – your optimism, your decisiveness, your empathy, your analytical mind – isn't accidental. It's essential. And when you pair self-awareness with intention, you step into the most powerful version of yourself.

But we don't stop at recognising what we're good at. We dare to look at what might hold us back – and meet it with courage, curiosity, and compassion. Because real strength lies not just in celebrating what's easy to see, but in owning what we're still working on. That's where the magic of personal growth happens.

Whether you're a leader seeking better ways to inspire, a parent wanting to connect more deeply, or simply someone curious about how to be your best self, this chapter invites you to reflect, reset, and remix. Because the moment you understand both your strengths and your potential limiters is the moment you begin to lead yourself intentionally.

Let's begin the journey of truly knowing ourselves – and, in doing so, give others permission to do the same.

In today's interconnected and rapidly evolving world, the significance of strengths in relation to personality diversity cannot be overstated. The following points explore how strengths enrich personality diversity and why understanding and leveraging them is essential for individual growth, team dynamics, and organisational success.

1. Defining Strengths and Personality Diversity

Strengths are the inherent capabilities, talents, and skills that individuals possess. For example, they can include natural tendencies from a personality perspective, such as:

- Analytical thinking – Green (Thinker)
- Supportive behaviours – Blue (Relator)
- Optimistic outlook – Yellow (Socialiser)
- Practical decisions – Red (Doer)

Some E-Colour personality styles are more likely to lead with:

- People focus – Yellow & Blue
- Task focus – Red & Green

Some personality styles tend to prefer:

- Action-oriented, fast-paced decisions – Red & Yellow
- Information-oriented, steady-paced decisions – Green & Blue

Personality diversity refers to the variety of personalities within a group, each bringing unique perspectives, behaviours, and approaches. What's important to recognise is that every personality style contributes strengths to the group. This diversity is rooted in differences of background, experience, and innate characteristics. E-Colours personality styles have helped bring couples, families, and working teams closer together. What follows is a perfect example.

E-Colours Impact in a Family Environment – Lewis Senior

One of the most remarkable benefits of the E-Colours framework is its ability to enhance family dynamics by fostering greater understanding and appreciation of different personality styles. A vivid example of this unfolded during one of our 'Seeing is Believing' experiential days at Cowboy Solution. Among the attendees was a family keen to help their teenage son and daughter gain a deeper understanding of their personalities and how these shaped their interactions as a family unit.

The father was predominantly Red/Green, the mother Red/Yellow, and the elder sister a blend of Red/Yellow and Yellow/Red. In contrast, the younger brother discovered his E-Colours were Blue/Green – a notable departure from the rest of the family. Throughout the day, he began to develop a clearer awareness of how his unique personality influenced his reactions to his parents and sister. For the first time, he could see why his perspective and demeanour often felt different from theirs.

By the end of the day, as the family prepared to leave, the usually quiet and introspective son walked to their car, then turned back to thank me again. He shared that, for the first time in his 18 years, he truly understood his parents and sister. It was a powerful and emotional moment that underscored the impact of self-awareness and mutual understanding.

Years later, we remain in touch. He still reaches out for advice and mentorship when he needs an outside perspective – a lasting testament to the transformative effect that day, and the E-Colours framework, had on his personal growth and family relationships.

2. Enhancing Individual Growth

Recognising and nurturing our strengths is essential for personal growth. When individuals understand their core strengths, they can use these abilities to overcome challenges, reach their goals, and pursue their passions. For example, someone with strong communication skills may thrive in roles involving negotiation, teaching, or public speaking. By focusing on their strengths, individuals often experience greater fulfilment and self-confidence, boosting motivation and engagement across different areas of life.

Additionally, recognising one's strengths allows for stronger alignment between personal and professional aspirations. This alignment creates more meaningful, rewarding experiences and reduces the risk of burnout. When individuals operate within their strengths, they are more likely to achieve a state of flow – a condition marked by deep focus and genuine enjoyment in their work.

3. Cultivating Effective Team Dynamics

In team settings, personality diversity is a powerful asset. Teams made up of individuals with different strengths tend to be more adaptive and innovative. Each team member contributes their unique abilities, leading to a more comprehensive and effective approach to solving problems. For example, a team with members who excel in strategic thinking, execution, relationship building, and influence is more likely to take a balanced and thorough approach to every project.

Diverse strengths also help cultivate a culture of collaboration and mutual respect. Teams that leverage a wide range of skills and perspectives are better equipped to manage conflict, as they can draw on their diverse perspectives to find creative and effective solutions.

How Our Personalities Can Disrupt Teamwork – A Story from Lewis Senior

Simon, a leader we work with whose E-Colours are predominantly Red/Yellow, is constantly seeking ways to improve his organisation, always on the lookout for new ideas to inspire his team and business partners. A few years ago, he experienced a valuable lesson that illustrates how adapting our approach is sometimes necessary to get the best results.

While leading a large organisation in London, Simon tasked Daniel, a highly capable and independent operations manager whose E-Colours are Red/Green, with designing a bonus scheme as part of a business partner's contract amendment. Daniel thrives when he's given clear direction and left to execute things in his own way.

The morning after delegating the task, Simon held a meeting and invited several team members to stay behind to brainstorm ideas for the bonus scheme. Daniel attended the meeting but remained silent throughout. After it ended, he followed Simon into his office, closed the door, and voiced his frustration.

To Simon's surprise, Daniel was visibly upset and asked, 'Do you trust me?' When Simon asked what he meant, Daniel explained that he felt undermined. Having been given responsibility for the bonus scheme, he didn't see the need for further input. From Daniel's perspective, Simon's well-meaning attempt to include the team came across as a lack of trust in his abilities.

This experience highlights an important point: without realising it, we can unintentionally disrupt teamwork or individual performance due to differences in personality styles and expectations. What works for one person or situation may not resonate with another.

4. Driving Organisational Success
Organisations that recognise and leverage the strengths of their employees are more likely to thrive in today's competitive landscape. By fostering a culture that values and nurtures personality diversity, companies can tap into a broader range of ideas and innovations. This diversity of thought is essential for solving complex problems and keeping ahead of industry trends.

Strengths-based organisations tend to experience higher employee engagement and better retention rates. When people feel that their unique contributions are appreciated, they are more committed to both their work and the organisation. This creates a more motivated and dedicated workforce, ultimately driving stronger performance and results.

For instance, Google, well known for its innovative culture, places a strong emphasis on diverse strengths within teams. By encouraging employees to lean into their unique talents within an environment of psychological safety, Google has maintained its position as a global leader in the tech industry.

5. Building Inclusive Cultures
Emphasising strengths within the context of personality diversity also helps promote inclusivity. When organisations focus on what individuals contribute rather than on their differences or potential limiters, they foster a culture where everyone feels valued and supported. This is particularly important in today's interconnected world, where teams often include individuals from a wide range of cultural and social backgrounds.

An inclusive culture values strengths and fosters psychological safety – an environment where employees feel comfortable expressing their ideas and taking risks without fear of judgement. This openness is vital for personal and team innovation and is an essential part of continuous improvement, encouraging the free exchange of ideas and constructive feedback.

6. Overcoming Potential Limiters
While strengths are vital, it is also important to acknowledge and address potential limiters associated with personality diversity. Other tools have historically identified people's 'weaknesses'; when Equilibria was founded, we originally referred to these as 'improvement opportunities'. However, the decision to rename them 'potential limiters' was a wise one. This shift came during a team-building session on Transocean's Pathfinder drill ship in Nigeria, when one of the catering crew approached us during a break and suggested that since Equilibria's vision is *REALISING POTENTIAL*, it would make more sense to rename 'improvement opportunities' as 'potential limiters'.

As mentioned previously, much of Equilibria's development has come from our clients' willingness to help us enhance our offering in the spirit of continuous improvement.

Our tendencies are only weaknesses if we choose not to address them. Using E-Colours personality diversity as a coaching tool is a courageous choice for anyone – facing your potential limiters and choosing to lean into your strengths requires time, effort, and energy.

Potential limiters can also result from over-reliance on certain strengths or from biases that undervalue specific talents. For example, a strong analytical thinker might struggle with ambiguity and creative processes, while a highly empathetic individual might find it difficult to make tough decisions.

Forward-thinking organisations and individuals can strive to create a balanced approach that not only leverages strengths but also mitigates potential limiters. This can be achieved through coaching, continuous learning, feedback, and development opportunities. For instance, mentoring programmes can help individuals expand their skill sets and address any capability gaps.

7. Becoming a Leader

There is no single personality style suited to just one role – it is all about managing your own strengths and potential limiters.

Remember Anne's story at the end of the last chapter? It is not the first time we have been asked, 'If I have limited Red (Doer) tendencies, does that mean I cannot become a leader?'

Looking back, we can see many leaders who displayed a range of personality styles and tendencies. So, the answer is a resounding 'no' – anyone, regardless of E-Colour combination, can become a confident and effective leader. It all comes down to how you leverage your strengths and manage your potential limiters.

Here are some examples of great leaders known for their diverse personality styles.

Visionary Leaders:

Steve Jobs – Co-founder of Apple Inc.
Known for his innovative vision and ability to anticipate future trends in technology and design.

Elon Musk – CEO of Tesla, SpaceX, X (formerly Twitter)
Renowned for his futuristic thinking and ambitious goals in space exploration, electric vehicles, and renewable energy.

Charismatic Leaders:

Martin Luther King Jr. – Civil Rights Leader
Remembered for his powerful oratory skills and ability to inspire and mobilise the civil rights movement.

John F. Kennedy – 35th President of the United States
Noted for his charismatic presence and his ability to inspire a nation through vision and speech.

Transformational Leaders:

Nelson Mandela – Former President of South Africa
Celebrated for his role in transitioning South Africa from apartheid to democracy, fostering unity and reconciliation.

Oprah Winfrey – Media Mogul and Philanthropist
Known for transforming the media landscape and empowering millions through her platform and philanthropy.

Servant Leaders:

Mahatma Gandhi – Leader of the Indian Independence Movement
Renowned for his non-violent resistance and his focus on serving the needs of the people.

Mother Teresa – Founder of the Missionaries of Charity
Admired for her selfless service to the poor and sick, embodying servant leadership.

Strategic Leaders:

Winston Churchill – Former Prime Minister of the United Kingdom
Known for his strategic mindset and leadership during World War II.

Angela Merkel – Former Chancellor of Germany
Respected for her pragmatic leadership through complex economic and political challenges.

Democratic Leaders:

Franklin D. Roosevelt – 32nd President of the United States
Known for leading collaboratively during the Great Depression and World War II.

Ellen Johnson Sirleaf – Former President of Liberia.
Praised for promoting peace, development, and democratic principles in Liberia.

Autocratic Leaders:

Margaret Thatcher – Former Prime Minister of the United Kingdom
Known for her firm, decisive leadership and transformative economic reforms.

Lee Kuan Yew – Founding Prime Minister of Singapore
Recognised for transforming Singapore into a prosperous global financial hub through strong, centralised leadership.

Coaching Leaders:

Bill Gates – Co-founder of Microsoft
Noted for his coaching style, fostering innovation and development within Microsoft, and mentoring emerging leaders through his philanthropic work.

Sheryl Sandberg – COO of Facebook
Known for her supportive leadership and advocacy for women in leadership roles.

Affiliative Leaders:

Herb Kelleher – Co-founder of Southwest Airlines
Celebrated for building a people-first corporate culture rooted in team spirit.

Howard Schultz – Former CEO of Starbucks
Recognised for nurturing a culture of care and focusing on employee wellbeing.

These leaders reflect a wide range of personality styles, each bringing unique strengths and approaches to leadership, proving that effective leadership can take many forms.

As further examples of leadership and the E-Colours, every individual brings a mix of tendencies: a top-colour Red may lead with direction, Yellow with inspiration, Green with strategy, and Blue with compassion.

8. **Recognising Strengths of a Yellow (Socialiser)**
   - Optimistic
   - Enthusiastic
   - Persuasive
   - Animated
   - Talkative
   - Stimulating
   - Influencing
   - People-orientated

9. **Recognising Strengths of a Blue (Relator)**
   - Supportive
   - Agreeable
   - Calm
   - Amiable
   - Thorough
   - Dependable
   - Loyal

10. **Recognising Strengths of a Green (Thinker)**
    - Perfectionist
    - Accurate
    - Persistent
    - Serious
    - Analytical
    - Orderly
    - Cautious
    - Logical

11. Recognising Strengths of a Red (Doer)
- Strong willed
- Practical
- Decisive
- Efficient
- Achiever
- Competitive
- Independent
- Strong ego

Conclusion of The Role of Strengths

The role of strengths in personality diversity is profound, influencing personal development, team dynamics, organisational success, and the cultivation of inclusive cultures. By recognising and applying our strengths, we can achieve personal fulfilment while contributing more effectively to teams and organisations. This, in turn, encourages innovation, boosts productivity, and supports a healthy organisational culture.

Embracing and developing strengths within the framework of personality diversity is not merely beneficial, it is essential in today's complex, dynamic, and ever-evolving world. Both individuals and organisations must commit to fostering environments that value and utilise the unique strengths of each person, ensuring long-term growth and success.

The Role of Potential Limiters in Personality Diversity

As we've discussed, personality diversity within teams and organisations brings a wide range of perspectives, strengths, and capabilities, which enhances innovation, problem-solving, and overall performance. However, alongside these strengths, potential limiters – innate or developed tendencies that may hinder effectiveness – play a key role in shaping team dynamics and outcomes. Understanding and addressing these potential limiters is essential for fully realising the benefits of personality diversity while avoiding its possible pitfalls. Let's explore why potential limiters matter and why awareness, balance, and intentional management are so important.

1. Understanding Potential Limiters

Potential limiters are characteristics or behaviours that can reduce an individual's or a team's effectiveness. These limiters can manifest in many ways, such as over-reliance on certain strengths, lack of adaptability, or difficulties in communication. In the context of personality diversity, potential limiters can arise from differences in cognitive styles, emotional responses, and interpersonal dynamics. As mentioned earlier, potential limiters are often labelled as weaknesses in other personality tools. However, the E-Colours view them as coaching opportunities because you can choose to take action to address them.

Here are examples of potential limiters:

- Procrastinating Green (Thinker)
- Stubborn Blue (Relator)
- Disorganised Yellow (Socialiser)
- Pushy Red (Doer)

These potential limiters do not diminish the value of an individual's strengths, but they do highlight areas where extra support or development may be needed.

2. Enhancing Self-Awareness and Personal Development

Awareness of potential limiters is crucial for personal development. Individuals who understand their own limiters can take proactive steps to address them, leading to more balanced and effective performance. Self-awareness allows individuals to seek feedback, pursue appropriate coaching and training, and adopt strategies to manage their challenges.

For example, an individual with a tendency toward Green perfectionism and procrastination, one strength and one potential limiter, might recognise the importance of setting realistic goals and deadlines, seeking support from colleagues, and practising self-compassion to reduce stress and improve productivity. By acknowledging and addressing their potential limiters, individuals can create a more balanced approach to development, strengthening both their capabilities and their areas for improvement.

3. Improving Team Dynamics

In team settings, potential limiters can significantly affect dynamics and outcomes. While diverse personalities contribute to a rich pool of ideas and approaches, unmanaged limiters can lead to misunderstandings, conflict, and inefficiency. Recognising and addressing these limiters is essential for fostering effective collaboration and cohesion.

For instance, a team with strong visionary thinkers but limited attention to detail might struggle with decisions and implementation. Conversely, a team of meticulous planners lacking creativity may find it difficult to innovate. By identifying these potential limiters, teams can adopt strategies such as role diversification, coaching, and open communication to maintain a more balanced approach.

Moreover, understanding each team member's potential limiters can help build empathy and mutual support. When team members are aware of each other's challenges, they can offer help, share knowledge, and create a supportive environment that leverages everyone's strengths while compensating for potential limiters. E-Colours also provides a universal language for quicker and more effective communication. For example, when Mark and Emma Wilkinson are having a conversation, Emma, a top colour Green, might say to Mark, 'Why don't you think about that a bit more?' – which could come across as a little abrupt. However, saying, 'Can you dip into your Green a little more?' is far more conducive to a harmonious discussion.

4. Driving Organisational Success
At the organisational level, addressing potential limiters is vital for sustaining long-term success. Organisations that recognise and manage these limiters can foster a culture of continuous improvement, resilience, and adaptability. This is particularly important in today's fast-moving business environment, where flexibility and innovation are key competitive advantages. Your people are your most important asset, so invest in them wisely, and you'll see the returns.

Organisations can implement a variety of strategies to manage potential limiters.

Training and Development Programmes: Offering targeted training helps employees develop skills that counterbalance their potential limiters. For example, leadership development can support analytical thinkers in enhancing their interpersonal skills.

Diverse Team Composition: In line with Equilibria's Ethics, we don't recommend forming teams solely based on E-Colours. However, some team members may need to tap into their lower percentages to encourage broader perspectives and greater diversity of thought.

Feedback and Coaching: Establishing a culture of regular feedback, along with individual and team coaching, helps employees become more aware of their limiters and receive guidance on how to address them.

Flexible Work Practices: Adopting flexible practices that accommodate different working styles and preferences can help reduce the impact of individual limiters.

5. Promoting Inclusive Cultures

Addressing potential limiters also contributes to promoting inclusivity within organisations. When organisations value and support the development of all employees, regardless of their limiters, they foster an inclusive environment where everyone feels respected and empowered to contribute.

For example, some individuals may offer exceptional strengths, such as attention to detail or innovative thinking, but may also struggle with traditional communication or social interactions. By recognising and supporting these limitations, organisations can fully harness their talent and create a truly inclusive culture.

6. Balancing Strengths and Limiters

While strengths are often celebrated, it is equally important to recognise that over-reliance on strengths can turn them into potential limiters. For instance, if a top colour Red overplays a strength and becomes overly competitive, or a top colour Blue becomes excessively loyal, these tendencies may become limiters, hindering team dynamics. Another example is a highly decisive leader who might struggle to collaborate or listen to others' input. Balancing our strengths and potential limiters involves recognising that every strength has a flip side and requires a measured approach to achieve Equilibria.

This balance can be supported through these strategies.

Role Flexibility: Allowing employees to take on different roles that challenge their limiters and broaden their skill sets.

Peer Support: Encouraging peer mentoring and collaboration to harness diverse strengths and address limiters together.

Continuous Learning: Fostering a culture of ongoing development where employees are encouraged to expand their capabilities and perspectives.

As we mentioned, something to be aware of is that overplaying a strength can often cause it to become a potential limiter. Another example might be a Red (Doer), who is naturally strong-willed, overplaying that strength and unintentionally preventing a Blue (Relator) from contributing to a group discussion.

7. Recognising Potential Limiters of a Yellow (Socialiser)
- Disorganised
- Excitable
- Manipulative
- Emotional
- Over talkative
- Vain
- Reactive
- Easily distracted

8. Recognising Potential Limiters of a Blue (Relator)
- Possessive
- Unsure
- Stubborn
- Slow to decide
- Insecure
- Reluctant to speak up
- Awkward
- Resistant to change

9. Recognising Potential Limiters of a Green (Thinker)
- Procrastination
- Picky
- Detached
- Too serious
- Critical
- Self-critical

- Fears criticism
- Judgemental

10. Recognising Potential Limiters of a Red (Doer)
- Pushy
- Insensitive
- Domineering
- Impatient
- Harsh
- Tough
- Unapproachable
- Poor listener

Young Mark the Yellow – A Story from Mark Wilkinson

As a child, I was known for being the life and soul of the classroom. Teachers often commented on my sunny disposition, boundless enthusiasm, and natural ability to lift the spirits of anyone feeling down. I was told I had an infectious laugh, endless ideas, and a curiosity that kept conversations lively and engaging. The other students enjoyed my energy, and even the quietest classmates were drawn to join in at times.

But I also faced challenges in the classroom. Teachers sometimes grew frustrated with my habit of talking during lessons, cracking jokes, or offering to help others in ways that often led us all off track. I found it hard to stay focused on one task, always wanting to jump from one exciting topic to the next. Other students, drawn in by my stories, would sometimes get distracted too, and I'd end up getting a gentle – or not-so-gentle – reminder to settle down.

As I got older, the mixed messages became confusing. I loved bringing energy to everything but started to feel like my enthusiasm wasn't always seen positively by everyone. Schoolwork often felt like a balancing act between expressing my joy and staying out of trouble. I wished there were a better way to understand this drive to share ideas and bring others along for the ride.

One day in school, I met an E-Colours Practitioner who introduced a concept called personality diversity. The Practitioner explained that my E-Colours style was led by Yellow, meaning my strengths included optimism, enthusiasm, and strong communication. They shared that these were amazing qualities, and that I could bring joy to groups, motivate people, and bring them together by encouraging collaboration. However, these strengths also came with some potential limiters, such as a tendency to get easily distracted, over-talkative, or sometimes unintentionally disruptive to others.

This information was a game-changer. For the first time, I saw that these personality tendencies weren't 'good' or 'bad' but instead strengths and potential limiters that could be managed more effectively. With the E-Colours' help, I started learning strategies to stay focused without dampening my enthusiasm. I really practised listening as much as talking, asking thoughtful questions, and pausing before speaking to give others space to contribute.

I also began embracing new habits, like setting goals for each lesson to stay on task and focusing on one idea at a time to avoid distractions. The classroom became a place where I could shine in new ways, sharing energy and knowledge while also respecting everyone else's needs.

As the school year went on, I noticed a huge difference. By understanding both my strengths and potential limiters, I became more confident, self-aware, and a more effective communicator – not only as a student but as a friend and teammate. This newfound balance helped me appreciate that the brightest qualities and strengths of each person, when guided thoughtfully, can be a gift to everyone.

This captures how early awareness of our strengths and potential limiters can help us harness our optimism, enthusiasm, and communication skills to be both expressive and effective as young people.

The truth is, this is the story I would have liked to tell if I'd been introduced to E-Colours at 10 years of age, instead of 40!

However, imagine the young people around you today being introduced to E-Colours early on. And for you, whether young or more experienced, it's never too late. Start exploring and applying personality diversity in your own life. Start today.

Do We Really Have All Four Personality Styles?

Equilibria's E-Colours framework outlines the four main personality styles: Red (Doer), Yellow (Socialiser), Green (Thinker), and Blue (Relator). We all embody these four tendencies to varying degrees, with each one represented by the percentages revealed in the Personality Diversity Indicator

(PDI) assessment. Initially, focusing on our primary and secondary E-Colours helps us to understand, remember, and apply the concepts more easily. The top two E-Colours offer valuable thoughts into our natural communication styles and behavioural tendencies, providing a solid foundation for personal development in areas such as communication, teamwork, leadership, and risk management – becoming an invaluable 'tool for life'.

However, understanding the percentages of our other two lower E-Colours offers a more complete view of our personality. Often, our lowest E-Colour can highlight areas where we might struggle or where growth may be needed. These areas represent opportunities for us to stretch our capabilities, improve our communication, and reduce friction in our interactions with others. Your E-Colours Premium Report, which includes your percentages for all four styles, contains a wealth of additional ideas. In Chapter 10, we will explore the Wells Model – a powerful analogy for understanding, managing, and accessing all four of your E-Colours personality styles.

The ability to recognise and manage different personality styles in everyday life has led to the Personality Diversity Indicator (PDI) being completed over 1.4 million times since its inception. This tool has inspired individuals and organisations – large and small – to engage Equilibria's coaches in live events across various sectors, including business, education, healthcare, sport, and non-profits. The widespread use of the PDI has produced a rich database that allows Equilibria to track personality tendencies across diverse cultures, age groups, and environments, something Lewis often refers to as our 'data lake' of information.

Can My E-Colours Change with Time?

It is possible for your personality style to evolve over time based on your experiences, reflections, and personal growth. It's natural for individuals to develop new perspectives, interests, and priorities as they move through life and encounter different situations. As we learn to leverage our strengths and manage our potential limiters, it's possible to see some learned behavioural changes that may lead to an updated PDI result. These changes can influence how you see yourself and others, as well as how you engage with the world around you.

As an example, Mark's E-Colours were originally Yellow/Blue. However, over time, through coaching, self-development, and intentional choices, he focused on developing his decision-making skills and managing his emotional responses. This eventually resulted in a shift from Yellow/Blue to Yellow/Red, although only by a couple of percentage points.

Do not be concerned about these changes. Embrace them. You are who you are, and there is no personality style that is better than any other. Everyone brings value.

Refresher on the Basic E-Colours Concepts

Basic E-Colour Concept

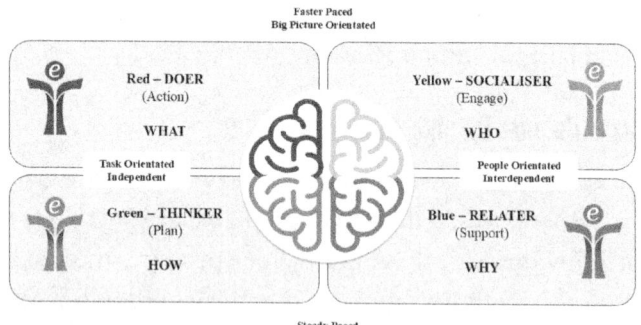

Faster Paced
Big Picture Orientated

Red – DOER
(Action)
WHAT

Task Orientated
Independent

Yellow – SOCIALISER
(Engage)
WHO

People Orientated
Interdependent

Green – THINKER
(Plan)
HOW

Blue – RELATER
(Support)
WHY

Steady Paced
Information Orientated

The Doer – The part of your personality that helps you to take action and get things done.

The Socialiser – The part of your personality that helps you interact and engage with others.

The Thinker – The part of your personality that helps you plan and analyse information.

The Relator – The part of your personality that helps you empathise with and support others.

Figure 6 – Refreshing the E-Colours
Copyright © 2025 Equilibria Services Pte Ltd. All rights reserved.

Dan's Story

> I didn't believe in E-Colors when I was first introduced to them because I didn't have the emotional intelligence to understand that not everyone in my team was motivated in the same way, or towards the same goal.
>
> After seeing E-Colors in practice – both in keeping front-line workers safe on job sites and directly impacting the efficiency of office-based teams – I'm grateful

my employer took the time to integrate E-Colors into our workplace. I fully believe the tangible benefits of E-Colors are reflected in my personality even years later.

– Dan Dickson (Red/Blue)
– Drilling Engineer and Operations Specialist, Canada

* * *

Remix Opportunities

- Know yourself.
- Know others.
- Once you've identified your own strengths and potential limiters, which area will you choose to work on and develop? For example:
  - **Red** – could decide to allow others to be involved in the decision-making process.
  - **Yellow** – could decide to be more organised, especially when interacting with others.
  - **Green** – could decide to act rather than overthink or procrastinate.
  - **Blue** – could decide to be less concerned about confrontation or what others think of you.

CHAPTER 6

GREEN TENDENCIES – THE THINKER

'Thinking is the hardest work there is, which is probably the reason why so few engage in it.'

— **Henry Ford (1863–1947)**, founder of Ford Motor Cars

This quote captures the thinking and analytical nature often associated with the E-Colour Green – the 'Thinking' personality style.

The world needs thinkers – not just to build what's next, but to make sense of what is.

In a world that often applauds speed, it's the thinkers – those who pause, ponder, and plan – who quietly shape the foundations we all stand on. Green tendencies, rooted in logic, analysis, and curiosity, bring depth to every decision and structure to every storm. They remind us that wisdom isn't loud – it's intentional.

This chapter is a celebration of the Green Thinker. Those who may not always be the first to speak, but whose words bring clarity when they do. Those who see patterns where others see chaos. Those who find joy not just in the answers, but in the journey of discovering them.

Yet the gift of thought can also be a weight – leading to over-analysis, perfectionism, or hesitation. Here, we explore the power of Green tendencies in action, and just as importantly, the transformative strength that emerges when a thinker chooses to step forward, press PLAY, and bring their knowledge into the world.

Whether you lead with Green or love someone who does, this chapter invites you to appreciate the quiet brilliance of the thinker. To honour the space between stimulus and response. To understand that patience, precision, and process are not delays – they are the very things that make progress last.

Let's take a breath, take a beat, and step into the powerful presence of Green.

The 'Thinking' personality style, referred to as Green in the E-Colours system, is the earthy individual who digs deep into the weeds, as described by the Chinese. This style is marked by a strong preference for logical reasoning, analysis, and systematic, strategic decision-making. Individuals who embody this style typically rely on intellect and rationality when processing information and making choices. They tend to favour data and time to reflect before deciding, making them steadier-paced and naturally independent.

Let's explore the Green (Thinking) personality style in more detail, examining its key characteristics and how it shows up in different aspects of life.

Characteristics of the Green (Thinking) Personality Style

Logical and Analytical: Greens prioritise logic and reason in their thought processes. They excel at dissecting problems, spotting patterns, and identifying practical solutions based on objective data and evidence.

Objective and Impersonal: Greens strive to remain objective and detached in their decision-making, focusing on facts and logic rather than emotion or personal bias.

Systematic and Organised: Greens prefer structured approaches to tasks and decisions. They often develop frameworks, checklists, or step-by-step plans to ensure thoroughness and efficiency. Thinkers are especially comfortable working with spreadsheets, for example.

Critical Thinkers: Greens are skilled at evaluating information critically, questioning assumptions, and seeking deeper understanding before drawing conclusions or taking action.

Problem Solvers: Greens thrive on tackling complex challenges. They enjoy situations that require logical reasoning and strategic thinking.

Detail-Oriented: Greens are meticulous, paying close attention to detail and aiming for precision in their work. This diligence helps them avoid errors and achieve high standards of accuracy.

Intellectually Curious: Greens possess a strong desire for knowledge and enjoy acquiring new information and skills that expand their understanding of the world.

Quirks & Tendencies of a Green (Thinker)

- Likes detail and gathering information
- Logical in their approach
- Likes to be given time to think and plan
- Can be judgemental of themselves and others, and think critically
- Views themselves as innovative thinkers
- Dislikes being rushed; appreciates time to think things through
- Likes discussing details with other people
- Prefers having a plan and sticking to it
- Dislikes being caught unprepared
- Enjoys creating systems to help themselves and others

Communication Styles of a Green (Thinker)

- Steady-paced
- Information-oriented
- Needs to know HOW
- Likes to explain
- Focuses on facts
- Active listener – asks a lot of questions
- Prefers personal space
- Less expressive with body language; can be perceived as lacking emotion at times
- Sceptical if people cannot provide data and facts

Body Language of a Green (Thinker)

- Uses fewer facial expressions
- Tends to avoid physical contact
- Gestures infrequently
- Moves with a steady, deliberate pace
- Displays patient, analytical expressions
- Moves with caution

Verbal Style Cues of a Green (Thinker)

- Focuses on facts, processes, and details
- Limits the sharing of feelings
- Tends to be formal and proper
- Speaks with little inflection
- Delivers speech in a consistent tone
- Sounds methodical
- May often say 'Well, technically...' or 'That's not exactly accurate'

Application in Different Areas

We recognise that individuals with different top E-Colours have natural tendencies that often align with their personalities. However, we also understand that personality diversity is nuanced, and people are not confined to rigid categories. This is why we use words such as 'can' and 'may' rather than definitive labels, allowing for individual differences, adaptability, and personal growth. That said, when people are happy in their work, they are often fulfilling their natural propensities.

Personal Life: In personal relationships, Greens may prioritise discussions grounded in facts and logic rather than emotions, which can occasionally lead to misunderstandings or a perceived lack of empathy. They typically approach personal goals with a methodical mindset, setting clear objectives and outlining steps to achieve them.

Professional Life: In careers that require analytical thinking, such as engineering, finance, or research, Greens tend to excel in roles that involve problem-solving and strategic planning. They contribute to team efforts by offering logical thinking, data analysis, and structured approaches to tasks.

Learning and Development: Many Greens thrive in academic settings where they can engage in intellectual challenges and structured learning. They are often drawn to disciplines such as mathematics, science, and philosophy, where logical reasoning is key.

A Guide to Managing Procrastination **and** Judgemental Tendencies **for Individuals with Predominant Top E-Colour Green Personalities**

For those whose top E-Colour is predominantly Green, a strong analytical mindset, attention to detail, and a commitment to quality often drive their behaviour. While these strengths promote high standards and thoroughness, they can also result in procrastination (due to over-analysis) and being judgemental when others don't meet those standards.

Managing these potential limiters requires self-awareness, intentional strategies, and using natural strengths to create better balance.

1. Increase Self-Awareness: Use the PAUSE Button to Prevent Over-Analysis.

Procrastination in Greens often comes from a desire to gather every detail before making a decision. This 'analysis paralysis' can hinder progress. To manage it, use Personal Intervention and press the PAUSE button when you notice yourself lingering too long on the details. The PAUSE button encourages you to assess whether more information is truly needed, or if action can be taken with what you already know.

2. Set Clear Deadlines to Overcome Procrastination.

Setting firm deadlines is essential to avoid procrastination, especially when perfectionism is a factor. Break large tasks into smaller, achievable milestones, each with its own clear deadline. This creates manageable steps that help move things forward, preventing projects from stalling due to an over-focus on gathering perfect information.

3. Cultivate Empathy and Open-Mindedness to Counter Judgemental Tendencies.

Top Colour Greens may hold high standards, which can lead to judgement when others fall short. Cultivating empathy by recognising that others may work differently or on different timelines can ease this tendency. Practising active listening helps you understand the perspectives of others and appreciate contributions that differ from your own.

4. Channel Energy into Productive Reflection, Not Overthinking.

If you're prone to overthinking, use reflection as a tool for growth instead of as a barrier to action. Set aside specific times to review your work, assess outcomes, or think through plans, rather than letting analysis interfere with active tasks. This structured approach to reflection can help you manage your desire for perfection without delaying progress.

5. Leverage Breathing Techniques to Stay Present and Focused
Greens can benefit from breathing techniques and strategies to manage and reduce over-analysis and judgement. When you find yourself stuck in thought or becoming overly critical, intentional breathing can help cultivate an attitude of acceptance and restore focus.

Square (Box) Breathing for Acceptance and Focus

- Your eyes may be closed or open.
- Inhale deeply through your nose for a count of four. If your eyes are closed, you can mentally trace the left vertical side of the "square" going up as you breathe in.
- Hold your breath for a count of four. Trace the top horizontal side, left to right.
- Exhale slowly through your nose or mouth for a count of four. Trace the right vertical side, going down.
- Hold your breath for a count of four. Trace the bottom horizontal side, going left, returning to where you started

Repeat this cycle 3-5 times when restlessness or overthinking builds. This will help you reset, allowing you to remain accepting and focused.

Thank you to E-Colours Practitioner Kerry Waters for the contribution on breathing techniques.

She can be contacted at:
kerry.waters@breathehouse.co.uk
https://kerrywaters.com/

6. Focus on Progress Over Perfection.
Greens often aim for perfection, which can lead to procrastination if they feel they can't achieve it immediately. Try shifting your mindset to value progress, even when it's imperfect. Small improvements add up, and progress often matters more than flawless execution. This perspective helps you act sooner and accept that perfection may evolve over time.

7. Reflect on Personal Progress to Gain Balance.
Regular reflection on your actions and decisions can reveal patterns where over-analysis or judgement may be slowing you down. Journaling or setting aside reflection time can help you identify when you're being overly critical or hesitant. Use these ideas to adjust your approach moving forward.

8. Leverage E-Colour Awareness in Team Settings.
Understanding how your Green tendencies interact with others' E-Colours can help reduce procrastination and judgement in teams. Collaborating with Red or Yellow personalities, who typically act more quickly, can help balance your desire for thoroughness. Recognising the strengths in others allows you to set more realistic expectations, avoid frustration, and avoid unnecessary criticism. For Greens, PAUSE & PLAY remains an especially valuable tool for managing procrastination and judgemental behaviours.

Applying PAUSE & PLAY (A Process Explored Further in Chapter 10)

PAUSE Opportunities

These are moments when you could consciously press your PAUSE button to avoid falling into limiting behaviours such as over-analysis or being overly judgemental.

1. When You Are Overthinking a Decision
PAUSE to recognise when you're caught in analysis paralysis. If you've gathered enough information but still hesitate to decide, press pause to break the cycle of over-analysis.

2. When You're Critiquing Others Too Harshly
PAUSE when you notice yourself being overly critical of others' work. Remind yourself that people have different approaches and consider whether your expectations are realistic or overly rigid.

3. When You're Feeling Overwhelmed by Details
PAUSE if you find yourself fixating on minor details that are delaying progress. Ask yourself whether the level of detail is necessary, or if you're losing sight of the bigger picture.

4. When You're Postponing Action in Fear of Imperfection

PAUSE when procrastination stems from fear that your work isn't perfect. Consider whether taking action now, even if imperfect, is more valuable than continued delay.

PLAY Opportunities

Once you've used the pause button to reflect and step away from limiting behaviours, PLAY helps you move forward with intentional actions that encourage progress.

1. Decisive Action After Gathering Enough Data
PLAY by setting a time limit for analysis. Once time is up, trust your process and act with the information you have. Progress is often more effective than waiting for perfection.

2. Empathy and Understanding
PLAY by making a conscious effort to empathise with colleagues or team members. Instead of judging their methods, look for the strengths they bring and how those strengths complement your own.

3. Break Tasks into Smaller, Actionable Steps
PLAY by dividing large projects into smaller, manageable steps. This helps you maintain focus and complete steps one at a time, making it easier to act and avoid procrastination.

4. Focus on the Bigger Picture
PLAY by keeping long-term goals in mind. When you're tempted to get lost in the details, refocus on how timely action supports the broader objective.

5. Reflection for Growth, Not Critique
PLAY by using reflection as a learning tool, not a source of harsh self-judgement. Celebrate progress and learn from what didn't go as planned, without being overly judgemental.

By mastering these PAUSE & PLAY moments, you can better manage procrastination and judgemental tendencies, allowing your strengths as a Green to come through in a more balanced, effective way.

A Green Story: Emma Wilkinson
A Story of Balance and Growth: Emma and Her Green Thinker Leadership

I am the Director of Bamboo Events Ltd, a thriving events company known for its meticulous planning and creative execution. My clients tell me that my calm, detail-oriented personality shines brightly in my work. With Green (Thinker) as my top E-Colour, I am the anchor of the organisation and the event. I must ensure every project runs smoothly, every budget is balanced, and every contingency is considered.

At the heart of my Green (Thinker) tendencies is my ability to analyse situations with precision. I thrive on structure, careful planning, and data-driven decisions. Whether it is a high-profile Life Remixed seminar or a corporate event, my approach is the same: every aspect needs to be planned to perfection. This mindset makes me the leader at Bamboo Events Ltd., and my clients trust me to deliver not just memorable occasions, but flawless ones.

My Green (Thinker) Strengths in Action

My Green E-Colour means I naturally lean toward:

- Attention to Detail: I ensure every contract is reviewed, every vendor is vetted, and every timeline is double-checked. My goal is to reduce risks and create a seamless client experience.

- Analytical Problem-Solving: When challenges arise, like a last-minute vendor cancellation, I keep calm and focused on finding logical solutions.

- Consistency: I value systems and processes. I create detailed checklists and workflows that my team follows, ensuring every event upholds Bamboo's impeccable reputation.

The Magic of Yellow: Appreciating Mark

At home, my relationship with my husband, Mark, is a wonderful contrast. With his Yellow E-Colour leading the way, Mark brings optimism, enthusiasm, and spontaneity into my structured world. Where my Green tendencies could sometimes lead to overthinking or analysis paralysis, Mark's cheerful encouragement reminds me of the importance of joy and flexibility. He also helps me to dip into my Red decision-making.

I've steadily learned to admire Mark's gift for seeing possibilities. His boundless energy and positivity inspire me to think outside the box, even in my business. For instance, when I'm hesitant to take on a new type of event, Mark's infectious 'Why not?' attitude gives me the courage to go for it.

Building a Life Together

Mark's Yellow energy adds a layer of fun and creativity to life. While I focus on the execution, Mark can bring bold ideas that help us create good things together. I appreciate his ability to rally the team, boost morale, and remind everyone why they love what they do.

For me, the key is balance. I now practise 'PAUSE & PLAY,' a concept that we both embraced early on in our relationship, to avoid falling too deeply into my Green (Thinker) tendencies. When my perfectionism risks stifling my creativity, I pause, reflect, and allow Mark's enthusiasm to guide me toward action.

In turn, I know Mark appreciates my ability to ground his sometimes-scattershot energy. I've helped him channel his ideas into actionable steps, and together, we've achieved success both at work and at home.

A Team Built on E-Colours

My Green (Thinker) strengths ensure that Bamboo Events Ltd delivers consistently high-quality results. My appreciation for Mark's Yellow tendencies enriches not just our marriage, but also my own leadership style. By embracing our differences and leveraging our E-Colours, we have created a life – and business – filled with harmony, creativity, and success.

– *Emma Wilkinson (née Knights)* (Green/Blue)
– Director, Bamboo Events Ltd, UK

Steve's Story

Curious and captivated by Life Remixed, I attended one of Mark's seminars where he spoke about his book and the transformative journey he'd undertaken, including understanding his own E-Colours and those of the team around him. I was hooked by his positivity and the way he exuded a sense of completeness in life. Since then, Mark has been coaching and guiding me for over a year, during which time he's also supported me in becoming an E-Colours Practitioner myself.

– *Steve Whiteside* (Green/Blue)
– Director, EMFS Group Ltd, UK

Adrian's Story

I will do my best to cage the Green in me and be brief:

- *Feedback – wow*
- *Inspiring*
- *Uplifting*
- *Can reflect on why people say E-Colours is life-changing*
- *PAUSE & PLAY buttons – used this with my 13-year-old daughter. Rather than remind her all stories have a start, middle and end which should align rather than ramble, I hit PAUSE and let her talk without interruption. My wife reminded me I can also do that with her… it's a work in progress.*

As I said after the session, I had never seen or heard of E-Colours before Sharon Smith mentioned it. I will admit I had reservations at first before the day started, but this tool is personal in ways I can't explain. For me, it is an inner reflection of the inner self and a tool to show how we can create our own blockers and frustration. The booklet and premium report are really reflective – we both read through them last night.

When you said 7-year-olds can do this, I thought of how beneficial this would be in the education system and how it's a must for teacher training. This would aid their approach and help deliver a better standard that all kids can benefit from. When my daughter comes home on a high, it could be because she has a teacher who may prove to be a high Yellow. When she comes home deflated, it could be because she has a teacher who may be more direct – like a high Red – look at me go now!

It would also be useful for kids labelled as having problem issues. I can see how these kids could do E-Colours and let them explain who they really are, and then use it to change the education approach for them.

I said to Sharon that I felt I was a dinosaur trying to live in a modern world ready to go extinct but now feel rejuvenated.

My wife and kids literally just told me how uplifted, happy, upbeat I am today – must have been a miserable sod before, so all I can say is thank you and I feel inspired. Also, I ordered Mark's Life Remixed book which will be coming later today. Thank you.

– Adrian Franklyn (Green/Red or Green/Blue)
– Safety Investigation Officer,
London Heathrow Airport, UK

Wayne's Story

Discovering E-Colours has been a real revelation. The power of this tool to understand not only oneself but others around you is nothing short of remarkable. The way it can bring complete strangers together in a room is a beautiful thing to witness. Learning Personality Diversity will improve your life.

– Wayne Perry (Green/Blue)
– Property Investor and DJ, UK

Steffy's Story

Thank you so much for today's wonderful session. I liked the straightforward approach you took throughout the session. While Mark – Yellow – is full of energy and proactive, I like how Emma (Green) is calm and patient. You really complement each other.

My experience being a Green/Blue: I can relate so much to the E-Colours and now know the importance of PAUSE & PLAY before I speak or take any action. I can very well think from other people's shoes now! E-Colours is a must-have session!

– Steffy Mary Tom (Green/Blue)
– HSE Officer, Dulsco, Dubai

Rebecca's Story

This information needs to be heard. Having done this work, we all communicate better, and we are seeing a reduction in accidents, incidents, and customer complaints – meaning our staff are more aware of great customer service as well as their own and others' safety.

– Rebecca Mupita (Green/Red)
– Managing Director,
Transdev Airport Services, UK

Dr. Zanovia's Story

E-Colors and the real-world resources have been a breath of fresh air. I have had the opportunity to apply this beautiful body of work in my professional life, as well as my personal life. As a Certified Practitioner and Trainer, the ability to help people become more self-aware and learn more about their colleagues is so enriching. I was able to train my department in 2019 and team members continue to request a refresher each year. Thank you for creating a common language for us! Looking forward to the future work and resources to come!

– Dr. Zanovia Gatson (Green/Red)
– E-Colors Practitioner, Houston, USA

* * *

The Green (Thinking) personality style brings valuable strengths to both personal and professional contexts, emphasising logical reasoning, systematic thinking, effective problem-solving, and a strong need for information. However, it is important for Greens (Thinkers) to balance their analytical approach with empathy and flexibility in order to navigate interpersonal relationships and adapt effectively to dynamic situations. Embracing a more holistic perspective that integrates both logic and emotional intelligence can further enhance their overall effectiveness and success, helping them move beyond potential overthinking and procrastination into decisive action and meaningful conversations.

* * *

Remix Opportunities

- If Green is your dominant E-Colour, and the paragraph above resonates with you, consider how you can continue to leverage your strengths while managing your potential limiters effectively.
- If your top E-Colour is Red, Yellow, or Blue, think about how you can best communicate with someone who shows the Green tendencies described above.

CHAPTER 7

YELLOW TENDENCIES – THE SOCIALISER

'Your network is your net worth.'

– **Porter Gale**, marketing expert, author, and public speaker known for her work in branding, networking, and social media

This quote highlights the value of relationships and social connections, which are often hallmarks of those with a Yellow (Socialiser) personality style.

Wherever joy walks in, connection follows. And often, it's led by someone with Yellow tendencies lighting the way.

There's a magic to Yellow personalities that's hard to miss and impossible to ignore. It's in the smile that brightens a meeting room. The story that pulls everyone in. The moment of spontaneous laughter that turns a stressful day into something better. Yellow – Socialiser – is not just a personality tendency. It's an energy. It's a gift.

This chapter is a celebration of that gift. Of the people who bring light into dark spaces. Of those who believe in possibilities, who say 'yes' more often than 'no', and who remind us that life, at its core, is about relationships.

But behind every spotlight moment is a choice. The choice to connect with intention. The choice to harness excitement without overwhelming. The choice to listen as much as you speak. Because when Yellow tendencies are guided by self-awareness, they don't just uplift the room – they transform it.

So, whether you lead with Yellow, or you're blessed to work or live alongside someone who does, this chapter invites you to see the beauty, the brilliance, and, yes, the boundless enthusiasm that Yellow brings. And it reminds us that being a beacon for others doesn't mean burning out. It means knowing when to PAUSE, when to PLAY, and how to keep showing up as your most authentic self.

The world needs your light. Let's make sure it shines with purpose.

The 'Socialiser' personality style, represented by Yellow in the E-Colours system and likened to the wind in Chinese philosophy for its fluid and unobstructed movement, is characterised by enthusiasm, energy, and a strong focus on building relationships. Individuals with this style are typically outgoing, persuasive, and comfortable in the spotlight. They thrive in environments where they can interact with others, share ideas, and form connections, making them invaluable in both social and professional contexts. During a recent E-Colours workshop, a top colour Yellow participant remarked, 'The real win is the friends we make along the way.'

Here's a closer look at the Yellow (Socialiser) personality style, its key tendencies, and how it often presents in different areas of life.

Characteristics of the Yellow (Socialiser) Personality Style

Outgoing: Yellows are naturally sociable and enjoy spending time with others.

Enthusiastic: They bring a high level of energy to their interactions.

Persuasive: Yellows are often skilled at motivating and influencing others.

Optimistic: They tend to focus on the positives and inspire others with their upbeat outlook.

Talkative: Yellows enjoy conversation. They thrive in social settings, often initiating discussions and engaging others with ease.

Influencing: Socialisers influence others through their vibrant communication style, relationship-building strengths, and ability to inspire collaboration and positivity. They create an atmosphere of trust and encouragement, helping others embrace new ideas and take action.

Creative: Yellows are imaginative and enjoy exploring new possibilities and approaches.

Quirks & Tendencies of a Yellow (Socialiser)

- Very people-oriented
- Has a positive and enthusiastic attitude toward life in general
- Likes to interact with and help others

- Good at engaging with and influencing people
- Likes to be liked
- Likes to be included
- Enjoys having people around them
- Has a warm and friendly disposition
- Dislikes negative people
- Enjoys coaching, mentoring, and influencing others in a positive way

Communication Styles of a Yellow (Socialiser)

- Faster-paced
- Focused on the big picture
- Needs to know WHO
- Likes to engage with people
- Prefers talking to listening
- Selective listener who can sometimes interrupt
- Comfortable being close to others
- Spontaneous and at ease with groups
- May unintentionally interrupt conversations

Body Language of a Yellow (Socialiser)

- Uses animated facial expressions
- Warm and friendly demeanour
- Comfortable with hugs
- Tends to act spontaneously
- Uses many hand and body movements
- Open body language; tends not to cross arms

Verbal Style Cues of a Yellow (Socialiser)

- Tells stories and anecdotes
- Shares personal feelings and opinions
- Uses informal speech patterns
- Can digress during conversations
- Speaks with noticeable inflection
- Uncomfortable with silence and may talk to fill it

Application in Different Areas

We recognise that individuals with different top E-Colours have natural tendencies that may align with their personalities. However, we understand that personality diversity is nuanced, and people are not confined to rigid categories. This is why we use words such as 'can' and 'may' rather than definitive descriptions, allowing for individual differences, adaptability, and personal growth. That said, it does seem that when people are happy in their work, they are often satisfying their natural propensities.

Workplace: In a professional setting, Yellows (Socialisers) bring energy and creativity to the workplace. For example, in a marketing team, a Yellow (Socialiser) may thrive in idea sessions, presenting campaign concepts, and engaging clients with their persuasive communication skills. Their ability to create a lively and uplifting environment often boosts team morale and productivity.

Family Dynamics: Within a family, Yellows often take on the role of the peacemaker and entertainer. They organise gatherings, make sure everyone feels included, and use their positivity to resolve conflicts. Their ability to connect with others helps strengthen bonds and create a joyful home life.

Education: In educational environments, Yellows can be engaging teachers or enthusiastic students. As teachers, they use their enthusiasm to create an interactive and dynamic classroom. As students, their energy and willingness to participate often make them active contributors in group discussions. However, a potential limiter for a top-colour Yellow is being easily distracted – something they can choose to work on.

Healthcare: In healthcare, Yellows can support patient care through their excellent bedside manner and empathetic communication. They build rapport easily, helping patients feel relaxed and heard. This ability to connect on a personal level can enhance patient satisfaction and trust in their care providers.

Sports Teams: On sports teams, Yellows are often the ones who lift spirits and boost team unity. Their enthusiasm can be especially helpful in high-pressure moments. They may also excel in roles that require quick thinking and adaptability, such as team captains or key players in dynamic sports like basketball or soccer.

Angelica – A Story from Lewis Senior

I had the pleasure of meeting Angelica (Yellow/Red) during her time working as both an FBI interrogator and a fundraiser for Cherish Our Children, a nonprofit dedicated to supporting underprivileged children worldwide. She was so impressed by Equilibria's work that she took a leave of absence from the FBI to join us at Equilibria for a year. During that time, she gained exposure to various industries, including the education sector, discovering how the E-Colours served as a foundational tool across multiple fields.

Her passion for righting wrongs, and a backstory involving the tragic loss of a teenage friend, eventually led her back to the FBI. She later acknowledged that her enhanced understanding of personality styles significantly improved her ability to gain quicker admissions during interrogations.

In collaboration with Mark and myself, Angelica decided to share her journey in her book, *Through These Brown Eyes*, now a bestseller we highly recommend. Her story is captivating and offers perspectives you might not expect. Her Yellow/Red personality shines through in how she intentionally navigates life's twists and turns, making her journey all the more inspiring.

A Guide to Managing Over-Talkative **and** Reactive **Tendencies for Individuals with Predominant Top E-Colour Yellow Personalities**

For individuals whose top E-Colour is predominantly Yellow, enthusiasm, spontaneity, and strong communication skills often drive behaviour. These strengths can boost collaboration and energise teams but may also lead to potential limiters, such as being over-talkative or reactive. Managing these tendencies requires self-awareness, intentional habits, and channelling energy in more productive ways.

1. Increase Self-Awareness: Use the PAUSE Button to Manage Reactivity (A Process Explored Further in Chapter 10). Reactivity in Yellows often stems from their spontaneous nature. You might respond quickly to situations or jump into conversations without fully processing your thoughts. Using the Personal Intervention technique to press the PAUSE button allows you to slow down before reacting impulsively. This gives you a chance to consider whether a more measured response would be more effective.

2. Set Clear Boundaries for Conversations.
Being over-talkative can sometimes overwhelm others or take the conversation off course. Set boundaries by focusing on active listening before speaking. Aim to speak only after others have had a chance to contribute, and keep your input to a few key points to maintain a balanced discussion.

3. Build Empathy by Actively Listening.
While Yellows are naturally social and engaging, they can sometimes dominate conversations, at times preventing others from sharing their ideas. Cultivate empathy by practising active listening. Focus on understanding others' perspectives before jumping in. This not only strengthens relationships but also reduces reactive responses.

4. Channel Your Energy into Structured Communication.
Yellows bring great energy to discussions but can sometimes lose focus. To stay on track, structure your communication by organising your thoughts before speaking. Consider the key message you want to share and express it clearly and concisely.

5. Use Breathing Techniques to Stay Grounded
When you feel the urge to jump into a conversation or react quickly, try using a simple breathing technique to calm your mind and body. This creates space for reflection and allows you to engage with greater intentionality. This method can help you slow down and stay present.

P-A-U-S-E Breath for Calm Communication

- Your eyes may be closed or open.
- Inhale deeply through your nose for 5 seconds.
- As you inhale, mentally say "P-A-U-S-E" until you reach the top.
- Release a relaxed exhale through your nose or mouth before you speak.

Practice this sequence before you prepare to respond in a conversation. Alternatively, repeat as often as you need when you feel the urge to interrupt or speak without fully processing your thoughts. It will help you stay composed, demonstrate active listening, and make space for others to contribute.

Thank you to E-Colours Practitioner Kerry Waters for the information on breathing techniques.

She can be contacted at:
kerry.waters@breathehouse.co.uk
https://kerrywaters.com/

6. Focus on Long-Term Gains from Thoughtful Contributions.
Shift your mindset from immediate participation to the long-term benefits of thoughtful communication. When you manage your enthusiasm and reactivity, you make room for more effective collaboration and build stronger relationships grounded in trust and mutual respect.

7. Reflect on Your Interactions to Identify Patterns.
Take time to review conversations where you felt reactive or talked too much. Identify any recurring patterns, such as

specific situations or topics that trigger impulsive behaviour, and adjust your approach. Journaling or discussing with a trusted colleague can help refine your communication style.

8. Leverage E-Colour Awareness in Team Settings.
Understanding how your Yellow tendencies interact with other E-Colours can help you manage over-talkativeness and reactivity in team environments. For example, individuals with high Blue or Green may process information more slowly or prefer deeper analysis before speaking. Being aware of this can help you adjust your pace and engagement level, fostering smoother collaboration.

Applying PAUSE & PLAY (A Process Explored Further in Chapter 10)

PAUSE Opportunities
These are moments when you could consciously press the PAUSE button to avoid falling into limiting behaviours such as over-analysis or being overly judgemental.

1. When You Feel the Urge to Speak Immediately
PAUSE when you notice a strong urge to jump into the conversation. Take a moment to reflect – consider whether it's the right time to contribute or if more listening is needed first.

2. When You Notice You're Over-Talking
PAUSE if you catch yourself dominating the conversation. Step back, create space for others to speak, and refocus your attention on listening.

3. When You're Reacting Emotionally or Impulsively
PAUSE when a strong emotional reaction begins to build. Taking a moment to hit PAUSE allows you to assess the

situation before responding in a way that might escalate things unnecessarily.

PLAY Opportunities

Once you've used the pause button to reflect and break from limiting behaviours, PLAY helps you move forward with intentional actions that encourage progress.

1. Structured and Focused Communication
PLAY by organising your thoughts before speaking, ensuring your contribution is clear and concise. This practice helps you channel your enthusiasm into more meaningful dialogue.

2. Encouraging Others to Share
PLAY by inviting others, especially those who are quieter or have different E-Colours, to contribute. Balancing your communication style with active engagement from others enriches the conversation.

3. Intentional Listening and Thoughtful Reactions
PLAY by listening closely and allowing yourself time to reflect before responding. This promotes better collaboration and reduces misunderstandings.

By managing the potential limiters of being over-talkative and reactive, you can make the most of your Yellow strengths and create more positive, productive interactions both at work and in your personal life.

A Yellow Story: Lewis Senior
As we gain deeper thoughts into our personality styles, each with its own strengths and potential limitations, we begin to

understand how life events are often directly influenced by these tendencies. As someone with a predominantly Yellow/Red personality style, I've always felt a strong desire to help others. Looking back, I now realise that, like most people, our strengths can become limitations when overused or unchecked.

In the early 2000s, I found myself juggling two significant roles within the same organisation. By day, I led a team of professionals tasked with sharing a new company culture across multiple organisations that had merged or been acquired. This role involved extensive travel and delivering three- to four-day workshops to large audiences. By night, I was fulfilling my duties as the company's Health, Safety, and Environment Manager.

This relentless pace continued for two to three years, during which I unknowingly fell into my own potential limiters. I found it difficult to say no, whether because someone asked for help or because I thought they needed it. It all came to a head in 2002, when I collapsed on the floor, convinced I was having a heart attack. In reality, I was simply exhausted and in urgent need of rest.

It took months to come to terms with the fact that no one had pushed me into this situation. I'd done it to myself by not setting clear boundaries. Thankfully, I've since learned the value of reflection and balance. Today, I'm proud to share a simple but powerful tool we've developed: the PAUSE & PLAY buttons. This simple but effective process allows anyone to PAUSE when they need to reset, and press PLAY when they're ready to re-engage.

One of the greatest privileges of this work has been introducing this practice into schools. By teaching children how to harness their strengths and manage their limiters, we give them tools to avoid future regrets and empower them to navigate life with confidence and self-awareness (see Chapter 13: E-Colours for Education).

Kerry's Story

I discovered the incredible E-Colours through my passion for house music, wellbeing science, and personal development, when I read Mark Wilkinson's book Life Remixed.

My curiosity piqued, I met Mark, who led me on a journey of personality discovery via the E-Colours technology. E-Colours revealed my Yellow/Blue personality style – which was truly like experiencing my reflection in a metaphorical mirror. So much about me and how I tick made sense, and I gained the awareness and tools to manage those tendencies better!

Seeing the opportunity to further help individuals and organisations be a force for positive change, I saw an obvious alignment with my work as a mindfulness and breathwork coach, and my corporate experience in business transformation. I am now an E-Colours Practitioner and proud member of this innovative, well-intentioned community.

Key elements that make E-Colours so impactful for me: data-driven ideas using information provided by you, well-established analytics, simple language and framework, and interventions that are easy to follow and embed. Simplicity overall – and an unquestionable 'a-ha' moment that hooks you right from the start. And not forgetting the recent inclusion of my simple

> *breathwork exercises – powerful supporting enablers for Personal Intervention and cultivating momentary presence in any situation. Thank you to Equilibria for allowing me to share these with our clients via your platform.*
>
> – *Kerry Waters* (Yellow/Blue)
> – E-Colours Practitioner & Breathwork Specialist, UK

Lloyd's Story

> *Through E-Colours I have learned how to deal with conflict in the workplace and, more importantly, how to get the best out of people who are wired entirely differently from myself.*
>
> – *Lloyd Cornwall* (Yellow/Red)
> – Director & Founder, Delicious International Food and Music Festival, Johannesburg, South Africa

Sharon's Story

> *E-Colours is a simple and engaging way to help you understand how you can get hurt. E-Colours teaches you self-awareness and so much more about yourself!*
>
> *Mark delivers this in an easy-to-understand way that empowers you to make safer decisions, understand your team, identify potential blind spots, and be mindful of your own actions.*
>
> – *Sharon Smith* (Yellow/Blue)
> – Head of Operational Safety Improvement, London Heathrow Airport, UK

Jason's Story

From my experience, I believe E-Colours has the capability to improve safety on construction sites. Could I or my workmates have acted differently on the day of my accident, had we known our E-Colours? Yes, it's possible. It's an incredible tool, and I look forward to seeing it implemented across UK organisations.

– *Jason Anker MBE* (Yellow/Blue)
– Global Inspirational Speaker & Author of *Paralysis to Success*, UK

Chris's Story

I met Mark and Emma Wilkinson at the SHE Show in 2024 and was immediately interested in what they, Hillmont Associates and Equilibria were presenting to us.

E-Colours and its application to personal and team safety is a real game changer. In a recent training session, understanding that each personality style sees and manages risk differently sparked great discussions in the JCB UK Safety Team. We are now planning for 2025, presenting this to our apprentices and their mentors, and embedding E-Colour practitioners into the business.

– *Christopher Briggs* (Yellow/Red)
– Group Health and Safety Director, JCB, UK

Lou's Story

Understanding my E-Colours has been revolutionary, and looking back at previous events in my life, it all makes perfect sense!

The way I found E-Colours is a story in itself. I visited a local cafe with my partner and came across Emma and Mark with their beautiful dog, Frankie the Frenchie. Mark, Sarah, my partner, and I are all top E-Colour Yellows, unbeknownst to myself and Sarah at the time. Naturally, we hit it off with lively chat and laughter. Emma, being top E-Colour Green, said very little.

Somehow, Mark and I got onto the topic of personality diversity indicators, and he told me about E-Colours. My Yellow shone brightly – I was all in and signed up for the Practitioner Course the following weekend!

Since then, I have delivered E-Colours workshops to numerous teams across my organisation and have consistently received positive feedback. People now understand and communicate with each other in the way each person needs, improving working relationships. This has been true in my own team, where colleagues often joke about how my lack of Yellow detail is balanced by the more analytical top E-Colour Green!

In my personal life, although both Sarah and I are top E-Colour Yellows, we have contrasting secondary colours – mine is Blue, hers is Red. That realisation was a true lightbulb moment. My sensitive Blue now doesn't feel as hurt by her forthright Red and her constant drive to move from one task to the next.

> *E-Colours have been transformative for me, and I will continue to weave it into my passions for sport and personal protection.*
>
> – *Lou Dutch* (Yellow/Blue)
> – Initial Training Manager,
> Police & Personal Trainer, UK

* * *

The Yellow (Socialiser) personality style is a powerful asset in any setting that values creativity, communication, and collaboration. By understanding and leveraging their strengths, while remaining aware of potential challenges, Yellows can make meaningful contributions to the success and wellbeing of the groups they belong to. Their unique mix of enthusiasm, creativity, and interpersonal skills makes them invaluable in both personal and professional environments.

* * *

Remix Opportunities

- If Yellow is your dominant E-Colour and the above paragraph resonates with you, reflect on how you can leverage your strengths while managing your potential limiters.
- If your top E-Colour is Red, Green, or Blue, consider how to communicate most effectively with someone who exhibits the Yellow tendencies described above.

CHAPTER 8

RED TENDENCIES – THE DOER

'In any situation, the best thing you can do is the right thing; the next best thing you can do is the wrong thing; the worst thing you can do is nothing.'

– **Theodore Roosevelt (1858–1919)**, former United States President

This quote reflects the proactive, decisive, and action-oriented nature commonly associated with the Red (Doer) personality style.

In a world full of hesitation, Red is the spark that gets things moving.

Red tendencies are the driving force behind action – the ones who see a challenge and say, 'Let's go.' The ones who don't wait for permission, because progress rarely comes from waiting. It comes from doing.

This chapter is a salute to the Red Doers. To the people who wake up ready to push forward. Those who cut through noise with clarity and turn vision into results. If you've ever found yourself frustrated by delay, inspired by momentum, or energised by goals that others find daunting – you might just be leading with Red.

But this chapter is also a reminder: the same fire that fuels achievement can sometimes burn too hot. The urgency to act can leave others behind. The instinct to move can miss the opportunity to truly listen. And that's where the power of intentional Red lies – in choosing to pause, to reflect, and to lead not just with action, but with self-awareness.

Whether you're a Red leader, a team member, a partner, or a parent, this chapter is your invitation to harness your boldness for good. To sharpen your strengths, soften your edges when needed, and channel your drive into something that inspires – not just results, but respect.

Because when Red is led by purpose and balanced by empathy, it becomes a force that doesn't just get things done – it gets the right things done, in the right way.

The 'Doer' personality style, represented by Red in the E-Colours system and likened to fire by Chinese philosophy for its intense and energetic nature, is characterised by strong willpower, practicality, decisiveness, efficiency, and a goal-oriented mindset. People with this personality style are typically independent and thrive in fast-paced environments where obstacles are few and progress flows smoothly.

This section offers a closer look at the Red (Doer) personality style, exploring its tendencies and how it manifests in various aspects of life.

Characteristics of the Red (Doer) Personality Style

Decisiveness: Reds are known for their ability to make quick, firm decisions. They're confident in their judgement and willing to take risks to reach their goals.

Goal/Result-Oriented: Reds are highly focused on setting and achieving goals. Their desire for success drives them to complete tasks efficiently.

Assertiveness & Direct Communication: Reds are assertive and direct in both their actions and communication. They express their opinions and needs clearly and directly. They value honesty and clarity in their interactions with others.

Independence: Reds prefer to work independently and take charge. They rely on themselves and prefer to have control over decisions and outcomes.

Efficiency: Reds value speed and effectiveness. They focus on completing tasks quickly and with practical, no-nonsense solutions.

Problem-Solving: Reds are natural problem-solvers who enjoy overcoming challenges. They favour a logical, hands-on approach to finding solutions.

Confidence: Reds exude confidence in their abilities and decisions. Their self-assurance often inspires and motivates others.

Quirks & Tendencies of a Red (Doer)

- Thrive on challenges and new opportunities
- Like results and being goal-oriented

- Expect competence and efficiency from others
- Focus more on tasks than people
- Can be impatient and may be perceived as tough, harsh, or unapproachable
- Like to get effective results quickly
- See the big picture quickly and clearly
- Adapt well to change and make decisions quickly
- Enjoy doing and achieving
- Dislike too much detail

Communication Styles of a Red (Doer)

- Fast-paced
- Big-picture focused
- Needs to know WHAT
- Likes to tell
- May not be the best listener
- Speed listens (can appear to be ignoring others)
- Prefers personal space
- May dominate the conversation
- Can become impatient if people don't get to the point

Body Language of a Red (Doer)

- Shakes hands firmly
- Makes steady eye contact
- Uses gestures to emphasise points
- May display impatience

- Likes to maintain distance and personal space
- Dislikes being touched

Verbal Style Cues of a Red (Doer)

- Tells more than asks
- Talks more than listens
- Makes strong, bold statements
- Tends to be blunt and direct
- Can use sharp, direct tones when emphasising a point
- Emails are often short and to the point – often just a single word or short sentence ('Yes.' 'No.' 'Thanks.')

Application in Different Areas

We recognise that individuals with different top E-Colours have natural tendencies that often align with their personalities. However, we also acknowledge that personality diversity is nuanced, and people should not be placed into rigid categories. This is why we use words such as 'can' and 'may' instead of definitive labels, making space for individual differences, adaptability, and personal growth. That said, it does seem that when people are content in their work, they are often expressing their natural propensities.

Workplace: In a professional setting, Red individuals thrive in roles where their decisiveness and goal orientation are valued, helping to drive company strategy and performance. They also excel in overseeing projects, ensuring tasks are completed efficiently and on time. Their leadership style is typically directive.

Family Dynamics: Within a family, Reds often take on household management, organising and overseeing daily activities to ensure everything runs smoothly. Their decisiveness supports key family decisions, such as financial planning, and helps resolve conflict quickly. Reds tend to set high standards and serve as role models – for example, by teaching children the value of hard work and determination. They foster a stable, supportive environment that encourages family members to pursue their goals and aspirations.

Education: In educational environments, Reds can deliver results quickly. They concentrate on meeting academic standards and improving overall school performance. In the classroom, their strengths help manage students and maintain a disciplined learning environment. Reds may also develop and implement programmes focused on outcomes and student achievement. They can mentor other educators, sharing practical strategies for effective teaching and leadership.

Healthcare: In healthcare settings, Reds can lead hospitals and healthcare organisations, ensuring efficient operations and high-quality care. They may drive improvements in patient care and clinical practices. Reds can also spearhead public health campaigns, ensuring programmes are effectively implemented and reach their goals. In medical emergencies, their decisiveness is crucial in coordinating responses and ensuring patient safety.

Sports Teams: On sports teams, Red individuals often become highly focused on results, pushing themselves to meet specific performance standards. They use their directive and competitive nature to motivate athletes and drive team success. Reds may manage sports teams with an emphasis on winning and maintaining discipline. They can also develop and oversee training programmes, ensuring athletes are well-prepared and performing at their peak. In addition, they may organise sports events and competitions, ensuring everything runs smoothly and efficiently.

A Guide to Managing Impatience and Poor Listening for Individuals with Predominant Top E-Colour Red Personalities

For individuals whose top E-Colour is predominantly Red, action, decisiveness, and results often drive behaviour. While these strengths can lead to success, they may also result in impatience and poor listening – especially when things don't move as quickly as expected or when others work at a slower pace. Managing these potential limiters requires self-awareness, intentional habits, and channelling your energy effectively.

1. Increase Self-Awareness: Use the PAUSE Button to Manage Impatience (A Process Explored Further in Chapter 10).
Impatience often arises from a desire for immediate results. To manage this, increase your self-awareness by using the Personal Intervention technique. Press the PAUSE button when you feel impatience rising. This gives you a chance to reflect before reacting, helping you determine whether immediate action is necessary or if patience will yield better outcomes.

2. Set Clear Priorities to Reduce Frustration.
Breaking larger goals into smaller, actionable steps with defined deadlines can help ease impatience. As someone driven by results, achieving small wins helps sustain momentum without feeling stalled by long-term projects. This structure allows you to focus on continuous progress, even when bigger outcomes take more time.

3. Practice Active Listening to Overcome Poor Listening Habits.

Reds often prioritise quick action, which can lead to poor listening during conversations. To counter this, practise active listening by making a conscious effort to understand rather than simply respond. Allow others to finish their thoughts before offering your input. This not only supports clearer communication, but also reduces frustration when things aren't moving as fast as you'd like.

4. Channel Your Energy into Focused Activities.

If impatience makes you feel restless, redirect that energy into short, focused physical or mental activities. A short walk, some stretching, or a quick mindfulness practice can help ground your energy, enabling you to approach tasks or conversations with greater patience and focus.

5. Use Breathing Techniques to Cultivate Presence.

When impatience or the urge to interrupt others arises, use breathing techniques to slow down and ground yourself. The 4-2-8 breathing technique can calm your nervous system and bring you back to the present moment, enhancing your ability to listen effectively and manage impatience.

4-2-8 Breathing for Patience and Focus

- Your eyes may be closed or open
- Inhale deeply through your nose for a count of four
- Hold your breath for a count of two
- Exhale slowly through your mouth for a count of eight

Repeat this cycle 3–5 times whenever impatience or restlessness builds. This will help you reset, allowing you to remain patient and focused.

Thank you to E-Colours Practitioner Kerry Waters for the information on breathing techniques.

She can be contacted at:
kerry.waters@breathehouse.co.uk
https://kerrywaters.com/

6. Focus on Long-Term Gains Rather Than Immediate Results.
Reds often seek quick results, but many meaningful outcomes require sustained effort and patience. Try shifting your focus to long-term benefits, recognising that some processes naturally take time. Reframing your perspective to value persistence can make it easier to remain patient, even when immediate progress isn't obvious.

7. Reflect on Your Listening Skills and Patience Levels.
Regular reflection plays an important role in improving both listening and patience. Take time to assess situations where impatience or poor listening may have hindered your progress. Noticing these moments can help refine your approach and highlight patterns that need adjustment. Journaling or self-reflection at the end of the day can be a useful practice.

8. Leverage E-Colour Awareness in Team Settings.
Understanding how your Red tendencies interact with other E-Colours can ease impatience and improve communication in teams. Individuals with predominant Blue or Green tendencies,

for example, may require more time to process information or make decisions. Being aware of these dynamics allows you to set realistic expectations, reducing frustration and creating smoother collaborations.

Applying PAUSE & PLAY (A Process Explored Further in Chapter 10)

PAUSE Opportunities
These are moments when you can consciously press the PAUSE button to avoid falling into limiting behaviours such as appearing pushy, impatient, or domineering.

1. When You Feel the Urge to Do / Act
PAUSE when you notice the impulse to jump into action. Reflect on the value of hearing the full perspective before moving forward.

2. When You Feel Frustration Building
PAUSE if you feel frustrated by a lack of immediate results. Use the pause to recognise small wins or incremental progress that can be acknowledged to ease the pressure for instant outcomes.

3. When You're Listening to Respond Rather Than Understand
PAUSE if you catch yourself preparing your reply before the other person has finished speaking. Focus on fully understanding their point of view first.

PLAY Opportunities
Once you've used the pause button to reflect and break from limiting behaviours, PLAY helps you move forward with intentional actions that support progress.

1. Active Listening
PLAY by choosing to engage in active listening. Let others speak without interruption and reflect back what you've heard to confirm understanding. This will help you manage impatience and improve collaboration.

2. Celebrating Small Wins
PLAY by celebrating short-term wins during long-term projects. Breaking big goals into smaller, actionable steps helps maintain momentum and progress, therefore reducing impatience.

3. Focused Physical Activities
PLAY by directing restless energy into focused physical activity, such as short walks or quick mindfulness exercises. This can help clear your mind, making it easier to listen and remain patient in demanding situations.

By managing impatience and improving listening, you strengthen your ability to lead effectively and build more harmonious relationships in both personal and professional environments.

A Red Story: Lewis Senior

In April of 2024, we celebrated a significant milestone – our 20th anniversary. As we prepared for the celebration, a deep sense of humility and gratitude filled our hearts and minds. Two decades had passed since we embarked on this journey, and it felt fitting to reflect on the many lives we'd touched and the relationships we'd built along the way.

To mark the occasion, we invited people to share short videos and reflections about their experiences with our work. The response was overwhelming; we received over 150 heartfelt messages, each telling a unique story. One video that particularly stood out came from Wendell Davis, whose E-Colours are predominantly Red/Green.

Wendell had been a friend for several years, dating back to his time as a supply chain manager for the Wells team in Nigeria. Our friendship deepened over time, and during my recent visit to Houston, I had the pleasure of joining him for early morning walks, where we discussed everything from work to life's challenges.

In his video, Wendell shared a harrowing experience that touched me — and anyone else who watched it. He described himself as someone whose personality is independent, task-focused, and direct, often preferring to work alone rather than engage in much human interaction. He acknowledged that this tendency sometimes made emotional connection a challenge.

However, Wendell recounted a life-changing moment that pushed him well beyond his comfort zone. A few years earlier, he had walked into a room in his home to find someone close to him standing on a chair with a noose around his neck. The shock struck Wendell deeply, and he realised this was a moment where he could either retreat into his usual self or rise to the occasion.

In that moment, Wendell made a choice completely outside of his typical comfort zone. He tapped into the Blue energy of his E-Colours, adopting a more empathetic and supportive approach. For over two and a half hours, he listened intently, allowing the individual to share their pain. Rather than seeking to be understood, Wendell focused on understanding.

His presence and commitment in that critical moment turned a potential tragedy into a chance for healing. His actions not only saved a life but also transformed his own perception of interpersonal connection.

Listening to Wendell's story, I was struck by the impact of the E-Colours in real life. It illustrated the importance of adaptability and emotional intelligence, even for someone who naturally prefers to be alone. Wendell had risen above his own tendencies and leveraged what could have been his limitations, ultimately saving the day.

As I reflected on his story, it became clear just how important it is to share the E-Colours with more people around the world. Wendell's experience was a testament to the transformative potential of understanding ourselves and others, and it underscored the value of empathy in our daily lives.

On the day of our anniversary celebration, I felt a renewed sense of purpose. Surrounded by friends, colleagues and supporters, I shared Wendell's story to remind everyone that each of us has the ability to make a profound impact, regardless of our personality. Together, we can continue to build a world where understanding, compassion, and collaboration thrive, paving the way for a brighter future.

Pete's Story

I'm a top E-Colour Red – very practical. Everything has to be matter of fact. At the time, I didn't understand my personality or PAUSE & PLAY – things that come from knowing your E-Colours. Understanding myself, rather than others, had to come first. You've opened a whole new world for me.

– *Pete Weston* (Red/Green)
– Managing Director, J&P Engineering, UK

Neill's Story

I honestly believe that working with E-Colours has helped me become a better colleague, team member, and manager. I regularly read through the PDI report and listen to what my colleagues tell me to make subtle changes, allowing me to adapt more quickly to the individual or situation. The entire QinetiQ Safety team is in a much better place now as a direct result of the E-Colours training that you delivered.

– *Neill Crawshaw* (Red/Blue)
– Head of UK Safety Excellence, Defence & Space, QinetiQ UK

Karin's Story

I've been a fan of E-Colours for almost two decades. I first encountered the tool while working on my first offshore oil rig off the coast of Nigeria.

As a safety coach, I work with the crew to develop their team dynamics, conversational skills, job planning, safety mindset, and leadership skills. Of course, everyone is different in all those areas, which makes for interesting discussions, interactions, and learning.

The power of E-Colours is helping people understand their differences and approaches in a healthy way. E-Colours is a catalyst that helps us identify our strengths and potential limitations. I love that it provides that awareness in a quick, ethical, easily digestible, and memorable way. Their 'aha' moments are a joy.

I've used different tools over the years, and E-Colours is my tool of choice. It gives us coaches confidence that we're working with our clients in a sound, ethical, and proactive manner.

I use my E-Colours as a reflection tool to help me become a better coach and leader. With a Red/Yellow style, I like to get to the point – which isn't always the most helpful approach. With this awareness, I can check myself to ensure I consider everyone's differences and play to both my strengths and theirs. It's not always easy, but it's worth it.

– *Karin Ovari* (Red/Yellow)
– E-Colours Practitioner & Leadership Coach, UK

Nico's Story

> *How can I explain to anyone that E-Colours will change the way you work, relate with others at work and at home, and rediscover yourself? Don't wait – please take the advice of this stranger: do your E-Colours premium report and start the most amazing journey. It will change your life.*
>
> – *Nico Fekete-Perez* (Red/Yellow)
> – E-Colours Practitioner, QSHE & Sustainability Manager, Hillmont Associates, UK

Andrew's Story

> *Big thanks for the E-Colours teambuilding session – it was well received by everyone I spoke to afterwards! It was the best three hours I've ever invested in a workshop. With a diverse international team, it will really help us work more effectively.*
>
> – *Andrew Tavener* (Red/Green)
> – Head of Marketing, Fleet Solutions EMEA, Descartes, UK

* * *

The Red (Doer) personality style is a powerful asset in any environment that values decisiveness and competitiveness. By understanding and leveraging their strengths while being mindful of potential limiters, Reds can contribute significantly to the success and wellbeing of the groups they are part of.

Their unique blend of decisiveness, efficiency, and practicality makes them invaluable in both personal and professional contexts.

* * *

Remix Opportunities

- If Red is your dominant E-Colour and the above paragraph resonates with you, consider how you can leverage your strengths while effectively managing your potential limiters.

- If your top E-Colour is Green, Yellow, or Blue, consider how you can best communicate with someone who demonstrates the Red tendencies described above.

CHAPTER 9

BLUE TENDENCIES – THE RELATOR

'True friends are like diamonds – bright, beautiful, valuable, and always in style.'

– **Nicole Richie**, American television personality, fashion designer, actress, and author

This quote highlights the value and rarity of true friendships. Just as diamonds are precious, enduring, and highly cherished, genuine friends are invaluable and timeless treasures in one's life. The comparison underscores the importance of nurturing and appreciating close, meaningful relationships.

In a world that moves too fast and speaks too loud, Blues remind us that listening is an act of love, and connection is our greatest strength.

There's something truly special about those who lead with Blue. They're the ones who show up, stay the course, and speak softly – yet whose presence is felt the most. They're not drawn to the spotlight, but they illuminate the path for others. They're the steady hands, the compassionate hearts, and the safe places where people feel seen, heard, and valued.

This chapter is a tribute to the Relators – to those who believe that kindness is a superpower, and that loyalty isn't a gesture, it's a promise. It's for the ones who carry emotional intelligence like a compass, and who instinctively build bridges where others see distance. Blue tendencies are the glue that holds teams together, families strong, and communities close.

But even the gentlest hearts must learn to protect their energy, to trust their voice, and to recognise that speaking up can be an act of courage – not conflict. When Blues combine their natural empathy with the intentional choice to engage, their influence becomes quietly transformative.

Whether you lead with Blue or love someone who does, this chapter encourages you to embrace the power of care, honour the beauty of sensitivity, and lead through connection. Because in a world that often rewards volume and speed, it's those who lead with heart who leave the most lasting legacy.

The 'Relator' personality style, referred to as Blue in the E-Colours system, embodies the qualities of someone who supports those around them – much like water surrounds and supports fish in the ocean, as described in Chinese philosophy. The Blue (Relator) personality revolves around building and valuing deep, meaningful relationships. People with this style thrive on forming strong bonds and are naturally inclined towards loyalty, empathy, and trust. Their world centres on people and the connections they make, and these relationships are the cornerstone of both their personal and professional lives.

At its core, the Blue (Relator) personality style is characterised by a profound need for connection. Blues are not typically drawn to superficial interactions; they seek depth in their relationships and tend to prefer a few close friends over a large network of acquaintances. This desire for intimacy and trust makes them reliable and supportive friends, colleagues, and partners.

Here's an exploration of the Blue (Relator) personality style, examining its characteristics and how it manifests in various aspects of life.

Characteristics of the Blue (Relator) Personality Style

Empathy and Understanding: Blue (Relators) have a strong ability to understand and share the feelings of others. They are excellent listeners and often provide a comforting presence, making them a go-to person for support and advice.

Loyalty: One of the most defining tendencies of a Blues is their loyalty. Once they form a bond, they are committed to maintaining it. They stand by friends and colleagues through thick and thin, making them reliable and trustworthy.

Trust-Building: Blues are naturally skilled at building trust. Their genuine interest in others and consistent, dependable nature create a strong sense of safety and trustworthiness.

Preference for Depth Over Breadth: Unlike some personality styles that thrive on networking or broad connections, Blues favour deeper, more meaningful connections. They invest time and energy into nurturing a select few.

Supportiveness: Blues are often the emotional backbone of their circles. They remember birthdays, check in during tough times, and are always ready to support and lend a helping hand.

Avoidance of Conflict: Blues are typically uncomfortable with confrontation and strive to avoid it when possible. Their aversion to conflict leads them to seek compromise and peaceful resolutions, further reinforcing their agreeable nature.

Patient and Tolerant: Blues tend to be patient and forgiving, even in challenging situations. This patience allows them to remain calm and understanding, contributing to their ability to maintain positive, agreeable relationships.

Quirks & Tendencies of a Blue (Relator)

- Acts as a peacekeeper/mediator, giving a balanced approach
- Likes to be given time to do research
- Prefers to work at their own pace
- Likes to do quality work and isn't too fussed about how long it takes
- Likes to do one job at a time
- Enjoys helping people
- Likes harmony both at home and at work
- Likes seeing and making people happy
- Is dependable and honest
- Does not like being left out or excluded
- Dislikes conflict
- Can withdraw from aggressive environments
- Attaches emotion where others may not make the connection

Communication Styles of a Blue (Relator)

- Steady-paced
- Information-oriented
- Needs to know why
- Likes to relate
- Good listeners – pick up facts and feelings
- Empathetic listeners – can appear to withdraw or 'go quiet' due to focus on listening
- Values trust and collaboration
- Can be reluctant to speak up, especially in large groups
- Does not like raised voices
- Does not like being rushed

Body Language of a Blue (Relator)

- Shakes hands gently
- Uses fewer animated facial expressions
- Tends to show feelings through expressions
- Makes intermittent eye contact
- Exhibits patience
- Uses steady, deliberate movements

Verbal Style Cues of a Blue (Relator)

- Does not like to speak in public
- Asks more than states
- Listens more than talks
- Communicates in a steady manner

- Uses gentler rather than forceful tones
- May use indecisive language

Application in Different Areas

We recognise that individuals with different top E-Colours have natural tendencies that may align with their personalities. However, we understand that personality diversity is nuanced, and people are not confined to rigid categories. This is why we use words such as 'can' and 'may' rather than definitive descriptions – allowing for individual differences, adaptability, and personal growth. That said, it does seem that when people are happy in their work, they are often satisfying their natural propensities.

Workplace: In professional settings, Blues are invaluable team members due to their ability to create and maintain strong, trusting relationships. Their natural inclination towards empathy and supportiveness makes them ideal for roles requiring collaboration and people management.

- **Team Dynamics:** Blues foster a collaborative atmosphere, ensuring team members feel valued and understood. Their supportive nature helps build a cohesive team where everyone is motivated to work towards shared goals.
- **Leadership:** As leaders, Blues are approachable and fair, leading with empathy and genuine interest in their team members' wellbeing. This builds high levels of trust and loyalty, boosting morale and productivity.
- **Customer Relations:** Blues excel in roles that involve customer interaction. Their ability to build strong

relationships with clients often leads to long-term loyalty and positive business outcomes.

- **Conflict Resolution:** Blues are adept at resolving conflicts, understanding different perspectives, and mediating discussions to find amicable solutions while maintaining a positive work environment.

Family Dynamics: Within the family unit, Blues play a crucial role in maintaining harmony and nurturing relationships. Their empathy and loyalty make them dependable and supportive family members.

- **Mediator:** Blues often act as mediators, resolving conflicts and ensuring all family members feel heard and understood.
- **Caregiver:** Their natural inclination to care for others makes them excellent caregivers – always attentive to the needs of their loved ones.
- **Emotional Support:** Blues provide a strong emotional support system, offering a calm presence and understanding during difficult times.
- **Family Activities:** They often organise family activities that promote bonding and togetherness, helping strengthen family ties.

Education: In educational settings, Blues contribute significantly to the learning environment through their supportive and empathetic nature.

- **Teachers:** As teachers, Blues create a nurturing classroom environment where students feel safe and supported.

Their ability to build strong connections fosters a positive learning atmosphere.

- **Students:** As students, Blues are collaborative and supportive classmates, often stepping into group roles that involve teamwork and peer assistance. They thrive in environments that value cooperation and respect.
- **Counsellors:** Blues make excellent counsellors, offering empathetic and understanding guidance to students, helping them navigate academic and personal challenges.
- **Parental Involvement:** As parents, Blues are actively involved in their children's education, helping create a supportive and encouraging home environment for learning.

Healthcare: In healthcare, the Blue personality style is highly beneficial, enhancing patient care and collaboration among healthcare professionals.

- **Patient Care:** Blues provide compassionate and empathetic care, building strong relationships with patients and ensuring they feel supported. This approach enhances patient satisfaction and outcomes.
- **Healthcare Teams:** Within healthcare teams, Blues help foster a collaborative and supportive environment, enhancing team dynamics and communication.
- **Support Roles:** Blues excel in support roles such as nursing, where their empathy and commitment to patient care make a real difference.
- **Mental Health:** In mental health professions, Blues' ability to build trust and offer empathetic support is essential for effective therapy and counselling.

Sports Teams: In sports, Blues contribute to team cohesion and morale, whether as players, coaches, or support staff.

- **Team Players:** As athletes, Blues are excellent team players, fostering a supportive and cooperative team environment. Their focus on relationships enhances team dynamics and performance.
- **Coaching:** As coaches, Blues emphasise teamwork, empathy, and individual player development. Their encouraging style builds trust and motivation within the team.
- **Support Staff:** In support roles, such as athletic trainers or team managers, Blues provide essential emotional and logistical support, helping ensure the team's wellbeing and success.
- **Conflict Resolution:** Blues play an important role in resolving conflicts within sports teams, promoting understanding and harmony among team members.

A Guide to Overcoming Reluctance to Speak Up **and** Feeling Unsure **for Individuals with Predominant Top E-Colour Blue Personalities**

For individuals whose top E-Colour is predominantly Blue, strong interpersonal skills, empathy, and a deep concern for others' feelings often shape your behaviour. These strengths promote harmony and cooperation, but they can also lead to potential limiters, such as reluctance to speak up and feelings of self-doubt. Managing these limiters requires self-awareness, intentional action, and leveraging your natural strengths to express yourself confidently.

1. **Use the PAUSE & PLAY Button to Manage** Reluctance to Speak Up **(A Process Explored Further in Chapter 10).**

   Reluctance to speak up often comes from a fear of disrupting harmony or offending others. Use the Personal Intervention technique to press the PAUSE button when you're feeling hesitant about expressing your thoughts. This PAUSE gives you a chance to reflect on the value of your input, which is essential for balanced team communication. Then press PLAY – and speak up!

2. **Set Clear Boundaries for Engagement.**

   Establishing clear boundaries for when and how you engage in conversations can help overcome uncertainty. Set small goals, like contributing at least once in meetings where you would normally stay silent, focusing on how your input could benefit the group.

3. **Practice Empathy for Yourself, Not Just for Others.**

   While Blues are naturally empathetic toward others, they often neglect their own needs and perspectives. Practice self-compassion by reminding yourself that your voice is just as important as others. Recognise that sharing your thoughts or concerns contributes to the group's overall success.

4. **Channel Your Energy into Thoughtful Contributions.**

   Blues may hold back for fear of saying the wrong thing. To counter this, channel your natural thoughtfulness into meaningful contributions. Before a meeting or discussion, take time to reflect on what you'd like to share, so you can approach the conversation with clarity and confidence.

5. **Use Breathing Techniques to Build Confidence**

   When feelings of uncertainty arise, grounding techniques like mindful breathing can help. Deep breaths slow your heart rate and calm your nerves. This helps shift focus from your insecurities to the message you want to deliver. This technique can help you regain composure and feel more centred.

   ## Coherent Breathing

   - Your eyes may be closed or open.
   - Inhale deeply through your nose for a count of five
   - Exhale slowly through your nose for a count of five
   - Repeat this cycle for as long as you are able in your environment. Aim for 5-6 breaths per minute which is your body's resonant frequency; the rate at which your heart, lungs and nervous system are most in sync.

Repeat this process when you feel nervous or unsettled. This will help you reset, allowing you to be calm and confident.

Thank you to E-Colours Practitioner Kerry Waters for the information on breathing techniques.

She can be contacted at:
kerry.waters@breathehouse.co.uk
https://kerrywaters.com/

6. **Focus on the Long-Term Value of Speaking Up.**

   Shift your mindset by focusing on the long-term benefits of contributing, rather than any momentary discomfort. Speaking up consistently builds confidence over time and ensures that your voice becomes a trusted part of team dynamics.

7. **Reflect on Times When Speaking Up Helped.**

    Reflection is a powerful tool for managing uncertainty. Think back to situations where speaking up made a positive difference. Journaling or talking it through with a trusted colleague can help you reinforce your strengths and recognise the positive impact of your voice.

8. **Leverage E-Colour Awareness in Team Settings.**

    Understanding how your Blue tendencies interact with the other E-Colours can help you feel more confident in team environments. Reds and Yellows may speak up more readily, while Greens might focus on details. Recognising these tendencies can help you find your voice without feeling overshadowed.

Applying PAUSE & PLAY (A Process Explored Further in Chapter 10)

PAUSE Opportunities

These are moments when you could consciously press the PAUSE button to avoid falling into limiting behaviours such as over-analysis or being overly judgemental.

1. **When You Hesitate to Speak**

    PAUSE when you feel reluctant to share your ideas in a group setting. Remind yourself that your contributions matter and that pressing your PAUSE button gives you space to reflect on the positive impact of speaking up.

2. **When You Feel Uncertain About Your Input**

    PAUSE if you begin to question the value of your contribution. Use this moment to remind yourself that your perspective is valuable, even if it differs from the group's.

3. When You Avoid Conflict to Maintain Harmony

PAUSE when you're tempted to stay silent in order to avoid conflict. While maintaining harmony is important, ensure that you're not sacrificing your own voice in the process.

PLAY Opportunities

Once you've used the PAUSE button to reflect and step back from limiting behaviours, PLAY helps you move forward with intentional actions that encourage progress.

1. Speaking Up with Confidence

After pausing, PLAY by contributing your thoughts. Start small if needed. Agreeing with someone or adding to someone else's statement can be a comfortable way to build confidence.

2. Setting Personal Engagement Goals

PLAY by creating simple goals for yourself, such as contributing your voice at least once per meeting or sharing feedback when asked. This creates a habit of engagement and boosts your confidence over time.

PLAY by practicing self-compassion. Show yourself the same patience and kindness you naturally extend to others. By managing reluctance to speak up and overcoming feelings of uncertainty, you'll express yourself more confidently and strengthen both personal and professional connections.

By mastering these PAUSE & PLAY moments, you can better manage reluctance to speak up and feeling unsure tendencies, allowing your Blue strengths to shine through in more balanced and effective ways.

'Please, we need to HEAR you!'

– Greens, Reds, Yellows

Caleb's Story

My name is Caleb Carroll. I live in Houston and my E-Colors are Blue/Yellow, with Green being my E-Color deficiency – which is a bit unique as I am an engineer, and being more analytical is a stereotypical expectation of most in my profession. While working through my career, I was asked to step out of a traditional engineering role and move into an operational supervisory role, as this was part of my career goals and development. I thought I was ready for it as well. This isn't uncommon within my company, a large international energy company based in Houston; however, the typical E-Colors for others asked to make this move are Red/Green, Green/Red, Red/Yellow, with the occasional Yellow/Red. As a Blue/Yellow, I was being asked to lead in executing well operations safely and efficiently – heavily equipped with great employees whose top E-Colors tended to be Red and/or Green, with some minor sprinkles of Blue and/or Yellow. I believe this is due to the complex nature of the work and the pace at which we need to make decisions to keep things progressing. Prior to learning about my E-Colors & Personal Intervention, I made the gross assumption that my leadership style would be a welcomed change within the team I was being asked to lead and develop. Little did I know that the conditioned response of the team had them expecting leaders with top E-Colors of Red and Green, with a hint of Yellow. A top colour Blue was very new and very different. I started the role and, for the most part, due to the strength of the team, we were quite successful in delivering safe and efficient operations. Team structure was tweaked with positive response from the team, at their request, and behaviours were aligned with our culture of safety and efficiency.

After working in the role for 8–9 months, the company took an employee survey throughout the organization, and the leaders were given the results to 'decode' and create actions for improvement. After looking at the results, I quickly learned that while my leadership style was appreciated by some, for others it was a major distraction. The survey showed a trend where my potential limiters were becoming actual limiters when trying to break through with some team members. This was a distraction for them and, therefore, a barrier for me in leading those individuals – they were not willing participants in our team, but merely compliant performers. My stubborn and resistance to change limiters as well as my slow to make decisions and procrastination were themes that I needed to correct. But I really didn't know how to manage these tendencies, as they had often been helpful in my previous role as an engineer during the planning phases of the well process. Serendipitously, I was selected for a Leadership Development course, where I learned about Personal Intervention and triggers. I had already been exposed to E-Colors, but mostly in terms of building awareness about myself and others. Personal Intervention, however, was a self-management tool – one that would really help me in my new role.

The coaching tips were not yet in the E-Colors pocketbooks, and I sure wish they had been. I still had an earlier copy. However, after learning about Personal Intervention and triggers in this course, I worked to identify my triggers and then tested alternative behaviours with my direct reports to help me keep potential limiters from becoming actual limiters. For me, one of my triggers was being asked for a quick decision – my tendency would be to slow it down and push the decision out, avoiding the stress of needing it now. I now use my PAUSE button and ask myself, 'What is needed from me, for my team to be successful, and when is it needed?' I also use my PLAY in this same scenario and ask, 'How can I help you and when do you need an answer?' or 'How can I support the decision to best serve you and the team?'

With a team full of people who filter information with their WHAT (Red) action and HOW (Green) questioning, this has helped me – and more importantly, helped the team – open their minds to different leadership styles and people who may think differently than them. This also helped get them to a place where they were willing to be led and supported by others who are different from them.

– *Caleb Carroll* (Blue/Yellow)
– Operations Manager, Wells International, USA

Greg's Story

I coach a diverse squad of young high jumpers, mostly in their mid to late teens. E-Colors has been an invaluable tool in helping me to be intentional in customising my communication style to each member of the team – both during training, when we are often working on problem-solving, and during competition, when I'm trying to find that one critical thought to optimise the performance of the next jump. It's been a game-changer for me as a coach.

– *Greg Engeler* (Blue/Green)
– Coach, Illawong Athletics, Australia

Ceri's Story

These sessions have made a big impact on our team. Understanding how each of us tick has helped us communicate effectively and ultimately work more effectively as a team. I honestly can't recommend them enough.

– *Ceri Hammuda* (Blue/Green)
– HSE Engineer, QinetiQ UK

Carolyn's Story

Thanks so much for the great E-Colors workshop. I think everyone who works in teams – as a member, or as a manager or leader – would benefit from this workshop. Either as a self-development tool for awareness, or as a team experience in organisations. The workshop really helped me gain a deeper appreciation of how important it is to flex and accept other idiosyncrasies when I have

> *more awareness. E-Colours would have been useful at school or university to help prepare us for the future, learning to be a more effective communicator rather than some of the more random things I no longer use!*
>
> – *Carolyn Steele* (Blue/Yellow)
> – Senior Manager, Professional Services Organisation, UK

* * *

The Blue (Relator) personality style is a powerful force for building strong, meaningful connections in both personal and professional settings. By leveraging their strengths – empathy, loyalty, and trust-building – Blues can cultivate deep and lasting relationships. When they actively manage their challenges, they maintain their wellbeing and remain the supportive, dependable individuals' others rely on. Through careful management of their emotional energy and selective engagement, Blues can thrive and make a positive impact on the lives of those around them.

* * *

Remix Opportunities

- If Blue is your dominant E-Colour and the above paragraph resonates with you, consider how you can leverage your strengths while effectively managing your potential limiters.
- If your top E-Colour is Red, Yellow, or Green, consider how you can best communicate with someone who demonstrates the Blue tendencies described above.

CHAPTER 10

MANAGING YOUR TENDENCIES – PERSONAL INTERVENTION

> 'Knowing yourself is the beginning of all wisdom.'
> – **Aristotle (384 BCE–322 BCE)**, Greek philosopher and polymath, born in Stagira, a city in Macedonia

This quote underscores the importance of self-awareness and understanding one's own tendencies as a crucial first step in Personal Intervention.

It's not who you are that holds you back – it's who you think you have to be. The moment you choose awareness over autopilot, everything begins to shift.

Every journey of growth begins with a decision – to no longer be a passenger in your own life. To notice the patterns. To understand the triggers. And to realise that the way you've always responded doesn't have to be the way you continue to.

This chapter is about that moment of choice.

Whether you lead with Red's decisiveness, Yellow's enthusiasm, Green's analysis, or Blue's compassion – or any combination in between – you have tendencies that serve you brilliantly… and tendencies that, unchecked, can get in your way. That's not failure. That's being human.

What sets intentional people apart isn't perfection – it's the willingness to pause. To step out of reaction and into reflection. To press PLAY not from habit, but from purpose. This is the heart of Personal Intervention.

In this chapter, we'll explore how to leverage your pause button as the most powerful tool in your leadership and your life. You'll learn how to interrupt unhelpful patterns, rewire your responses, and choose the kind of person, teammate, leader, or partner you truly want to be.

Your E-Colours tell the story of your potential. It's what you do with that awareness – how you manage your tendencies – that determines whether you realise your full potential.

So, breathe deep. Be honest. And step forward, not just as the sum of your personality tendencies, but as an intentional, evolving version of yourself.

This is where the transformation begins.

The Concept of Personal Intervention

Personal Intervention is a powerful tool for managing our natural tendencies. By deepening our understanding of this concept, we can enhance self-awareness and make more intentional, conscious choices.

The idea emphasises that intentional results come from responding thoughtfully rather than reacting impulsively. The PAUSE and PLAY buttons serve as valuable tools to support better decision-making.

Our character is shaped by our morals, ethics, and beliefs. By learning to pause and play on our inherent personality tendencies, we gain greater perspective on the choices we make. Personal Intervention uses these buttons to guide how we respond to different situations, helping us adopt a more mindful and intentional approach to life.

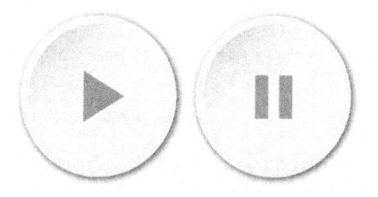

Figure 7 – Personal Intervention – PAUSE & PLAY Buttons
Copyright © 2025 Equilibria Services Pte Ltd. All rights reserved.

For example, people who identify as Red (Doer) or Yellow (Socialiser) often benefit from using the PAUSE button more frequently, as they tend to speak openly and act quickly. Conversely, those with Green (Thinker) or Blue (Relator) tendencies often find the PLAY button helpful in encouraging them to speak up or vocalise their thoughts and feelings more openly. Here's an example.

Greg Engeler's Story – Personal Intervention and the Use of the PAUSE & PLAY Buttons

> *I can think of a couple of times when I could have been more intentional regarding feedback. I pushed PAUSE instead of PLAY when a colleague didn't see the bigger picture – facilitating an outcome that met the requirements of a particular geography (Thailand), but was not in my company's broader best interests. My Blue/Green vulnerability is that I want to avoid conflict, and I'm always concerned that I don't have all the facts. The next time a similar situation happened, I pushed PLAY and inserted myself into the process early so that I could guide this person to a better outcome – very Blue/Green.*
>
> *– Greg Engeler* (Blue/Green)
> *– Product Engineering Specialist, Australia*

Understanding and Applying E-Colours & Personal Intervention

Step 1: Identify your personality tendencies and percentages by completing the E-Colours online questionnaire at www.equilibria.com/PDI-home/ and obtain a Premium Report.

Step 2: Review your Premium Report in detail to gain a better understanding of your strengths, potential limiters, and the distinction between personality and character – refer to Chapter 3, Figure 4.

Step 3: Recognise the difference between personality-driven reactions and character-driven responses.

Step 4: Enhance your performance by consciously choosing to respond rather than react. Be aware of and use your internal PAUSE & PLAY buttons to guide your behaviour.

Step 5: Book a coaching session with Lewis Senior or Mark Wilkinson in order to debrief the Premium Report.

For many, simply becoming aware that they have access to PAUSE & PLAY buttons is a transformative experience.

Dan's Story

As you know, this concept/tool goes hand in hand and can be used more effectively if you have some formal understanding of the E-Colors. In a nutshell, the PAUSE & PLAY concept helps me manage my own 'reactions' based on my personality, as well as my 'responses' based on my character; am I being reasonable with my reaction/response to this person or situation? The more I understand my personality tendencies and my own character, the more effectively I can use this tool.

When I use the PAUSE & PLAY Personal Intervention technique, it means I'm generally self-aware of my own tendencies and can be more intentional in how I act and interact with others in a variety of situations. It simply and effectively helps me respond, rather than react, in a more thoughtful, deliberate, conscious way. As a Green/Red, I often PAUSE myself when I start overanalysing something or become overly critical of something or someone. It's even natural for me to be self-critical on a variety of things, and so sometimes I have to PAUSE myself from negative thinking in that aspect.

I also need to press PAUSE at times to slow down, as I can take action or make decisions without fully considering or involving others' input. Some areas where the tool has helped me press PLAY include listening better, seeking others' input (not just my own), being more collaborative, staying open to new ideas, and considering other people's emotions in the work I do.

When you have a team who understands these concepts and applies them in practice, it really makes a world of difference. There are many examples in my career where I wish I had pressed PAUSE or PLAY. For me, I have more examples of when I should've PAUSED – lol.

One such time where I should have PAUSED was when I needed support from the office on a critical activity that took place over the weekend. We had an unplanned event occur during this activity and needed some specialized input. The individual was on their day off and had a difference of opinion on the criticality of the need. It just so happened that some other management folks were offshore at the time, and I quite literally gave them my opinion of displeasure about how we don't have the support needed to run a 24/7 business and that it wasn't acceptable. It was the wrong time and place for it, and I certainly reacted out of frustration vs responding to it. As someone who is detailed, a perfectionist and a get-it-done personality, I could have hit my PAUSE button and approached the entire situation differently, which could have resulted in a more productive conversation with all involved.

– Dan Snyder (Green/Red)
– Offshore Installation Manager, USA

Through Personal Intervention, we can achieve more desirable outcomes in any given situation by recognising when we're triggered and by preparing to respond rather than react.

As human beings, we often react to issues, events, or touch points based on our personality.

These reactions are typically instinctive and do not always lead to a positive result.

Learning to self-monitor and shift from reaction to response can lead to better outcomes.

Understanding our own personalities, as well as those of the people we live and work with, improves our ability to respond appropriately to both people and tasks.

By practicing Personal Intervention, we take a step closer to *REALISING POTENTIAL* – at work, school, and in our social environments.

The next few sections are designed to help you understand how Personal Intervention can support your success in managing natural reactions.

Rick Foote's Story – Personal Intervention and the use of the PAUSE & PLAY Buttons

> *I attended a conference recently where a presenter shared a professional opinion that I took exception to. Rather than push my PAUSE button, I approached that individual after their session and shared my displeasure. I greatly regretted doing that and wished I'd approached them later privately after some reflection. In hindsight, I was overly sensitive to criticism of my profession – my Green (Thinker) tendencies not being managed.*
>
> *Here's the rub. The same individual had shared that same opinion with me at a dinner the previous evening.*

In that situation I should have pushed my PLAY button and constructively shared my differing perspective with them right then. Instead, I was reluctant to speak up in that setting and let things fester until I reacted in a more public setting the next day.

The good news is that we did talk later... one on one... and all is well. But it was a learning moment for me regarding managing my potential limiters.

– *Rick Foote* (Green/Blue)
– Senior Consultant, FIT, USA

E-Colours & Personal Intervention

The use of Personal Intervention and the PAUSE & PLAY buttons is essential in managing predictable E-Colour tendencies. Below are some coaching and remix opportunities that link personality tendencies to the PAUSE & PLAY concept.

Blue (Relator) – Press PAUSE:
- To stop dwelling on things beyond your control
- To be open to changes in decisions and actions
- To avoid assuming that others think and feel the same way you do

Blue (Relator) – Press PLAY:
- To speak up and contribute your views and feedback
- To actively ask for clarification if you're unsure
- To share what's on your mind with others

Yellow (Socialiser) – Press PAUSE:
- To focus and ensure understanding before taking action

- To give others a chance to voice their opinions
- When you feel a strong emotional reaction coming on

Yellow (Socialiser) – Press PLAY:
- To be more organised and less reactive
- To plan more and focus on details
- To practise intentional listening and give thoughtful responses

Green (Thinker) – Press PAUSE:
- When you begin analysing
- On being over critical – of yourself and others
- On over thinking a decision

Green (Thinker) – Press PLAY:
- To try new things and be more open to others
- To accept others who don't work to your standards
- To keep the long-term goals in mind

Red (Doer) – Press PAUSE:
- To slow down and make sure there's shared understanding before acting
- To give control to others and let them decide
- To remember that not everything is as obvious to others as it is to you

Red (Doer) – Press PLAY:
- To listen and seek out feedback and input
- To be more collaborative and involve others in tasks and decisions
- To celebrate short term wins in long term projects

Can you imagine the positive impact this can have on behavioural safety, psychological safety, teamwork, and intentional leadership? Your effective use of the PAUSE & PLAY buttons can help manage potentially unsafe or challenging situations, as well as navigate everyday life successfully.

Why Use Personal Intervention?

The goal of Personal Intervention is to encourage proactive decision-making, allowing a balanced individual to:

- Approach and engage with others positively
- Control your personality-based reactions into character-based responses
- Assert their own rights and needs appropriately
- Give reasons for actions and positions
- Express frustrations effectively without harming others and property
- Show the capacity to empathise
- Negotiate and compromise appropriately
- Have positive relationships in all areas of life
- Cope with setbacks and rejection with resilience
- Improve safety and risk management
- Not easily be intimidated by bullies – see Chapter 13
  - Develop and sustain a 'Psychologically Safe Environment' – see Chapter 11

Personal Intervention gives us the ability to choose the right response in any situation rather than reacting from a subconscious habit.

We can now choose to PAUSE or PLAY when faced with a challenge, interrupting unhelpful reactions and avoiding negative consequences that come from poor choices in words, actions, or inactions.

Reid Mann's Story – Personal Intervention and the Use of the PLAY & PAUSE Buttons

There are so many times I wished I would have pushed PAUSE.

In general, learning to push PAUSE has saved me minutes, hours or even days in some cases, I am confident. Understanding the other person's perspective and personality first has taught me to keep my lips zipped until I think the entire situation through or sleep on it. In most cases, nothing needs to be said at all, and in the others, constructive feedback is given rather than a thoughtless, emotional reaction that normally equals a negative outcome.

I am Green/Red, with Red (Doer) being right behind Green (Thinker). I like a plan, I want things done now, and I naturally don't like unforeseen events or waiting for results. The PAUSE & PLAY buttons are one of the best, if not the best, tools I have ever been exposed to in both my career and personal life.'

– *Reid Mann* (Green/Red)
– General Manager, Expanse Electrical, North Dakota, USA

Breathwork & Personal Intervention

The breath is the physiological bridge to our nervous system. The nervous system influences our thoughts, emotions and behaviour. Our thoughts and emotions, Strengths and Potential Limiters determine how we act and communicate every waking moment of our lives.

The breath communicates with the body every time we breathe, but what it says depends on how we breathe. The messages that are sent thereafter determine what we think, how we feel, and what we say and do – and all of this is done at rapid speed. As such, conscious control of our breath through breathwork and mindfulness plays a perfect supporting role for embedding E-Colours Personal Intervention. Drawing upon the innate intelligence of your breath through the exercises provided will maximise your ability to PAUSE & PLAY, and to respond instead of reacting in any situation.

> 'Breath is the bridge that connects life to consciousness, which unites your body to your thoughts.'
>
> – Thich Nhat Hanh

Thank you to E-Colours Practitioner Kerry Waters for the information on breathing techniques.

She can be contacted at:
kerry.waters@breathehouse.co.uk
https://kerrywaters.com/

The Intersection of E-Colours, Personal Intervention, and Safety

In industries where safety is critical, the human element often plays a major role in managing risk and preventing incidents. Understanding how different personality styles interact with safety protocols can dramatically improve outcomes. When E-Colours are combined with the concept of Personal Intervention, using the PAUSE & PLAY framework, they become powerful tools in promoting safer practices.

The PAUSE Button: Reflective Practices in Safety

1. **Self-Awareness Through E-Colours**

    The PAUSE button encourages individuals to take a moment to reflect on their own behaviours and decision-making processes before acting. Understanding your E-Colour percentages can help you recognise when you might be rushing into decisions – for example, the Red (Doer) and Yellow (Socialiser) may overlook details, the Green (Thinker) may hesitate due to over-analysis, or the Blue (Relator) may prioritise harmony over necessary conversations. PAUSING allows for more thoughtful decision-making, reducing the likelihood of safety oversights.

2. **Assessing Situations Accurately**

    PAUSING also involves assessing the situation from multiple angles. For instance, someone with a predominant Green (Thinker) E-Colour might naturally PAUSE to gather more data before proceeding. This can be especially valuable in safety-critical situations where detailed analysis is needed. However, a Red (Doer) E-Colour individual may need to consciously PAUSE to consider whether their drive for immediate action is overlooking potential risks.

3. **Understanding Group Dynamics**

   The PAUSE button is also useful in team settings, where understanding group dynamics is crucial. For example, a Blue (Relator) E-Colour individual might be inclined to maintain group harmony, potentially at the expense of addressing safety concerns. PAUSING helps them reflect on the importance of speaking up, even if it disrupts the status quo, to ensure that safety remains the top priority.

4. **Encouraging Intentional Communication**

   Miscommunication is a common source of safety issues. PAUSING before communicating allows individuals to tailor their messages to the E-Colours of their audience, ensuring the message is clear, understood, and acted upon. For example, a Green (Thinker) E-Colour might need to simplify their detailed explanations for a Red (Doer) E-Colour colleague who prefers concise, direct communication.

5. **Intervening in Potential Risks**

   Personal Intervention often requires individuals to PAUSE and consider the best course of action before stepping in. E-Colours can help guide this process by helping people recognise their natural intervention style. For instance, a Blue (Relator) E-Colour might hesitate to intervene for fear of causing discomfort, while a Red (Doer) E-Colour person might jump in too abruptly. PAUSING helps both styles adjust their approach for more effective outcomes.

The PLAY Button: Taking Action in Safety and Risk Management

1. **Proactive Engagement**

   The PLAY button encourages individuals to take proactive steps in managing safety and risks. After PAUSING to reflect, they can engage their strengths and the strengths of others to address the situation effectively. For instance, a Red (Doer) E-Colour may take swift, decisive action, while a Blue (Relator) ensures the wellbeing of all involved as they press their PLAY button.

2. **Leveraging Personality Strengths**

   E-Colours can guide how individuals apply their strengths and manage potential limiters in safety interventions. For example, a Green (Thinker) E-Colour might excel at creating detailed safety procedures, while a Yellow (Socialiser) could be key in communicating those protocols in a way that energises and motivates the team.

3. **Improving Team Collaboration**

   The PLAY button also involves active participation with the team. Recognising the E-Colours of colleagues can help align actions with each person's strengths. For example, a Blue (Relator) might open a safety discussion, a Green (Thinker) could present supporting data, a Red (Doer) might map out next steps, and a Yellow (Socialiser) might energise the group and address concerns.

4. **Continuous Improvement**

   Playing with E-Colours isn't just about the action – it's about learning from it. After each intervention, individuals can reflect on the outcome and how their E-Colour tendencies influenced the process. This continuous improvement cycle ensures that interventions become more effective over time.

5. **Promoting a Safety Culture**

    The PLAY button also contributes to building a broader culture of safety across the organisation. E-Colours help leaders engage and motivate diverse personality styles. For example, a Red (Doer) might drive results by setting clear safety goals, while a Blue (Relator) might focus on building a supportive environment where everyone feels responsible for safety.

Case Study 1: Application in Equilibria

At Equilibria, the integration of E-Colours & Personal Intervention, using the PAUSE and PLAY buttons, plays a crucial role in enhancing safety and risk management:

PAUSE: Before implementing new safety measures or when faced with a risky situation, Equilibria teams PAUSE to consider the most appropriate way forward. This reflective practice ensures that the measures are comprehensive and take into account different perspectives and potential risks based on people's natural personality tendencies. By understanding how an individual might get hurt, it becomes easier to recognise how different E-Colours perceive risk.

PLAY: Once safety measures are established, or it's clear that it's safe to proceed, Equilibria encourages active participation from all E-Colours in carrying them out. For example, a Red (Doer) might drive the initiative, a Green (Thinker) ensures every detail is followed, a Blue (Relator) supports everyone's efforts, and a Yellow (Socialiser) keeps the team engaged and motivated.

Equilibria coaches its clients to recognise when Personal Intervention is necessary and how to do so effectively, based on their E-Colour tendencies. This ensures that safety concerns are addressed promptly and appropriately, with each person playing to their strengths while managing their potential limiters.

Case Study 2: E-Colours & Personal Intervention in Emergency Services (EMS)

E-Colours has made a significant impact on the EMS programme at San Jacinto College in Houston. By Q4 2018, all students and faculty had completed Leadership Institute training. Since its introduction, the programme has seen a reduction in medical errors during simulations, thanks to students' understanding of the 'PAUSE-Task-Responsibility' concept.

What's been most revealing is how quickly EMS students recognise the benefits of understanding themselves better – and how using Personal Intervention can have a profound effect on their self-confidence.

Each student is now more aware of their potential limiters and understands the importance of pressing their PLAY button to speak up when they observe a dangerous action or see the need for further intervention. This has led to greater personal accountability, and the programme has introduced a critical thinking exam review using the E-Colours lens, which has helped students improve their exam performance.

There has also been a drop in the number of students dominating class discussions, as they've learned to press PAUSE and make space for others to contribute. Students report feeling more comfortable communicating with their peers in class, without fear of embarrassment if they get something wrong.

Teenagers, Drugs, and Alcohol Abuse

One of the most profound privileges of introducing the E-Colours into school systems was the opportunity to connect with students aged 11 to 16 in residential treatment centres. This chance came through South-West Schools in Houston, Texas, where we first implemented Equilibria's personality diversity tools, as they held the education contract for nine centres across the state. The E-Colours and accompanying tools quickly became essential in helping these young people navigate their path toward self-awareness and better cope with the challenging world around them.

Many of these students, recovering from alcohol and drug addictions, embraced the E-Colours as their coping mechanism. To our amazement and sincere gratitude, they openly shared that after learning about Personal Intervention, they chose to press their PAUSE buttons and rejected the idea of suicide.

Hearing these raw, powerful, and life-saving confessions was both humbling and eye-opening, driving us with even greater urgency to bring the E-Colours to a broader audience.

In conversations with these students, we often asked how they had initially fallen into substance abuse at such a young age. Two responses came up most frequently.

1. 'I couldn't live up to my parents' expectations.' When we asked, 'What are your parents' expectations?' they

often replied, 'I don't know – they've never actually told me.' This highlights the importance of encouraging parents to engage in 'mutual expectations' discussions with their children and loved ones, a point we emphasise every time we share this story.

2. The second response often came from students with dominant E-Colours of Yellow or Blue. They would explain, 'You know my E-Colours – I like to be liked, and it's hard for me to say 'no.' Plus, I don't like conflict, so I just go along with the crowd.'

Remarkably, once these students understood the power of the PAUSE & PLAY buttons, they began to show newfound confidence, leading to more positive and constructive life choices.

Behavioural and Psychological Safety

Integrating the concepts of Personal Intervention and the PAUSE & PLAY buttons with the E-Colours provides a powerful framework for improving safety and risk management within organisations. By introducing self-awareness and team-awareness, encouraging proactive engagement, and promoting a culture of continuous improvement, these practices help ensure that safety becomes more than a set of rules – it becomes a dynamic, inclusive process where every individual's contribution is valued. Equilibria's approach to safety in heavy-duty and high-risk industries demonstrates the effectiveness of these principles, showing that when personality diversity is understood and applied through E-Colours, safety and risk management becomes not just more robust, but also more human-focused.

Taking Personal Intervention Forward

Most behavioural scientists believe it takes three weeks to a month to form a new habit. Practice makes permanent. The use of our PLAY and PAUSE buttons will only come naturally when we've refined the process in a way that works for us individually.

From what we've seen, tools such as our Personal Intervention E-Colour wristbands help facilitate the habit. By wearing your E-Colours and having the PAUSE & PLAY buttons visible on your wrist, you create a tangible reminder to activate them when needed.

Each time you catch yourself about to react, take note of what triggered the impulse, how you were about to react, and what you did instead to respond.

Remember the outcome after you responded. Within a month, you'll likely find yourself reacting less and responding more, naturally.

Jennifer Majano's Story – Personal Intervention: Using the PAUSE & PLAY Buttons

My partner Erick and I were having a conversation the other day. While Erick was talking, I felt the urge to interrupt and finish his sentence or add my thoughts. As a Blue/Yellow, I'm very aware of my E-Colors and know I should PAUSE my thoughts to fully listen when others are talking. I am aware that I should wait until a person is done talking. In my case, interrupting Erick led him to say, 'I wish you would just listen and let me express what I have to say instead of interrupting me.' I realised again that I should have just PAUSED and listened to Erick. I realised that even if we have been together for almost 15 years – my high school sweetheart – it doesn't matter how comfortable you are with someone; interrupting is still not okay. I should be patient and keep practicing when to PAUSE to fully listen to what others have to say.

– Jennifer Majano (Blue/Yellow)
– Manager of Financial Planning and Analysis, USA

Cowboy Solution and the E-Colours of Champions – Lewis Senior

One of the most remarkable examples of the power of understanding our personality diversity technology, expressed through the E-Colours, came from an unlikely place: a ranch in Texas, just north of Houston, run by Dr Don Hutson. Known as the Cowboy Solution, this centre specialises in teaching people the art of effective communication – using horses as their trainers. As you can imagine, horses – unlike people – respond only to genuine, consistent communication. They aren't swayed by hierarchy, status, or social expectations. For them, it's all about clarity and trust.

At the time, many employees from one of our anchor clients were training at the Cowboy Solution, and being familiar with Equilibria, arrived wearing their E-Colour wristbands to show their personality styles. Curious, Dr Hutson began asking about the significance of the colours. He was pointed in my direction, and I soon found myself on a trip to the ranch, joined by one of our E-Colour champions from a nearby school.

We met with Dr Hutson and introduced him to the Equilibria E-Colours model. He immediately recognised the potential to enhance communication and understanding. I left him with a selection of our materials – booklets explaining the E-Colours and PAUSE & PLAY wristbands designed to help people become more aware of their reactions and learn to respond with intention.

A couple of months later, I returned to the ranch and was astonished by what I saw. Every horse at the Cowboy Solution had been assigned an E-Colour and wore a matching wristband on its fetlock – essentially, its 'ankle'. Don and his assistant, Sara, had fully embraced the concept, integrating the E-Colours into their training to help people better recognise and adjust to personality differences, even among the horses.

As word spread, the E-Colours concept reached the Texas A&M University equestrian team. One of the riders' mothers, impressed by what she'd seen at the Cowboy Solution, contacted us. Her daughter was a member of Texas A&M's competitive team, and they faced a particular challenge: while they performed well at home, riding their own horses, they struggled at away events where they were assigned unfamiliar horses. She wondered if the E-Colours could help the team adapt more effectively.

We accepted the invitation and soon began working with the Texas A&M equestrian team and their coaching staff. We helped them recognise not only their own personality styles but also how to observe and interpret the E-Colours of the horses they would ride. Before each away competition, they had only a few minutes to observe a new horse, ride it briefly, and then enter the ring. Developing the ability to quickly read and adjust to each horse's unique personality became an invaluable skill.

Within three years, the Texas A&M team had transformed their competitive approach. By applying personality awareness to understand each horse, they went from struggling in away events to capturing the NCEA National Championship. It became a powerful example of how willing individuals, equipped with E-Colours knowledge, can achieve exceptional results, even in the high-pressure world of collegiate equestrian sports.

E-Colours Observations for Equines – Cowboy Solution, Texas

Red Horses

Based on observations at Cowboy Solution, where the horses have been assigned their top E-Colours, the Red horse is characterised by these tendencies, needs, and rewards.

- **Personality Tendencies:** Strong-willed, confident, alert, and often impatient when standing still. They are eager to be first, with noticeable excess energy. Behaviours include head tossing, stamping, fidgeting; and they may appear confrontational or ego-driven.
- **Needs and Rewards:**
- Red horses want to please and prefer immediate rewards upon completing tasks.
- They respond best to clear, concise vocal rewards and firm physical rewards that are simple and direct.
- They dislike seeing attention given to other horses or people right after them, as they want to feel they're the best.
- Encouragement should come from the whole team, not just the rider.

If this reflects your experience with such horses, it may offer a useful perspective on handling and interacting with them effectively.

Green Horses

Based on the observations at Cowboy Solution, the Green horse is characterised by these tendencies, needs, and rewards.

- **Personality Tendencies:**
    - Accurate in responding to cues and detail-oriented, with a strong focus on tasks – but they require clarity of purpose.
    - Enjoy performing tasks but show little emotional interest in the rider.
    - Persistent, but prone to panicking and overreacting to minor stimuli.
    - Cautious, guarded, and ego-driven, often appearing detached or bored.
    - Highly focused unless over-corrected.
- **Needs and Rewards:**
    - Respond best to calm, straightforward verbal praise and soft pats (avoiding the face).
    - Strongly value personal space and expect it to be respected after completing a task.
    - Their greatest reward is peace: acknowledgment of their effort followed by being left alone.

This description offers helpful strategies for engaging effectively with Green horses. Let us know if you'd like to compare them with other E-Colours.

Yellow Horses

Based on observations at Cowboy Solution, the Yellow horse is characterised by these tendencies, needs, and rewards.

- **Personality Tendencies:**
  - Relationship-oriented rather than task-driven, seeking to please the rider.
  - An interactive 'people pleaser' who enjoys being involved.
  - Welcoming of new experiences and comfortable with personal space being invaded – often expecting the same from others.
  - Alert, interested in interactions, and generally relaxed.
  - Possesses a short attention span.
- **Needs and Rewards:**
  - Thrives on enthusiastic verbal praise and warm, friendly physical reassurance.
  - Must feel included and in frequent contact, needing encouragement from all team members, not just the rider.
  - Dislikes standoffish or detached behaviour, which can cause disengagement and loss of trust.

This description highlights the importance of maintaining a close, interactive, and positive approach when working with Yellow horses.

Blue Horses

Based on the observations at Cowboy Solution, the Blue horse is characterised by these tendencies, needs, and rewards.

- **Personality Tendencies:**
  - Strives not to displease the rider, showing a calm, agreeable, and dependable nature.
  - A people pleaser – composed and patient – yet may display passive-aggressive tendencies.
  - Insecure and reliant on the rider for frequent reassurance.
  - Content with repetitive tasks and not motivated by competition.
  - Tolerates personal space being invaded but does not actively seek it out.

- **Needs and Rewards:**
  - Requires early cues to allow time for processing – soak time is important.
  - Responds poorly to harsh cues; persistence is more effective.
  - Thrives with fair and gentle treatment, though may need stronger cues for motivation – without being pushed too far, as this can cause them to shut down.
  - Works best under supervision with manageable expectations – overburdening can lead to disengagement.

These indicators emphasise a balanced, reassuring, and patient approach when handling Blue horses.

Let us know if you'd like to explore more about these or other horse E-Colour tendencies!

Remixing Life with PAUSE & PLAY – Mark Wilkinson

I had travelled the world as an international DJ, captivating audiences with my house music beats, pianos, vocals, and electronic energy. The music pulsed through the crowd, and I could feel the room lift as everyone moved in rhythm. But while the music thrived on continuous play, over the years I noticed how relentless that energy was – not only for my career but also for my wellbeing.

After many years on the road and in the industry, I reached a turning point. I got ill, took a break, shifted gears, and focused on writing *Life Remixed*, a book about transformation, resilience, and finding purpose beyond the turntables and the dancefloor. That journey led me to answer the E-Colours questionnaire, where I discovered more about my personality, my strengths, and the areas I needed to work on – described as my potential limiters. This exploration introduced me to the PAUSE & PLAY model, a concept that deeply resonated with my life in music and beyond.

The idea of PAUSE & PLAY was simple but profound. Just as DJs control the night and the flow of music by mixing beats together, hitting PAUSE or PLAY at the right moments, each person can learn to manage their own reactions, impulses, and strengths. I quickly realised that, as a top colour Yellow, I naturally brought energy, enthusiasm, and optimism to my life and work – qualities that were vital to my success. However, the E-Colours model helped me identify some potential limiters too, like a tendency to be emotional, easily distracted or overly talkative, which could at times overwhelm others or cloud my own focus.

I began practicing the PAUSE & PLAY technique to use my strengths more effectively. When faced with new projects or big decisions, I learned to PAUSE and assess my approach, noticing if my enthusiasm was pushing me too quickly into action. Then I would choose to PLAY with intention, directing my energy more purposefully. This process became my internal DJ mixer, helping me manage my instincts instead of letting them manage me.

In the music industry, I saw clear parallels to the importance of pacing and balance. Just as DJs shape their sets with pauses, crescendos, and drops to keep the crowd engaged, I began shaping my own rhythm in life. I recognised that PLAY moments were essential for sharing my talents and connecting with audiences, but the PAUSE moments were just as important – for recharging, reflecting, and resetting my direction.

Over time, I noticed a shift in how I approached both my personal and professional life. By managing my personality tendencies with this new awareness, I found it easier to focus on what truly mattered. The PAUSE & PLAY model allowed me to create inner harmony – blending my strengths and managing my limiters to achieve success beyond what I'd known as a DJ.

In the end, *Life Remixed* wasn't just about my experiences, it was about finding a new rhythm, one that combined passion with intention and energy with balance. My journey became a remix in itself – of music, personality, and purpose, crafted through the powerful blend of understanding and applying PAUSE & PLAY.

Paul's Story

E-Colours has truly been a game changer for my personal and professional growth, providing me with invaluable thoughts into my personality and how I interact with the world around me. By significantly heightening my self-awareness, it has enabled me to understand and address long-standing questions about myself.

I previously viewed certain personality tendencies as insurmountable weaknesses, accepting them as 'it is what it is.' I now know, through working with E-Colours, that these are not weaknesses – they are potential limiters that need to be effectively managed. I'm actively employing the Personal Intervention PAUSE & PLAY tools. It's a work in progress, but one that's yielding incremental daily improvements.

The change I've seen in myself and the power I've witnessed in E-Colours led me to become an E-Colours Practitioner, so that I can help others realise their potential – empowering them to adapt, develop, and thrive.

– Paul Davis (Blue/Red)
– E-Colours Practitioner, Director & Partner, Davis&, Dubai

Brian's Story

E-Colours is an amazing journey of beautiful discovery and continues to grow and get even better! It has revolutionised the way we operate as a family – all members knowing our E-Colours and being able to grow even more as a loving, caring unit. Thank you so very much, Lewis and Mark.

— Brian Merchant (Yellow/Blue)
— Police Trainer and E-Colours Practitioner, UK

* * *

Remix Opportunities

After reviewing the examples below of how different personalities apply PAUSE & PLAY, how do you intend to use Personal Intervention in both your home and work life?

The Red Doer:

I have to hit my Red PAUSE button when I know others are working their hardest but aren't keeping up with me. That also means hitting my Blue – PLAY button to calm down, step back, support them, and understand where they're coming from.

The Yellow Socialiser:

I use my Yellow PAUSE button when I catch myself talking and not listening to other suggestions that may be out there.

The Blue Relator:

I tend to ramble about my thoughts or ideas and sometimes try too hard to get people to see things my way. I'm learning to hit my Blue PAUSE button to organise my thoughts and be more open to change.

The Green Thinker:

I need to learn to use my Green PAUSE button. I'm always thinking about a better, simpler, more orderly way to do things. I struggle to turn off my Green PLAY button even at home.

CHAPTER 11

UNDERSTANDING AND APPLYING PSYCHOLOGICAL SAFETY USING THE E-COLOURS & PERSONAL INTERVENTION

'Psychological safety is not about being nice. It's about giving candid feedback, openly admitting mistakes, and learning from each other.'

– **Dr Amy Edmondson**, renowned scholar, professor, and author, is widely recognised for her work on psychological safety and team dynamics

Psychological safety doesn't start with policies or programs. It begins the moment someone feels seen, heard, and valued – exactly as they are.

Imagine walking into a room where you don't have to pretend. Where your questions are welcome, your mistakes are met with curiosity instead of judgement, and your voice – no matter how different – is not only allowed but required. That's psychological safety. And it's not just a nice-to-have. It's the foundation of every high-performing, deeply connected, and truly human team.

But this doesn't happen by accident. It's built, brick by brick, through awareness, intention, and courageous conversations. That's where the E-Colours & Personal Intervention come in – not as abstract ideas, but as everyday tools for transformation.

In this chapter, we'll explore how understanding ourselves and others through the lens of personality diversity opens the door to trust. How pressing the PAUSE button helps us respond with intention instead of reaction. How choosing PLAY invites others to do the same. And how, together, we can create environments where people don't just survive – but thrive.

You'll hear how a simple framework turned silence into breakthrough at a renewable energy firm, and how a zoo became a model for connection by embracing personality diversity in every conversation, at every level.

Because when people feel psychologically safe, they bring their ideas, their energy, and their full selves. And that's when innovation happens. That's when trust grows. That's when teams become families, and workplaces become communities.

So let's reimagine what's possible – starting with the simple decision to understand ourselves, and each other, a little better.

Introduction to Psychological Safety

Psychological safety has emerged as a critical factor in fostering a productive and innovative work environment. It is the belief that one can speak up, express ideas, and admit mistakes without fear of retribution. The E-Colours & Personal Intervention framework, developed by Equilibria, adds another dimension by offering tools to better understand personality diversity and improve self-awareness and communication.

Equilibria has chosen to explore psychological safety through the lens of personality diversity. The combination of psychological safety, E-Colours, and Personal Intervention can transform teams – leading to more effective collaboration, reduced risk, and enhanced performance. This book explores the significant impact these concepts have on workplace dynamics and how they can be used together to foster a thriving organisational culture.

Understanding Psychological Safety

Definition and Importance: Psychological safety refers to a shared belief that the work environment is safe for interpersonal risk-taking. The concept was popularised by Amy Edmondson, a professor at Harvard Business School, who highlighted that psychological safety is a key driver of learning, innovation, and growth within teams.

The Four Stages of Psychological Safety: Psychological safety can be broken down into four distinct stages:

- **Inclusion Safety:** The foundation of psychological safety is where individuals feel they belong.
- **Learner Safety:** Where employees feel safe to ask questions, make mistakes, and learn.
- **Contributor Safety:** Allows employees to contribute to the team using their unique skills.
- **Challenger Safety:** The most advanced stage, where employees feel secure enough to challenge the status quo.

Psychological Safety and Performance: Numerous studies have shown that teams with high psychological safety consistently outperform those without it. This is because psychological safety promotes open communication, creativity, and resilience – all of which are essential for navigating the complexities of today's work environment.

Introducing E-Colours & Personal Intervention

How E-Colours Enhances Self-Awareness: Self-awareness enables individuals to better manage their behaviour and interactions with others, leading to more effective teamwork and collaboration.

The Role of E-Colours in Team Dynamics: Teams that understand and appreciate the diverse E-Colours within the group are better equipped to leverage each member's strengths and manage potential limiters. This understanding fosters a more inclusive environment, where all voices are heard and valued – closely aligned with the concept of psychological safety.

Personal Intervention – PAUSE & PLAY Concept: Personal Intervention, through the use of the PAUSE & PLAY buttons, offers practical tools that align with the psychological safety framework. They represent the idea that individuals can choose to reflect before acting – PAUSE, or proceed with intention and awareness – PLAY.

The Intersection of Psychological Safety with E-Colours & Personal Intervention

Building Psychological Safety with E-Colours & Personal Intervention: E-Colours & Personal Intervention provide a powerful foundation for creating and maintaining psychological safety within teams. By promoting self-awareness and a better understanding of others, this approach supports individuals in navigating diverse communication styles, reducing misunderstandings, and building trust.

- **Communication**: E-Colours & Personal Intervention support open and honest communication by helping team members understand their colleagues' preferred communication styles and how they might interpret feedback or criticism.

- **Conflict Resolution**: Knowing the E-Colours & Personal Intervention of team members can assist in resolving conflicts more effectively by offering ideas into their underlying motivations and concerns.

Psychological safety can be strengthened through E-Colours & Personal Intervention, adding significant value to any organisation.

A Culture Transformed – The Story of a Renewable Energy Company

A global organisation known for its innovation was quietly struggling with a hidden issue: psychological safety. Employees hesitated to speak up, fearing criticism or judgement. This silent barrier stifled creativity and hindered the company's growth.

Enter Suzie, the new HR director. Having recently completed training in the E-Colours methodology and Personal Intervention model, she quickly noticed a pattern: team members often reacted to situations based on their personality tendencies, leading to misunderstandings and conflict. Determined to foster a safer environment, she proposed a bold initiative – embedding E-Colours & Personal Intervention into the company's culture.

Step 1: Awareness

Suzie began by introducing the E-Colours online questionnaire to the entire organisation. Employees were encouraged to explore their personality tendencies and percentages. The results revealed a broad mix: Yellows (Socialisers) who thrived on energy and ideas, Blues (Relators) who valued harmony, Reds (Doers) who drove results, and Greens (Thinkers) who sought clarity and precision. Suzie emphasised that no E-Colour was 'better' than any other. The focus was on understanding and valuing these differences.

Step 2: Education

Using the information from their Premium Reports, Suzie held interactive workshops to help employees recognise their strengths and potential limiters. She highlighted the crucial difference between personality – how we act naturally, and character – how we consciously choose to act. This distinction became the foundation of their training sessions and started to embed in their company culture.

Step 3: Reactions vs Responses

One of the most transformative lessons was learning to distinguish between automatic, personality-based reactions and intentional, character-driven responses. In a memorable session, an engineering team re-enacted a tense project meeting. Initially, participants reacted based on instinct/personality: interrupting, withdrawing, or avoiding conflict. With the help of the PAUSE & PLAY method, they learned to step back, reflect, and respond thoughtfully. The change was palpable.

Step 4: Building Psychological Safety

As employees practiced Personal Intervention, the impact was felt across the organisation. Leaders who had previously reacted with impatience began to press the PAUSE button and respond with empathy. Teams used the PLAY button to initiate conversations about challenges without fear. Gradually, trust deepened, and a sense of safety emerged.

A defining moment came during a company-wide meeting. A junior analyst named Alex pressed his PLAY button and shared a bold idea for improving a key process. Before the E-Colours initiative, Alex would have kept quiet. But now, supported by the culture of psychological safety, his idea triggered a breakthrough that ended up saving the company millions of dollars.

The Outcome

Within a year, the company's transformation was unmistakable. Engagement scores soared, innovation flourished, and employee turnover dropped dramatically. Teams collaborated more cohesively, using their understanding of E-Colours to balance strengths and navigate challenges with confidence.

Suzie's initiative demonstrated that psychological safety wasn't just a leadership trend – it was a tangible outcome driven by self-awareness and intentional behaviour. The organisation became a leading example of how E-Colours & Personal Intervention could turn a struggling workplace into a thriving, innovative community.

Practical Applications

Using E-Colours & Personal Intervention to Enhance Psychological Safety: E-Colours & Personal Intervention can play a vital role in risk management by helping teams recognise and address the cognitive biases and blind spots that may lead to poor decision-making.

The PAUSE & PLAY Concept: In risk management, Personal Intervention using the PAUSE & PLAY buttons is a tool that aligns with both psychological safety and the E-Colours framework.

Psychological Safety and Risk Management: Psychological safety allows team members to speak up when they notice potential risks, which is essential for effective risk management. When employees feel safe to raise concerns, organisations can address issues before they escalate into more serious problems.

E-Colours in Hospitality – Lewis Senior

Houston-based hotel management company American Liberty Hospitality (ALH) took a deep dive into Intentional Leadership with Equilibria throughout 2018. The process began with the Executive Team revisiting the vision, mission, and values of ALH, which has a 50-year history of owning, operating, and developing hotels. They recognised that their culture was mostly passed down from employee to employee, and while that was encouraging, it was more accidental than intentional.

The senior leadership team embraced the challenge to grow through self and team awareness, leveraging E-Colour combinations and diversity of thought. The programme elevated team performance both collectively and individually while remaining sustainable for the future. Importantly, ALH leaders appreciated that the training upheld the company's existing culture and values – it didn't change the company's deep history and roots, but spotlighted and reinforced them.

The training came at a pivotal time in the ALH journey. For many decades, operations had been directed solely by the family ownership. But with continued growth, the corporate office staff has grown considerably, and decision-making responsibilities are now shared among key executive team members.

The E-Colours training was instrumental in getting the ALH Executive Team aligned around a shared approach to Intentional Leadership. Since the monthly sessions in 2018, the team has introduced the Equilibria Personality Diversity Indicator (PDI) to hotel-level associates and has been amazed by the enthusiasm and natural alignment with the hospitality industry. Associates at all levels are eager for the Equilibria tools and concepts, which affirm that personality diversity is a good thing. It's simple: when employees are better equipped to interact with people, they are more successful in this industry. That success breeds victories at the guest level, which then transcend to all other levels.

ALH also created custom, co-branded collateral that incorporates Equilibria content – tangible pieces that reinforce the concepts and communicate the permanence of the programme. One such piece, the size of a hotel key card, displays the E-Colour concepts in a quick-reference format.

A Culture of Continuous Improvement

Continuous Learning and Psychological Safety: Psychological safety is essential for cultivating a learning culture where employees feel encouraged to share knowledge, experiment, and learn from failures. This ongoing cycle of learning is critical for organisational resilience and innovation.

E-Colours & Personal Intervention as a Tool for Continuous Improvement: E-Colours & Personal Intervention supports continuous improvement by offering a structured approach to self-assessment and team development. Regular reflection on E-Colours, combined with active use of the PAUSE & PLAY buttons, helps individuals and teams identify opportunities for growth and development.

Integrating E-Colours & Personal Intervention and Psychological Safety in Leadership Development: Leaders play a vital role in fostering psychological safety and using E-Colours & Personal Intervention within their teams is key to continuous improvement. Leadership development programs that incorporate both elements can equip leaders with practical tools to build high-performing, resilient teams.

Challenges and Best Practices

Overcoming Resistance to Change: As noted previously, introducing concepts like psychological safety, E-Colours, and Personal Intervention into an organisation can be met with resistance or scepticism. We look to explore strategies for overcoming these challenges, including securing leadership involvement, providing consistent training and coaching, and demonstrating the value of these ideas through ongoing programmes.

Best Practices for Sustaining Psychological Safety, E-Colours & Personal Intervention: Maintaining the benefits of psychological safety and E-Colours & Personal Intervention requires ongoing investment. Best practices include regular training, embedding an E-Colours Coach or Practitioner, integrating these concepts into performance reviews, and celebrating successes that arise from their application.

E-Colours at the Houston Zoo – Lewis Senior

Home to over 6,000 animals and attracting more than two million visitors annually, the Houston Zoo is among the fastest-growing zoos in North America. As Houston's top visitor attraction, it serves as a vibrant space to connect communities with wildlife and inspire efforts to protect global biodiversity.

This level of success demands extraordinary collaboration. Behind the scenes, a committed team works tirelessly to care for animals, educate the public, and maintain the Zoo's status as a must-visit destination for Houstonians and tourists. With over 450 employees across 22 departments and various shifts, strong communication and efficient decision-making are vital.

Equilibria partnered with the Zoo to strengthen leadership and team dynamics. Starting with the leadership, Equilibria focused on identifying strengths and areas for development, laying the foundation for improved engagement. One of Equilibria's coaches, experienced in education and nonprofits, worked with the Zoo's training manager to co-design a programme tailored to the organisation's needs. The initiative began with leadership, who participated in a series of sessions designed to integrate Equilibria principles into daily practices. Supervisors and team leads followed, with the ultimate goal of introducing all Zoo staff to the programme.

A key component of the initiative was the Personality Diversity Indicator (PDI), which participants completed before their sessions. This tool helps individuals identify their E-Colours, a framework that categorises personality and communication styles.

This straightforward yet powerful approach enhances self-awareness, enabling more intentional choices in collaboration and communication. As the programme gained traction, staff began incorporating E-Colours into daily routines – wearing badges, updating email signatures, and even sporting wristbands across Zoo grounds.

The E-Colours initiative nurtured a culture of self-awareness and intentional behaviour, empowering employees to embrace personality diversity. Ongoing team activities continue to strengthen decision-making and cross-departmental communication.

To ensure the programme's long-term sustainability, selected staff members became E-Colour Champions through a 'train-the-trainer' model. These Champions, supported by advanced coaching from Equilibria, are now equipped to train new employees and reinforce the programme over time. Equilibria now provides support on an as-needed basis, with the programme led by those who live and model its principles daily. As the Houston Zoo cements its status as a leader in wildlife conservation, it has also prioritised internal trust and communication. By leveraging its human capital, the Zoo has strengthened its internal culture, ensuring its team is equipped to make intentional, impactful decisions. Equilibria is proud to have played a role in that transformation, helping the Houston Zoo shine as a global example of leadership and collaboration.

Future Trends and Innovations

The Role of Technology in Enhancing Psychological Safety, E-Colours & Personal Intervention: Advancements in technology, such as AI-driven assessments and virtual reality training, present new opportunities to enhance psychological safety and the application of E-Colours & Personal Intervention.

These tools provide more personalised ideas and create immersive learning experiences.

The Evolving Workplace and Psychological Safety: The workplace is undergoing a significant transformation. With the rise of remote and hybrid teams, traditional office dynamics are giving way to virtual collaboration and flexible schedules. While these changes bring undeniable benefits, they also introduce new challenges, particularly around maintaining connection, trust, and effective communication among globally distributed teams.

Why Psychological Safety Matters: Psychological safety – the belief that team members can speak up, share ideas, and take risks without fear of embarrassment or retribution – has always been essential to high-performing teams. In today's changing workplace, its significance is even greater.

- **Remote Disconnect:** Without the face-to-face interactions of traditional offices, misunderstandings and feelings of isolation can increase. Psychological safety helps bridge this gap by fostering open communication and trust.
- **Diverse Teams:** As workplaces become more global, teams often include people from varied cultural backgrounds and perspectives. Psychological safety ensures these differences are embraced rather than stifled.

Innovation Demands: Thriving in a fast-paced, competitive environment requires bold, creative ideas. Psychological safety encourages employees to think outside the box and share their thoughts freely.

The Role of E-Colours & Personal Intervention: This is where E-Colours & Personal Intervention come into play. These frameworks offer practical strategies to address the challenges of modern workplaces.

- **Understanding Personality Tendencies:** E-Colours enables team members to recognise their own and others' communication styles and tendencies. This awareness reduces conflict and misunderstanding, especially in remote settings where nonverbal cues are limited.
- **Building Empathy:** By identifying different personality strengths and potential limiters, teams learn to value diverse perspectives and foster mutual respect.
- **Proactive Behaviour:** Personal Intervention, through the use of PAUSE & PLAY, empowers individuals to respond thoughtfully rather than react impulsively, even under pressure. This is particularly valuable in fast-paced or high-pressure virtual environments.

A Future of Connected Teams: As the workplace continues to evolve, psychological safety will remain a cornerstone of success. E-Colours & Personal Intervention equip teams with the skills to navigate this complexity, providing the tools needed to stay connected, collaborative, and resilient. They provide a framework for creating inclusive cultures where every voice is valued and where innovation thrives.

The evolving workplace is a challenge, but it is also a tremendous opportunity. By prioritising psychological safety and embracing tools that enhance self-awareness and intentional action, organisations position their teams not just to adapt, but to excel in this new era.

Mel's Story

> *Anyone even considering using E-Colours – don't think twice, just do it! What an impact it's had on our diverse, geographically spread team. The progress we've made in the last twelve months using E-Colours has been transformational. Thank you, Mark and Emma.*
>
> – Mel Butler (Blue/Yellow)
– Senior Health and Safety Manager, Excellence and Engagement, QinetiQ UK

The interplay between psychological safety, E-Colours, and Personal Intervention offers a powerful approach to enhancing workplace effectiveness. By fostering an environment where individuals feel safe to express themselves, and where personality diversity is recognised and appreciated, organisations can unlock the full potential of their teams. As the workplace continues to evolve, the integration of these concepts is essential for building resilient, high-performing organisations.

* * *

Remix Opportunities

As you review the information connecting psychological safety, E-Colours, and Personal Intervention, what steps can you take to achieve these results?

- Create an environment of psychological safety for the people you interact with.
- Consider and share with others what *you* need in order to feel that you are in a psychologically safe environment.

CHAPTER 12

PRACTICAL APPLICATIONS OF THE E-COLOURS & PERSONAL INTERVENTION

> 'Between stimulus and response there is a space. In that space is our power to choose our response. In our response lies our growth and our freedom.'
>
> – **Stephen Covey**, author of *7 Habits of Highly Effective People*

This quote underscores the importance of not only acknowledging personality diversity but also actively valuing and integrating it into our interactions and collaborations.

Awareness is where the journey begins. Action is where transformation takes root.

You've explored the information, understood the tendencies, felt the resonance of your E-Colours, and perhaps had more than a few 'aha' moments along the way. But here's the truth: awareness, on its own, is never enough. It's what you do with that awareness that changes lives – yours and those around you.

This chapter is the bridge between theory and impact. Between knowing and becoming. Between understanding yourself and using that understanding to shape stronger relationships, safer environments, and more resilient teams.

From oil rigs and construction sites to classrooms and hospital wards, boardrooms, dog sleds in the tundra, and even music festivals – E-Colours & Personal Intervention have proven their worth not just as tools, but as lifelines. Because whether you're leading others, working alongside them, or simply trying to show up better each day, the ability to communicate intentionally, resolve conflict constructively, and respond rather than react… is everything.

In the pages that follow, you'll find real-world stories and practical steps for living your E-Colours with purpose. You'll learn how to delegate, how to listen, how to lead, and perhaps most importantly, how to PAUSE. You'll see how psychological safety can be built conversation by conversation. How trust grows not from grand gestures, but from daily decisions to understand before being understood.

And you'll realise that what started as a personality indicator can become a personal legacy. So, let's go beyond awareness. Let's get practical. Let's remix who we are – intentionally.

Unlocking the Full Potential of E-Colours & Personal Intervention

In a world where understanding human behaviour is key to success in both personal and professional spheres, the E-Colours system and the concept of Personal Intervention provide powerful, transformative tools. However, their full potential is only realised through consistent, practical application in daily life.

Personalities Remixed explores how the E-Colours framework, when moved beyond theory and integrated into real-world scenarios, can revolutionise the way individuals and teams operate. Through practical examples, you'll learn how to effectively harness your own and others' personality strengths, while managing potential limiters. Whether it's improving communication, strengthening leadership, minimising risk, resolving conflict, fostering psychological safety, building a more inclusive and productive work environment, and creating a harmonious family life, this book illustrates the practical steps needed to make the E-Colours & Personal Intervention an integral part of everyday interactions.

Through practical application, the abstract becomes concrete, and the theoretical becomes transformative. *Personalities Remixed* is your companion in bridging the gap between knowing and doing, helping you integrate E-Colours & Personal Intervention into all areas of life using Equilibria's actionable intelligence:

- The Wells Model
- Intentional Communication
- How Can I Get Hurt? – Physically and Emotionally
- Intentional Leadership Behaviours
- How to Delegate to Me
- If You Want Me to Listen
- When Working with Me
- Effective Form of Recognition
- Conflict Resolution
- Doubt & Resistance

- Premium Reports
- Alignment Reports
- Essential Leadership Cycle
- Intentional Leadership
- Advanced Error Reduction in Organisations (AERO)

* * *

THE WELLS MODEL

When using a model to envisage something, particularly in the context of tools like E-Colours & Personal Intervention, it involves creating a conceptual framework that allows you to visualise and anticipate outcomes based on certain variables or behaviours. This approach is particularly effective in understanding how different personality tendencies interact in real-life situations and in anticipating the effects of these interactions.

For example, consider a team made up of individuals with diverse E-Colour styles. By using a model that maps out these personalities, you can begin to visualise how team dynamics might evolve. This model helps anticipate potential challenges and offers strategies for mitigating the issues through Personal Intervention. Taking this proactive approach enables you to craft more effective, cohesive teams by anticipating and addressing problems before they arise.

The expression 'A picture is worth a thousand words' has been attributed to many sources, but is most widely associated with an advertising campaign by Fred R. Bernard in the 1920s – *Printers' Ink*.

Consider someone's four E-Colours shown as four distinct water wells (see Figure 8).

Figure 8 – The Wells Model – In Calm Waters
Copyright © 2025 Equilibria Services Pte Ltd. All rights reserved.

The top E-Colour shown is **Green** (Thinker). Due to their natural tendencies, being higher up the well makes it easier and more instinctive to access the strengths associated with a Green. It is also easier and quicker to access the potential limiters associated with a Green.

The second E-Colour shown is **Yellow** (Socialiser). Although it will be slightly more challenging to access the strengths and potential limiters compared to that of the top Green, they are still readily available and play a part in this person's personality tendencies.

The third E-Colour is **Red** (Doer). These strengths remain accessible, though it takes more deliberate effort to engage them, and the potential limiters may be less relevant.

The fourth and lowest E-Colour is **Blue** (Relator). As this personality style gets deeper in the well, accessing its strengths requires even more effort, and the potential limiters become even less relevant.

By now, you can likely see how the model functions: the higher the percentage of a particular E-Colour, the easier it is to access these strengths and potential limiters. The lower the percentage, the more challenging it is to access those strengths and potential limiters.

In moments of smooth sailing and minimal stress, we can effectively harness the full spectrum of E-Colour strengths and potential challenges. This requires skillfully managing personal tendencies and employing techniques such as Personal Intervention, which empower individuals to activate their PAUSE & PLAY buttons.

Figure 9 – The Wells Model – In Choppy Waters
Copyright © 2025 Equilibria Services Pte Ltd. All rights reserved.

However, life isn't always so accommodating. Pressures, stress, conflict, and tight deadlines often create the 'turbulent waters' we must navigate. In stressful moments, the Green E-Colour well could almost overflow, exaggerating strengths and potential limiters. This is when the internal PAUSE & PLAY buttons become even more important to manage our RESPONSES.

At Equilibria, we help build high-performing environments by equipping individuals with tools to navigate these challenging situations. Even a simple tool – like an E-Colour wristband, designed to create a PAUSE or PLAY moment for the wearer – can help steer you toward the most effective course of action.

* * *

INTENTIONAL COMMUNICATION

Intentional communication with E-Colours & Personal Intervention is about being mindful and consciously deliberate in how you interact with others, based on an understanding of their E-Colours and your own.

Here is a simple guide to help you with intentional communication.

Red (Doer): an independent personality, task-oriented, likes to tell, and asks the questions 'WHAT?' and 'WHEN?'

If you recognise the following Red communication style (verbal and visual):

- Displays impatience
- Likes to keep their distance
- Tends to be blunt and to the point

Consider the following approach when communicating:

- Be clear, specific, and brief
- Present the information logically
- Offer alternatives and choices for decision-making

Blue (Relator): an interdependent personality, people-oriented, likes to relate, and asks the question 'WHY?'

If you recognise the following Blue communication style (verbal and visual):

- Displays openness and a steady, measured pace
- Can be reluctant to speak up in large groups
- Has a calm and patient demeanour

Consider the following approach:

- Start with a personal comment to break the ice
- Show sincere interest in them as a person
- Listen to understand and respond thoughtfully

Green (Thinker): an independent personality, task-oriented, likes to explain, and asks the question 'HOW?'

If you recognise the following Green communication style (verbal and visual):

- Comes across as autonomous or independent
- Asks for pointed information
- Looks for facts and data, not stories

Consider the following approach:

- Approach them in a direct and logical way
- Provide solid, practical information
- Give thorough detail

Yellow (Socialiser): an interdependent personality, people-oriented, likes to engage, and asks the question 'WHO?' – and often, 'Can I get involved?'

If you recognise the following Yellow communication style (verbal and visual):

- Displays openness and willingness to engage
- Tends to talk more than listen
- Speaks on a variety of subjects in a friendly tone

Consider the following approach:

- Be sociable, relatable, and friendly
- Avoid overwhelming them with detail
- Invite their opinions and ideas

Ultimately, intentional communication using E-Colours & Personal Intervention is about fostering more positive, productive interactions by minimising misunderstandings, improving collaboration, and fostering a more supportive environment. It's about aligning your communication style with others' preferences to achieve the best possible outcomes.

A Musher's Reflection on E-Colours: Lessons from the Icy Tundra – Lewis Senior

The following heartfelt account comes from a musher who worked with Equilibria coaches in the icy reaches of Ells River, Canada. Through these experiences, he developed a deeper appreciation for the dynamics between himself and his team of huskies, guided by the E-Colours framework.

> *Lewis, I received your email this morning, and once again, Equilibria has made us feel like a million bucks. Highlighting Happy in your Operational Excellence moment was incredibly touching – it made us feel special and appreciated. We'd be honoured if you shared it with your team.*
>
> *I can't begin to describe how many times that dog drove me crazy, yet just as often, he saved the morale of our teams. Looking back, I now realise that because Happy's dominant E-Colour is Yellow, his need for sociability is essential for him to thrive. Without understanding it at the time, we naturally placed him in situations where his strengths became an asset rather than a hindrance.*
>
> *From an E-Colours perspective, Happy was utilised to the best of his ability – aligned with who he was and what he was naturally good at. On challenging trails, he was always part of the team tackling the toughest stretches. By mid-afternoon, when spirits were low, Happy would lift everyone up, ensuring we always made it back home.*
>
> *Encouragement, like direction, is often better received by the team when it comes from one of their own. With dogs, I've noticed they speak the same language and communicate on a shared level. It's incredible to witness this dynamic.*

For instance, some dogs excel at maintaining order among their peers, stepping in to correct others before issues escalate into bad habits. These dogs are often very team-oriented, and exclusion from the group genuinely affects them emotionally.

Young dogs, on the other hand, sometimes lack the discipline to stay focused, particularly if their tasks aren't engaging enough. When paired with mature dogs with strong work ethics, these younger ones quickly learn that goofing off isn't acceptable. Watching them absorb this lesson from their peers is inspiring – they'll often glance back at me for approval. When I show support for the correction, they accept it without resentment. If I were to issue the same discipline myself, there's a good chance it would hurt their feelings and diminish the effectiveness of the lesson.

Top E-Colour Green dogs excel in this role, turning corrections into an art form. They instinctively know when and how to intervene, though they sometimes forget they're dealing with puppies still exploring the world.

Then there's Jack, our steadfast top E-Colour Blue dog. Over the years, he has never let me down. He's relentless in his work ethic, sometimes to the point of overworking to compensate for weaker team members. Jack has taught countless puppies the value of a 'head down and work' attitude. He leads by example rather than position, embodying what it means to inspire through action. It brings tears to my eyes to think how our lack of understanding early on nearly ruined such a remarkable dog. That's a lesson I'll carry with me forever.

Equilibria's E-Colours programme has not only made us better mushers but also better breeders, and ultimately, better people.

Thank you for giving us the tools to understand and nurture the incredible personalities within our team.

* * *

HOW CAN I GET HURT? (PHYSICALLY AND EMOTIONALLY) – Lewis Senior

Having worked in the oil and gas industry since the mid-1970s, I have witnessed countless incidents, injuries, and fatalities that left me continually questioning what we might have been missing. As HSE manager for a large drilling contractor, I was assured of our senior leadership's commitment to investing in safety equipment, programmes, and processes to protect our workforce. Yet, during a series of mergers and acquisitions in the early 2000s, a string of fatalities deeply affected me on both a personal and professional level.

A pivotal moment occurred in Nigeria in 2004, following a tragic incident on one of our most modern oil rigs. While trying to understand what we were missing, during conversations with the crew, a supervisor with some understanding of personality diversity posed a simple yet profoundly impactful question: 'Why don't you ask us the obvious question – how can we get hurt?' This straightforward yet powerful query triggered a major realisation and became the foundation for a new approach to safety. It became clear that this question applied not only to safety and risk management, but also to teamwork, effective communication, and recognising both physical and emotional harm.

In high-risk environments, this question often takes on even greater weight, evolving into 'How could I get hurt, maimed, or killed?' – a sobering reflection that often leads to meaningful and consistent answers.

The question 'How Can I Get Hurt?' has since become a core element of the E-Colours & Personal Intervention process. It fosters self-awareness and promotes thoughtful reflection before acting or making decisions, especially in high-pressure situations. When used in pre-task meetings, this question opens the door to vital conversations. Once participants identify potential risks, the discussion naturally progresses to: 'So how could I or we prevent it?' – establishing a strong foundation for proactive and effective safety practices.

E-Colours & Personal Intervention Process

1. **Understanding Self-Awareness**

    When faced with a situation that might provoke a strong emotional REACTION, asking yourself, 'How Can I Get Hurt?' helps you PAUSE and consider the possible negative outcomes of your natural REACTION. This question encourages you to reflect on the potential emotional, relational, or professional consequences before REACTING impulsively. By giving yourself a moment of awareness, you are now better positioned to RESPOND and cause a better outcome.

2. **Recognising Your E-Colours Tendencies**
    - Each E-Colour is associated with its own set of strengths and potential limiters. For instance, someone with dominant Red (Doer) tendencies might REACT quickly or assertively under stress, while someone with strong Green (Thinker) tendencies might overanalyse and become paralysed by indecision.

- By asking 'How Can I Get Hurt?', you bring attention to the possible pitfalls of your predominant E-Colours. This allows you to RECOGNISE when your natural tendencies could lead to conflict, misunderstanding, or other forms of pain or harm – and choose to RESPOND accordingly.

3. **Encouraging Personal Intervention**
   - Personal Intervention means consciously interrupting automatic REACTION patterns to choose a more mindful, appropriate course of action. Asking 'How Can I Get Hurt?' triggers this process, prompting you to consider alternative RESPONSES that better fit the situation and the people involved.
   - For example, if you're inclined to REACT with impatience – a potential Red (Doer) tendency – this question might help you pause, reassess the situation, and choose a calmer RESPONSE, avoiding unnecessary conflict, strain, and emotional or physical injury.

4. **Promoting Empathy and Perspective-Taking**
   - The question also encourages you to consider the impact of your REACTION on others, not just yourself. Asking 'How Can I Get Hurt?' often leads you to consider how others could also get hurt, leading to a more empathetic and considerate approach.
   - This is especially valuable in risk management, teamwork, and relationships, where the goal is to create constructive interactions and avoid unnecessary tension or harm.

5. **Enhancing Decision-Making**
   - Ultimately, 'How Can I Get Hurt?' serves as a tool for improved self-awareness and decision-making. It helps you weigh the risks of your natural tendency to REACT

against the potential outcomes, and choose a more thoughtful path that minimises harm and maximises positive results by RESPONDING.
- This allows you to act in alignment with your values and goals, rather than out of habit or emotion.

If you can predict it, you can manage it – and what better way to make a prediction than by asking the right questions? 'How Can I Get Hurt?' is one such question. People know themselves best, so rather than guess, just ask. Since 2004, this and other key questions have helped us build a robust data lake of responses, allowing us to continually and scientifically validate the use of personality diversity in raising awareness.

These documented responses, drawn from ongoing research, are based on both primary and secondary E-Colours. Remarkably, no matter where we work in the world, the answers have become strikingly predictable for each personality style.

Here is what people have told us from a Top E-Colour perspective.

Yellow (Socialiser) – 'How Can I Get Hurt?'

- Jumping in to help someone
- Not listening to instructions
- Getting distracted
- Being overly creative
- By being overconfident
- By taking on too much to please others
- By not following the procedure or process

Blue (Relator) – 'How Can I Get Hurt?'

- By relying on others
- Not asking questions, as I don't like confrontation
- By not being included, or inserting myself
- Working under pressure
- Being distracted by my own thoughts
- When being or feeling rushed
- By assigning emotions to situations

Red (Doer) – 'How Can I Get Hurt?'

- Through my impatience
- Being unaware of my surroundings
- By taking risks
- Being too focused on the task
- Not listening to all the instructions
- Acting out of annoyance
- When it's someone else's fault

Green (Thinker) – 'How Can I Get Hurt?'

- When taking something for granted
- When there's no proper plan
- By a lack of sufficient information
- Experiencing a loss of control
- When others don't follow the plan or procedure
- When the task becomes too complicated
- By being judged harshly

By introducing these discussions into the high-risk industries we serve worldwide, we see a marked increase in self-awareness among participants, leading to a reduction in accidents and incidents. Whether individuals agree or disagree with the specifics shared, the critical point is initiating these conversations. Doing so raises awareness and empowers people to identify and articulate how they might be at risk and to implement preventative measures.

'How Can I Get Hurt?' is a powerful question within the E-Colours & Personal Intervention framework. It's where it all began for Equilibria – to the best of our knowledge, no other personality tool has ever asked this question. It raises self-awareness and awareness of others, encourages deliberate and constructive actions, and helps people navigate difficult situations with greater mindfulness and care, leading to better outcomes both personally and professionally.

Continuous Research

Since the initial question was asked, Equilibria has continued to pose multiple questions to individuals completing their PDI questionnaires – another key differentiator from any other personality tool on the market.

We use a database approach to verify and validate our ongoing research into personality diversity. Through online surveys, completed after individuals finalise the Personality Diversity Indicator (PDI), Equilibria gathers data points that continue to grow our research. Currently, over 1.4 million PDIs have been completed, each contributing valuable input to the database.

Oliver's Story: A Fiery Lesson in E-Colours

My E-Colours are Red/Green and I am a firefighter. I've learned that my strengths – being direct, decisive, and action-focused – can also become my biggest challenges and potential limiters. Let me share how understanding my E-Colours and using my pocketbook helped me through one of the toughest situations I've faced.

It was a warehouse fire involving volatile chemicals. Normally, I'd charge in, relying on instinct and adrenaline. But I had my pocketbook with me – a tool I've come to trust. It reminded me of how I could get hurt if I wasn't careful:

- *Taking risks without calculation*
- *Letting impatience get the better of me*
- *Becoming too focused on the task and losing awareness*
- *Being improperly positioned*
- *Ignoring my surroundings*

With those words in my mind, I approached the fire differently. I stopped to assess the building's integrity and planned a safer route. Normally, impatience would push me to move faster, but I kept my pace deliberate and steady, pausing to check for hazards.

While setting up the hose, I caught myself becoming overly focused. A falling ember grazed me, snapping me back into awareness. That moment could've been a disaster, but because I remembered to stay mindful of my surroundings, I repositioned safely.

I stayed low, shielding myself, and took an extra second to update my team about a shift in the fire's behaviour. That moment of awareness helped the entire team adjust tactics, containing the fire before it reached the hazardous materials.

When I emerged, covered in soot but successful, my captain said, 'Well done, Oliver. You kept a cool head.' For me, that moment was a realisation: being 'top E-Colour Red' isn't about rushing in, it's about channelling my boldness wisely.

By understanding my E-Colours and using my pocketbook as a guide, I turned what could've been recklessness into a safe and successful mission. That's the power of knowing yourself and taking control of how you RESPOND.

At Equilibria, we now refer to our pocketbooks as the 'take it out of your pocketbook' moment, and this story is a perfect example.

– Oliver, Firefighter (Red/Green)

* * *

INTENTIONAL LEADERSHIP BEHAVIOURS

Let's look at how E-Colours can help create intentional leaders.

1. **Enhanced Self-Awareness**

    - **Understanding Personal Strengths and Potential Limiters:** E-Colours help leaders recognise their natural tendencies and identify areas for growth. For example, a leader with dominant Red (Doer) E-Colours might be highly action-oriented but could benefit from being more aware of their impact on others.

- **Adjusting Leadership Style:** By understanding their own E-Colours, leaders can refine their approach to better align with their team's needs, resulting in more effective and balanced leadership.

2. Improved Communication

- **Tailoring Communication:** Leaders who understand their own and their team members' E-Colours can communicate more effectively by adjusting their style to match the preferences and strengths of their team. For instance, they might offer more data to Green (Thinker) personalities or adopt a more collaborative tone with Yellows (Socialisers).

- **Reducing Misunderstandings:** Awareness of E-Colours & Personal Intervention allows leaders to anticipate potential communication barriers and to address them proactively, reducing the likelihood of misunderstandings and conflicts.

3. Enhanced Decision-Making

- **Balanced Perspectives:** Leaders can promote E-Colour awareness within their team to make more well-rounded decisions. By considering different perspectives – Red's Doing, Blue's Relating, Green's Thinking, and Yellow's Socialising – leaders can approach problems from multiple angles.

- **Strategic Adaptation:** Personal Intervention techniques enable leaders to PAUSE and reflect before RESPONDING, leading to more thoughtful and strategic choices that consider the impact on all stakeholders.

4. Team Collaboration

- **Building Stronger Relationships:** By understanding and appreciating the E-Colours of team members, leaders can create an environment where diverse strengths are acknowledged and leveraged. This encourages a more cohesive and collaborative team dynamic.

- **Conflict Resolution:** Leaders trained in E-Colours & Personal Intervention skills are better equipped to address conflicts by addressing underlying issues and finding solutions that align with various team members' needs and styles.

5. Boosting Motivation and Engagement

- **Recognising Individual Needs:** E-Colours help leaders identify what motivates each team member, allowing for a more tailored approach. A Red (Doer) may prefer autonomy, while a Green (Thinker) might value detailed feedback. This will increase motivation and engagement.

- **Personalised Development:** With E-Colours awareness, leaders can provide targeted development opportunities that align with each team members' strengths and growth potential, creating a more motivated and high-performing team.

6. Promoting Resilience and Adaptability

- **Navigating Challenges:** Personal Intervention techniques help leaders manage stress and navigate challenging situations more effectively by encouraging thoughtful RESPONSES rather than defaulting to REACTIVE behaviours.

- **Embracing Change:** Leaders who are mindful of their E-Colours and use Personal Intervention techniques are better equipped to lead their teams through uncertainty, modelling resilience and adaptability.

Our observations since the inception of Equilibria in terms of the leadership styles of the top E-Colours are as follows.

Yellow (Socialiser) – My leadership style tends to be INSPIRATIONAL:

- **Paints the VISION**
- Creates and shares the team or organisational vision
- Coaches individuals to strengthen team performance
- Invests time in those who show reciprocal interest
- Aims to foster an inclusive team environment

Blue (Relator) – My leadership style tends to be COMPASSIONATE:

- **Maintains VALUES**
- Sets team or organisational values and ethics
- Creates an environment of respect, participation, and collaboration

- Demonstrates loyalty to the team and overall vision
- Holds people accountable for their behaviours

Red (Doer) – My leadership style tends to be DIRECT:

- **Drives the MISSION**
- Defines and communicates clear goals and objectives
- Establishes and maintains performance standards
- Holds others accountable for results and outcomes
- Focuses on tasks and expects consistent effort

Green (Thinker) – My leadership style tends to be STRATEGIC:

- **Plans the STRATEGY**
- Defines roles, processes, procedures, and success metrics
- Monitors performance to ensure consistency
- Places importance on the methods used to achieve outcomes
- Sets high standards and strives for excellence

E-Colours & Personal Intervention positively impact leadership behaviours by increasing self-awareness, improving communication, encouraging collaboration, and promoting thoughtful decision-making. These tools enable leaders to navigate complex team dynamics with empathy and effectiveness, ultimately leading to a more productive and harmonious work environment.

* * *

HOW TO DELEGATE TO ME

Using E-Colours & Personal Intervention to delegate tasks effectively means recognising the different personality styles within the E-Colours framework and tailoring your approach to align with each individual's strengths and preferences. Here's how you can apply these tools to delegate tasks across various personality styles.

1. **Tailoring Delegation**
   - **Red Doer:**
     - **Delegation Style:** Give clear, concise instructions and define specific goals. Allow them to take charge and make decisions.
     - **Personal Intervention:** Use PAUSE & PLAY to avoid overwhelming them with too many details. Give them the freedom to act quickly and decisively.
   - **Yellow Socialiser:**
     - **Delegation Style:** Offer opportunities for creative input and collaboration. Highlight how the task connects to team goals and vision.
     - **Personal Intervention:** PAUSE to avoid limiting their creativity with rigid rules. PLAY by involving them in brainstorming and open discussion.
   - **Green Thinker:**
     - **Delegation Style:** Provide thorough instructions, clear expectations, and a structured plan. Allow time for analysis and questions.

- ○ **Personal Intervention:** PAUSE to ensure you're providing all necessary details and avoid overwhelming them. PLAY by staying open to feedback and adjustments based on their analysis.
- **Blue Relator:**
  - ○ **Delegation Style:** Emphasise how the task supports team harmony and relationships. Be supportive and open to their input.
  - ○ **Personal Intervention:** PAUSE to avoid applying too much pressure. PLAY by providing reassurance and showing appreciation for their contributions.

2. Applying Personal Intervention

- **Assess the Situation:** Before delegating, use Personal Intervention to determine the best approach for everyone. Factor in each team member's E-Colours and how they might RESPOND to different styles of delegations.
- **Adapt Your Approach:** Be flexible – adjust your delegation style to match the individual's needs or preferences. This might mean giving more guidance, more freedom, or added support.
- **Monitor and Adjust:** Continue applying Personal Intervention after delegating to monitor progress and adjust as needed. Check in with team members regularly to ensure comfort and progress.

3. Creating a Supportive Environment

- **Encourage Feedback:** Create an environment where team members feel safe giving input on the delegation process. Use their feedback to improve how you delegate tasks in the future.

- **Recognise Strengths:** Acknowledge the strengths each E-Colour brings to a task. This fosters a positive work environment and motivates team members.

By understanding the E-Colours and using Personal Intervention, you can adapt your communication to align with different personality styles. This helps ensure that tasks are clearly heard, properly understood, and genuinely valued, resulting in more effective interactions and better overall outcomes.

A Story of Delegation and the HOP Principles – Lewis Senior

Ella, whose E-Colours are Green/Red, is a seasoned project manager who faced a critical challenge: a tight deadline on a client deliverable. Even though her natural style was somewhat perfectionist and occasionally critical, she decided not only to press PAUSE on doing the work herself or handing it to her most trusted veterans, but to press PLAY on involving less experienced team members – and to adopt and apply recently learned Human and Organisational Performance (HOP) principles.

Error is Normal: Ella began by framing the tasks realistically. 'Mistakes might happen, and that's okay. The goal here isn't perfection but learning and delivering together,' she told the team. This mindset encouraged open communication, and one of the newcomers, Sam, immediately asked clarifying questions instead of silently guessing.

Blame Fixes Nothing: When a small misstep occurred – a data entry error that delayed some calculations – Ella focused on resolution rather than blame. She called a quick meeting to review what happened and walked Sam through the correction process. 'This isn't about fault; it's about finding ways to prevent similar issues,' she reassured the team. Sam left the meeting feeling supported and more confident.

Systems Influence Behaviour: Ella ensured the team had the tools and clarity they needed. She provided clear instructions, access to templates, and scheduled regular check-ins. When one team member struggled with an outdated software tool, Ella quickly arranged for an updated version. 'Success depends on the system supporting you,' she reminded the group, helping set them up for a smoother workflow.

Response Matters: As tasks progressed, Ella maintained a constructive tone. When a section of the report was completed ahead of schedule, she praised the effort in a team meeting. Conversely, when another section needed revision, she gave actionable feedback, focusing on opportunities for improvement. Her balanced RESPONSES kept the team engaged and motivated to take ownership of their work.

Learning and Improving is Essential: At the project's conclusion, Ella held a debrief session. She asked everyone to reflect on their challenges and achievements, emphasising the value of the experience. 'Delegation isn't just about offloading tasks,' she said. 'It's about growth – for me as a leader, and for you as team members. Every task is a chance to improve.'

Outcome: By applying the HOP principles and managing her own strengths and potential limiters, Ella created a supportive, growth-oriented environment. The project was delivered on time, and her less experienced team members emerged more confident, capable, and ready for future challenges. Ella reflected on the process with pride. By embracing the HOP principles, she not only delivered a successful project but also strengthened her team.

* * *

IF YOU WANT ME TO LISTEN

Using E-Colours & Personal Intervention to get different personality styles to listen to you involves tailoring your communication to align with their preferences and needs. Here's how to apply these concepts to effectively engage and gain the attention of various E-Colours.

1. **Tailoring Your Communication**
   - **For Red E-Colours:**
     - **Be direct and concise:** Get straight to the point with clear, actionable information. Highlight the benefits and outcomes.
     - **Personal Intervention:** PAUSE to ensure you're not overexplaining or going off track. PLAY by respecting their time and focusing on results.
   - **For Yellow E-Colours:**
     - **Be engaging and enthusiastic:** Use energetic language and involve them in the conversation. Share ideas and collaborative opportunities.

- **Personal Intervention:** PAUSE to avoid too much detail. PLAY by welcoming their ideas and keeping things upbeat.
- **For Green E-Colours:**
  - **Be detailed and organised:** Present structured information with supporting data. Provide clarity to back up your message.
  - **Personal Intervention:** PAUSE to ensure you're being thorough. PLAY by being open to their need for more information and providing thorough RESPONSES.
- **For Blue E-Colours:**
  - **Be empathetic and supportive:** Show you value their feelings and their impact on the team. Use a warm, considerate tone.
  - **Personal Intervention:** PAUSE to make sure you're addressing their concerns and not putting undue pressure on them. PLAY by showing genuine interest in their perspective and demonstrating how your message benefits the team.

2. **Applying Personal Intervention**
   - **Assess the situation:** Before speaking, use Personal Intervention to consider the best approach for your audience.
   - **Adapt your message:** Tailor your communication style based on the individual's E-Colours. This means adjusting your tone, level of detail, and engagement strategies.
   - **Monitor RESPONSES:** Watch how they respond and be ready to adjust your approach if needed. Use Personal

Intervention to shift your strategy if you notice signs of confusion or disengagement.

3. **Creating a Positive Listening Environment**
   - **Encourage openness:** Foster an environment where everyone feels comfortable freely sharing their thoughts and listening. Invite questions and be open to different perspectives.
   - **Show appreciation:** Thank them for listening and contributing. Positive reinforcement can help maintain their attention and engagement.

4. **Building Relationships**
   - **Develop trust:** Build strong relationships by consistently respecting their communication preferences and showing that you value their input. Trust enhances listening and collaboration.
   - **Be consistent:** Apply these principles consistently in your interactions to build a reputation as a considerate and effective communicator.

* * *

WHEN WORKING WITH ME

Using the E-Colours can be incredibly helpful in understanding how best to work with you, especially in communication, decision-making, and collaboration. Here's how the E-Colours can be applied.

1. **Discovering Your E-Colours**
   - The first step is to discover your own E-Colours.

- Knowing your predominant E-Colours helps you better understand your natural tendencies, strengths, and areas for growth.

2. **Tailoring Communication**

    - If your predominant E-Colour is **Red**, you likely prefer direct, concise communication and appreciate action-oriented discussions. When working with you, it's most effective to be straightforward, focus on results, and avoid unnecessary detail.
    - If you are primarily **Yellow**, you might enjoy enthusiastic, lively interactions and value recognition and positive feedback. In this case, maintaining a positive tone and allowing space for creative input can be helpful.
    - A predominant **Green** person values detailed information, structure, and logical reasoning. It's important to provide thorough explanations and allow time for analysis when working with you.
    - If **Blue** is your predominant colour, you likely value harmony, empathy, and personal connection. When working with you, it's important to be supportive, listen actively, and focus on building strong relationships.

3. **Adapting to Decision-Making Styles**

    - Knowing your E-Colours can also give you awareness into your decision-making style. For example, a Red might prefer quick decisions based on instinct, while a Green might prefer to weigh all options carefully.
    - By understanding these preferences, your colleagues can adapt their approach to better align with your style, helping decision-making run more smoothly.

4. **Enhancing Team Collaboration**

   - The E-Colours can highlight potential areas of conflict or synergy within a team. For example, understanding that a Red and a Blue may have different approaches to resolving conflict can help in finding common ground.
   - Teams can use E-Colours to ensure diverse viewpoints are included and to make the most of the unique strengths each member brings.

5. **Promoting Self-Awareness and Growth**

   - Understanding your own E-Colours helps you become more aware of your strengths and notice where you may need to adapt. For instance, if you're a Red and tend to lead most discussions, you might consciously make more space for others to contribute.
   - Similarly, knowing your E-Colours can help you recognise when your natural tendencies might not be the most effective and adjust accordingly.

6. **Applying the Platinum Rule**

   - The Platinum Rule says, 'Treat others the way they need to be treated.' Using E-Colours helps others understand your preferences and adjust their behaviour to better align with your style.

By incorporating E-Colours into your relationships, you can create a more understanding and effective environment that makes the most of everyone's strengths.

When Working with Me – A Green and Yellow Collaboration – Lewis Senior

John, a top E-Colour Green known for his thoughtful, analytical nature, sat down with Ava, a top E-Colour Yellow bursting with energy and creativity. They were preparing to co-lead a team project and wanted to establish a smooth working dynamic.

'Alright, Ava,' John began with a small smile, 'before we dive in, let me explain a bit about how I work best. Knowing your Yellow energy, I think we can make this a really strong partnership.'

'Sounds fun! Let's hear it,' Ava said eagerly.

John nodded. 'For starters, I value clarity and structure. When we're working together, it helps if you can be clear, specific, and straight to the point when sharing ideas. I know you're full of creativity, but I work best when everything is laid out logically.'

Ava nodded, scribbling notes. 'Got it. Less brainstorm clouds, more bullet points.'

'Exactly. I also like to have choices and alternatives laid out. If there's a decision to be made, presenting me with clear options is really helpful. It supports my need to analyse and think things through before acting.'

'Okay,' Ava said. 'What about flexibility? I like to bounce between ideas sometimes.'

John chuckled. 'I know you do, and I'll try to keep up. But I work best with a plan and a schedule. If we agree on something, I really need us to follow through. Consistency is important to me.'

'Noted,' Ava replied. 'What else?'

John leaned forward. 'I see tasks as problems to be solved, so I might not always focus on the people side the way you do. But I respect your ability to connect with others. Just know my approach may seem more task-driven than social.'

'Totally makes sense,' Ava said. 'I'll remind you to step out of "task mode" when we need some team bonding time.'

'Perfect,' John said with a grin. 'And one last thing – if you want to grab my attention or build rapport, start with something personal to break the ice. I appreciate sincerity, so showing genuine interest really goes a long way.'

Ava smiled. 'Deal. And if I need to bounce ideas quickly, I'll give you a heads-up so you can get ready.'

John nodded. 'Sounds like a plan. Together, I think we can balance your creative spark with my structure to get great results.'

Their collaboration flourished, with John's focus keeping them grounded and Ava's energy driving the team forward. By understanding each other's strengths and communication styles, they created a partnership built on respect and mutual growth.

* * *

EFFECTIVE FORM OF RECOGNITION

Using the E-Colours to identify effective forms of recognition involves understanding the unique preferences and motivations associated with each personality profile. Tailoring recognition to these preferences can make it more meaningful and impactful. Here's how you can use the E-Colours to recognise individuals effectively.

1. **Red (Doer)**
   - **Motivations:** Reds are often driven by achievement, results, and the need for action.
   - **Effective Recognition:**
     - **Direct Praise:** Recognise them publicly for their accomplishments and contributions, especially in front of peers or superiors. This could be during meetings, in company-wide emails, or at award ceremonies.
     - **Opportunities for Advancement:** Reds value recognition that comes with tangible rewards, such as promotions, bonuses, or added responsibilities that reflect their leadership potential.
   - **Challenge and Responsibility:** Assign them high-stakes projects or leadership roles to show confidence in their ability to deliver.
2. **Yellow (Socialiser)**
   - **Motivations:** Yellows thrive on interaction, enthusiasm, and being part of a dynamic environment.

- **Effective Recognition:**
  - **Public Acknowledgment:** Celebrate their achievements with energetic recognition, like team meetings or social media shout-outs. They enjoy being the centre of attention and thrive on engaging celebrations.
  - **Personalised Recognition:** Make it specific. Highlight individual contributions, creativity, or their impact on morale.
  - **Social Gatherings:** Plan team events such as lunches or happy hours where their contributions can be celebrated in a fun, social setting.

3. Green (Thinker)
   - **Motivations:** Greens value accuracy, quality, and thoroughness. They're motivated by knowledge and being recognised for their expertise.
   - **Effective Recognition:**
     - **Detailed Feedback:** Provide thoughtful, well-worded recognition. Written notes that outline their contributions and impact can be very effective.
     - **Professional Development:** Offer learning opportunities such as training, workshops, or conferences. They appreciate growth-oriented recognition.
     - **Private Acknowledgment:** While they may not seek the limelight, they value genuine, private recognition that acknowledges their hard work and dedication.

4. Blue (Relater)
   - **Motivations:** Blues are driven by harmony, trust, and meaningful relationships. They value recognition that reinforces belonging and connection.

- **Effective Recognition:**
  - **Personal Touch:** Take time to thank them personally, whether in conversation or with a handwritten note. Authenticity matters to Blues.
  - **Team-Oriented Praise:** Recognise how their efforts support the team, especially their contributions to creating a collaborative environment.
  - **Inclusive Practices:** Invite them to participate in team-building activities or community service events. They appreciate recognition that emphasises teamwork and collective effort.

General Tips for Using E-Colours in Recognition

- **Understand Individual Preferences:** Most people have a dominant E-Colour, but secondary colours also shape their preferences. Recognising these nuances allows for more tailored and effective recognition.
- **Balance Recognition Styles:** In a diverse team, it's important to use a variety of recognition tendencies to cater to different personality styles. This ensures everyone feels valued in a way that resonates with them.
- **Use the Platinum Rule:** Treat others the way they need to be treated. By recognising each person's E-Colour, you can adjust your recognition methods to align with individual preferences, fostering a more inclusive and motivating environment.

By leveraging the E-Colours to understand and match individual recognition preferences, you can build a more personalised and effective approach to appreciating and motivating your team.

Recognition – A Blue and Yellow Conversation: Recognition Matters – Lewis Senior

Sophia, a top E-Colour Blue, sat across from Max, a top E-Colour Yellow, during a team recognition meeting. They had been paired to brainstorm ways to celebrate their achievements, but first, Sophia wanted Max to understand what recognition meant to her.

'Max,' Sophia began gently, 'I know you thrive on bold, public recognition – celebrations, trophies, and applause, right?'

Max grinned. 'You got it. If you're going to recognise my hard work, make it big.'

Sophia smiled. 'I admire that energy, but I'm a little different. For me, recognition feels most meaningful when it's personal and sincere. I value authenticity over spectacle.'

Max raised an eyebrow. 'So, no big speeches or team shout-outs?'

'Not really,' Sophia replied. 'I prefer something more private – like a thoughtful one-on-one conversation. A simple "thank you" or acknowledgement of my effort means a lot. It shows me you've truly noticed what I've contributed.'

'That's fair,' Max said, leaning back. 'What else works for you?'

Sophia thought for a moment. 'Feedback. If I've done something well, tell me why it mattered. And if I need to improve,

I'd appreciate hearing that, too. It's not about perfection – it's about understanding how I can grow.'

Max nodded slowly. 'So, specific feedback over general praise?'

'Exactly,' Sophia said. 'And fairness is huge for me. When everyone's efforts are recognised equally, I feel part of the team – not just someone striving alone. Recognition is also about fostering collaboration, not competition.'

Max grinned. 'Got it. Genuine, specific, and fair. And no fireworks.'

Sophia laughed. 'Right. But don't get me wrong, seeing you light up from your kind of recognition inspires me, too. Maybe we can strike a balance that suits the whole team.'

Max slapped the table. 'Sounds like a plan. I'll work on my quieter side for you, Sophia, as long as you don't mind the occasional loud cheer for me.'

Sophia nodded. 'Deal.'

The conversation left both with a deeper appreciation for each other's styles, creating a stronger foundation for their collaboration. By understanding and respecting Sophia's preference for personal, sincere recognition, Max helped foster a culture of inclusivity and mutual respect.

* * *

CONFLICT RESOLUTION

Using the E-Colours in conflict resolution can significantly enhance understanding and empathy, leading to more effective outcomes. Each E-Colour represents a distinct communication style, decision-making approach, and response to conflict. By aligning conflict resolution strategies with these tendencies, you can address issues more constructively and help all parties feel acknowledged and respected. Here's how the E-Colours can be applied to conflict resolution.

1. Red (Doer)
Conflict Resolution Strategies:

- **Be Direct and Concise:** When resolving conflicts with a Red, get straight to the point. They appreciate clear communication and may become frustrated with long-winded discussions.

- **Focus on Solutions:** Reds are solution-focused and prefer to move forward quickly. Emphasise actionable steps and specific outcomes rather than analysing the problem at length.

- **Acknowledge Their Need for Control:** Reds often like to feel in control. Allow them input in the process and offer choices where possible to support their autonomy.

2. Yellow (Socialiser)
Conflict Resolution Strategies:

- **Maintain a Positive Tone:** Yellows respond well to an upbeat, optimistic approach. Keep the conversation light and avoid a negative tone.

- **Focus on Relationships:** Emphasise the value of strong relationships and team harmony. Yellows value social connections and are often willing to compromise to preserve them.

- **Use Empathy and Active Listening:** Show genuine interest in their emotions and perspective. Validating their concerns helps to build rapport and trust.

3. Green (Thinker)
Conflict Resolution Strategies:

- **Provide Detailed Explanations:** Greens appreciate clear, logical explanations and data-driven discussions. Share relevant details and avoid vague statements.

- **Take a Methodical Approach:** Greens prefer a structured, step-by-step resolution. Outline the steps to be taken and agree on a timeline for resolving the conflict.

- **Allow Time for Thought:** Greens often need space to process information. Avoid pressuring them for immediate responses and give them space to think things through.

4. Blue (Relater)
Conflict Resolution Strategies:

- **Create a Safe Environment:** Blues need to feel emotionally safe in order to open up. Approach them in a non-threatening, open manner and encourage them to share their perspectives.

- **Prioritise Emotional Wellbeing:** Address the emotional elements of the conflict. Acknowledge their feelings, comfort level, and show empathy to foster trust.

- **Collaborate on Solutions:** Blues appreciate collaborative approaches that involve everyone in finding a solution. Emphasise cooperation and consensus-building to ensure they feel included and valued.

General Tips for Using E-Colours in Conflict Resolution

- **Understand the Underlying Motivations:** Each E-Colour has different core motivations that influence how they perceive and respond to conflict. By understanding these, you can address the root causes more effectively.
- **Adapt Your Communication Style:** Tailor your communication to match the preferred style of each E-Colour. Use clear, concise language with Reds, empathy and support with Blues, and detailed explanations for Greens, and use a friendly tone for Yellows.
- **Use the Platinum Rule:** Treat others the way they need to be treated. By considering the E-Colours, you can adjust your conflict resolution approach to align with individual preferences and promote constructive dialogue.
- **Encourage Mutual Understanding:** Use the E-Colours to help each party understand the other's perspective. This reduces misunderstandings and promotes empathy, leading to more effective resolutions.
- **Facilitate Compromise and Collaboration:** By recognising the strengths and needs of each E-Colour, you can guide the conflict resolution process towards a mutually beneficial outcome, ensuring all parties feel heard and respected.

By leveraging the E-Colours in conflict resolution, you can create a more personalised and effective approach – one that promotes understanding, empathy, and collaboration across the team.

Creative Sparks Fly at the Delicious Festival in South Africa

The Delicious Festival in Johannesburg was just a few weeks away, and the energy in the planning room was electric. Lloyd, the festival's Creative Director, paced around the table, his Yellow/Red personality style on full display. His enthusiasm radiated as he sketched his vision for this year's festival layout.

'Picture this,' he said, his voice brimming with excitement. 'A seamless flow where the food stalls blend into the performance areas. No barriers, just a free-spirited experience! It'll feel like one giant celebration.'

Stephanie, the services manager, adjusted her glasses and folded her arms.

Her Green/Red personality style shone through her measured, no-nonsense demeanour. 'Lloyd, that sounds exciting, but it's not practical,' she said, her tone calm but firm. 'We need defined zones for crowd control and clear paths for vendor logistics. Your plan could create chaos.'

The room fell silent. The rest of the team exchanged nervous glances. Everyone knew Lloyd and Stephanie were both brilliant, but their differences sometimes led to heated debates.

The Tension Builds

'Chaos?' Lloyd said, leaning forward. 'Steph, it's a festival, it will work itself out. People come here to have fun, not walk through barricades!'

Stephanie's jaw tightened. 'And what happens when people can't find the bathrooms or the lines for food stretch across the performance areas? Fun doesn't mean disorganised.'

Their voices grew louder, each determined to defend their perspective. The team could feel the tension rising, and it seemed like a resolution was nowhere in sight.

Lloyd then replied, 'Let's take a step back. We're both passionate about making this festival incredible, but let's not forget we're a team. Take some time to reflect, and we'll revisit this tomorrow.'

Lloyd and Stephanie agreed to disagree, retreating to their respective offices to cool off.

Coming Back Together

The next morning, Lloyd suggested an E-Colours conflict resolution session with his success coach, Mark Wilkinson. Within an hour, Mark introduced the notion of personality diversity and the potential for conflict between them even though they were both looking for the same result, to create an unforgettable experience for their attendees.

After the online coaching session, Lloyd entered the boardroom, this time with a calmer demeanour. Stephanie was already there, her laptop open and a cup of coffee in hand.

Lloyd broke the ice. 'I get it now – structure is important to your top Colour Green. I don't want my Yellow vision to cause headaches for you or the team.'

Stephanie looked up, a smile on her face. 'And I've been thinking too, Lloyd. Your ideas are what make this festival special. I don't want to stifle that creativity.'

With the tension diffused, they began collaborating.

The Compromise

Stephanie proposed a solution: 'What if we use creative markers, like art installations or themed signage, to define zones? That way, people still feel the freedom you want, but we maintain order.'

Lloyd's eyes lit up. 'I love it! We could use arches to indicate food areas and creative lighting to subtly guide people through different sections. It's functional and still fun.'

They worked together to refine the plan, finding ways to balance Lloyd's vibrant ideas with a more structured approach.

The Festival Comes Alive

When the Delicious Festival opened, the layout was a hit. Visitors moved effortlessly through the space, marvelling at the vibrant design and clever zoning.

Lloyd's artistic flair was everywhere, from the colourful installations to the dynamic flow of the event. Meanwhile, Stephanie's meticulous planning ensured everything ran like clockwork.

In that moment, they knew their differences weren't weaknesses – they were their greatest strength. Together, they created magic.

Bridging the Gap: The Power of Necessary Conversations – Conflict Resolution – Lewis Senior

A couple of years ago, I found myself needing to have a difficult, yet necessary, conversation with a team member who was at odds with his colleagues. This individual was known for his technical skills and high productivity, but lately, there had been growing misalignment in his approach to teamwork. It was creating a ripple of frustration among others, though no one had directly addressed it. I was asked to facilitate an honest discussion, which required careful thought to ensure it would be constructive.

I began by taking a THINKING (Green) approach, gathering the facts. I reviewed recent project feedback and specific examples of the issues that had been raised, wanting to enter the conversation with a clear picture of the impact his actions were having. By grounding myself in the details, I felt better prepared to address specifics, rather than making generalised statements that could come across as criticism.

Next, I shifted my focus to RELATING (Blue). I reminded myself to approach the conversation with empathy, recognising he was likely unaware of how his actions were affecting others. When we sat down to talk, I opened by acknowledging his strengths and what he brought to the team. 'You've been doing great work technically, and the team really appreciates that,' I said, aiming to establish a foundation of mutual respect. As we spoke, I listened deeply, trying to understand his perspective and motivations. It became clear that he felt isolated from the team's decision-making process, which explained some of his recent behaviours.

Once we established this understanding, it was time to SOCIALISE (Yellow) – to communicate in a way that would encourage collaboration. I shared some of the feedback I'd gathered, framing it as an opportunity for growth rather than a list of complaints. 'What if we work on building stronger lines of communication so everyone feels included?' I suggested, inviting him into the process of finding solutions. This approach shifted the tone of the conversation, and he became more open, expressing his own ideas for improving teamwork.

Finally, we moved to DOING (Red). Together, we discussed clear steps for moving forward, focusing on actions that could strengthen his relationship with the team. We agreed to hold regular check-ins to maintain open dialogue and brainstorm ways to make his technical leadership more collaborative. This allowed him to see how he could lead technically while still fostering a team-focused environment.

Looking back, that conversation became a turning point – for him and for me. By using the THINK-RELATE-SOCIALISE-DO framework, we not only resolved an immediate challenge, but also deepened trust and enhanced the coaching relationship. Over time, his engagement with the team improved, and he became a respected leader who balanced his technical expertise with a clearer understanding of team needs. That experience reinforced for me that necessary conversations, using the E-Colours wisely, and approached thoughtfully, can drive real transformation and growth – for individuals and the team.

* * *

DOUBT & RESISTANCE
The Pathway to Appreciation
Implementing something new is often faced with challenges that begin with doubt and resistance.

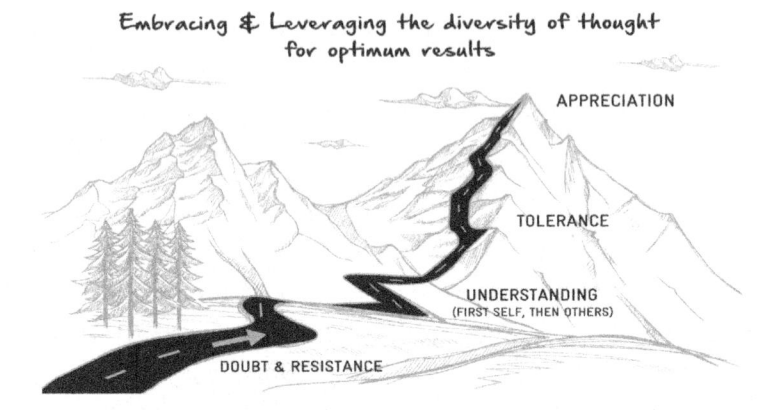

Figure 10 – The Pathway to Appreciation
Copyright © 2025 Equilibria Services Pte Ltd. All rights reserved.

* * *

Mark Wilkinson: As we mentioned in Chapter 1, there are times when, in explaining our personality diversity technology and ethics to new people, we encounter a degree of doubt or resistance. This quote from Tony Robbins often captures what it feels like to describe something that has had a meaningful impact on you, to someone who hasn't yet experienced it: 'I'm trying to explain to you what a rose smells like, when you've never smelled a rose!'

At one point, Andy Ward was sceptical. Later, he sent Lewis and I the photograph below.

Figure 11 – Andy Ward's Hand Tattoo

Andy's Story

Having known Mark Wilkinson for many years in the music industry, and after reaching out to him for advice during some pretty dire financial struggles in the past, I was more than happy to look at 'this thing that might help you,' one day after he got in touch. I'd been having a bit of a rant on my Facebook wall about 'Why are people such idiots?' and 'Why is it so hard for them to understand even simple instructions?' – though my actual language was a lot more colourful than that.

My first introduction to Mark's 'new' direction as a Success and E-Colours Coach was an online course, and I was immediately blown away by how accurately my Strengths and Potential Limiters as a top colour Red were described. It laid out all the issues I'd been facing when communicating with those around me – whether at work or at home.

My initial feeling of resistance turned into full commitment, and my life has turned around completely. I started joining Mark in everything he did involving E-Colours and his Life Remixed *book clubs, and I'm beyond grateful that I later became a coaching client of Mark's – and eventually a certified E-Colours Practitioner.*

As a 12-month coaching client of Mark's, he helped me understand myself better and kickstarted my journey of self-discovery and improvement through E-Colours. My relationships with everyone around me have improved, and honestly, there are way too many things to mention that have turned around in my life – financially, physically, spiritually. A few highlights: I'm now two years alcohol-free; I got back into running marathons; my wife and I have invested in two more properties in Spain (something I would never have considered before); and my website and graphic design clients keep rolling in – paying rates I never thought possible! All this came from understanding myself, overcoming limiting beliefs, and 'Living with Intention.'

Using my new skills, I now reach out to others when I see their frustrations and offer to help. And as you can see, I even got the tattoo!

– *Andy Ward* (Red/Yellow)
– Inspire & Be Inspired – 100 Day No Alcohol Challenge – Vocal Booth Weekender – Vocal Booth Radio, UK & Spain

Managing Doubt & Resistance

Handling doubt and resistance when using the E-Colours involves addressing concerns, offering clarity, and demonstrating the value of the system. It's essential to approach resistance with empathy, openness, and flexibility to help individuals better understand and appreciate the benefits of E-Colours.

Here are some strategies for managing doubt and resistance effectively.

1. **Acknowledge and Validate Concerns.**
    - **Listen Actively:** When individuals express doubt or resistance, listen to their concerns without interrupting

or dismissing them. This shows respect for their feelings and helps you understand the root of their resistance.

- **Validate Their Feelings:** Acknowledge that their concerns are valid and that it's natural to have questions or reservations about a new approach or tool. This validation can reduce defensiveness and open the door to more constructive dialogue.

2. **Provide Clear Explanations and Context.**

- **Explain the Purpose and Benefits:** Clearly articulate the purpose of the E-Colours and how it can support individuals and teams. Highlight how understanding personality preferences improves communication, teamwork, conflict resolution, and productivity.
- **Share Real-Life Examples:** Use real-life examples or success stories to show how the E-Colours have positively impacted individuals or teams. Concrete examples help make the benefits more relatable and tangible.

3. **Demonstrate the Value of the E-Colours.**

- **Use Data and Research:** If available, provide data or research supporting the effectiveness of the E-Colours system. Evidence-based information helps build credibility and reduce scepticism.
- **Encourage a Trial Period:** Suggest trying the E-Colours on a trial basis to let individuals experience the benefits firsthand. Seeing the positive impact in action can alleviate doubt and resistance.

4. **Address Misconceptions.**

- **Clarify Misunderstandings:** Some resistance may stem from misconceptions about the E-Colours. For example, individuals may think it's a form of labelling or oversimplifying personalities. Clarify that the E-Colours are a tool for self-awareness and communication – not a rigid classification.

- **Emphasise Flexibility:** Reinforce that the E-Colours are intended to provide awareness, not to box people into fixed categories. Everyone has a blend of colours and can adapt their behaviour depending on the situation.

5. **Involve and Empower Individuals.**

   - **Involve Sceptics in the Process:** Engage those who are doubtful in discussions or activities related to the E-Colours. Active participation can help them see its value and practical application.
   - **Learning About Others:** Resistance often comes from individuals feeling they already know themselves – and that's fine. The E-Colours also offer a way to understand others better.
   - **Empower Individuals to Choose Their Involvement:** Encourage people to explore the E-Colours at their own pace. This respects their autonomy and reduces the sense of being pushed into something unfamiliar.

6. **Create an Open and Inclusive Environment.**

   - **Promote Open Dialogue:** Provide a safe space for open dialogue where individuals feel comfortable voicing concerns or asking questions about the E-Colours.
   - **Encourage Feedback:** Invite suggestions on how to make the E-Colours more accessible and relevant to the team. This inclusive approach builds trust and fosters engagement.

7. **Lead by Example.**

    - **Model E-Colour Principles:** Demonstrate how you use the E-Colours in your interactions and decision-making. Leading by example reinforces your belief in the system and commitment to its ethics.

    - **Share Personal Experiences:** Talk about your own journey with the E-Colours – and how it helped you understand yourself and improve your relationships. Personal stories can be powerful and relatable.

8. **Use the E-Colours to Tailor Your Approach.**

    - **Adapt to Individual Preferences:** Use your understanding of the E-Colours to adjust your approach to resistance. For example, provide detailed information and data for Greens, prioritise connection for Blues, keep communication direct and solution-focused for Reds, and make the process engaging and upbeat for Yellows.

By using these strategies to handle doubt and resistance, you can create a more open, supportive, and understanding environment that encourages individuals to explore the benefits of the E-Colours and incorporate them into their personal and professional lives.

The Impact of E-Colours on an Upward Mentoring Programme – Lewis Senior

An upward mentoring programme offers valuable benefits, especially when viewed through the lens of E-Colours, a personality framework that promotes self-awareness and stronger interpersonal dynamics. In the scenario described, a younger, less experienced mentor named Sarah – whose top E-Colour is Blue (Relater), reflecting empathy, loyalty and a focus on relationships – provides feedback to a seasoned, task-driven leader named George, whose dominant E-Colour is Red (Doer), marked by decisiveness, goal-focus, and directness. This dynamic reveals several key advantages and considerations.

Benefits of an Upward Mentoring Program

1. **Enhanced Self-Awareness for Leaders**
   - Leaders with dominant Red tendencies may prioritise tasks and efficiency over interpersonal considerations. Feedback from a Blue upward mentor can highlight the impact of their communication style on team dynamics and morale.
   - This increases the leader's awareness of how their actions are perceived, helping them build stronger relationships.

2. **Enabling Open Communication**
   - Upward mentoring promotes a culture where honest feedback flows in both directions. This is especially valuable for Red personalities, who may not naturally invite or expect constructive input from subordinates.

3. **Mutual Growth**
   - The mentor gains confidence in expressing themselves to authority figures, overcoming potential deference – especially where cultural norms emphasise hierarchy, as with the Blue mentor.
   - The mentee benefits from nuanced perspectives that may challenge their own.

4. **Bridging Generational and Cultural Gaps**
   - Younger mentors bring fresh perspectives, while seasoned leaders offer context and experience. This exchange fosters understanding across age and cultural divides, as illustrated by the Blue mentor succeeding in a hierarchical setting.

5. **Improved Emotional Intelligence**
   - Leaders like George, who are direct and task-focused, can develop greater empathy and relational skills, balancing their natural decisiveness with the people skills brought to light by an upward mentor like Sarah.

6. **Positive Organisational Impact**
   - As shown by George's adoption of the upward mentoring process in his new organisation, success stories can inspire wider implementation, creating a ripple effect that improves leadership culture and team engagement.

Personality and Willingness for Upward Mentorship

- **Blue – relational-focused personalities:** Naturally value mentorship and are more inclined to encourage upward feedback.
- **Green – information-focused personalities:** Value upward mentorship, not for emotional support or affirmation, but as a source of credible, well-reasoned guidance that aligns with their intellectual curiosity and need for clarity.
- **Yellow – social and expressive personalities:** Open to new ideas and enthusiastic about collaboration, they often embrace upward mentorship with ease.
- **Red – task-focused personalities:** Though potentially resistant at first due to their direct and authoritative

style, once mutual expectations are set, they may come to appreciate the efficiency and clarity such programmes bring to improving their leadership effectiveness.

It is important to understand that some personality styles are naturally more open to upward mentorship than others.

Essential Success Factors

Clear Expectations

- As demonstrated by George and Sarah, outlining mutual expectations from the start ensures clarity and reduces discomfort.

Courage and Commitment

- For a Blue upward mentor, addressing direct Red behaviour means stepping outside their comfort zone. Success relies on mutual trust and a shared commitment to growth.

Cultural Awareness

- Acknowledging cultural dynamics and sensitivities, such as deference to elders or hierarchical norms, is vital.

Would you, considering your own E-Colours, welcome an upward mentor into your world?

Doing so requires openness to feedback – both positive and constructive – and a willingness to embrace different perspectives. The success of such a programme lies in its ability to challenge leaders to grow beyond their default tendencies, fostering a collaborative and self-aware organisational culture.

* * *

PREMIUM REPORTS

Equilibria provides three different Personality Diversity Indicator (PDI) Reports: Free, Basic, and Premium.

Report Details	FREE Report	BASIC Report	PREMIUM Report
Report length	1 Paragraph	1 Page	33 Pages
Discover your E-Colour combination (top 2 E-Colours)	☑	☑	☑
Basic understanding of what the top 4 E-Colours represent		☑	☑
Pie chart providing your full E-Colours make up and percentages		☑	☑
Basic self-awareness overview and limited self-management tips		☑	☑
Advanced self-awareness review (Professional and Personal environments)			☑
Advanced self-management section, including Personal Intervention			☑
E-Colours trigger recognition sheets and practical application protocols			☑

Figure 12 – Personality Diversity Indicator Reports
Copyright © 2025 Equilibria Services Pte Ltd. All rights reserved.

The Premium PDI Reports (approximately 33 pages)

Features include:

- Giving you a thorough framing of personality tendencies and behavioural awareness
- Raising your self-awareness in both work and personal environments
- Giving you an advanced understanding of Personal Intervention (a self-management tool)
- Pointing out coaching and self-management opportunities

- Helping you understand top E-Colour triggers so you can apply what you've learned at any point, even if you do not know the other person's E-Colours
- Providing communication protocols to help you apply new concepts and enhance your personal effectiveness
- Providing a tool for life

* * *

ALIGNMENT REPORTS

E-Colours Interactive Alignment Reports Bundle: the ultimate tool to enhance your interpersonal skills and build stronger relationships. If you are holding a performance review for a member of your team, or if you're facing a personality-based challenge with someone in your life, and you know your own E-Colours but not those of the other person, you can complete an E-Colours observation report via the Equilibria website. At the end of this short 15-minute process, you'll be offered the opportunity to purchase an E-Colours alignment report (single or all 12) that provides detailed information about your style and how to align with the style of the other person.

Jon's Story

> *The creation of the alignment reports is good timing. I just used this as part of an annual performance review. It was one of the most productive reviews I have ever done.*
>
> – *Jon Feldkamp* (Green/Red)
> – General Manager of Automation,
> Expanse Electrical, USA

There are 144 Alignment Reports – 12 for each of the 12 E-Colour combinations – containing in-depth knowledge on how to align and interact effectively with each of the 12 E-Colour personality styles, with all tips tailored specifically to your own natural E-Colours style.

Each report includes an introduction, an overview of both styles, techniques for aligning with the other style, and a conclusion.

E-Colours Interactive Alignment Report Features

Comprehensive Personality Overview

- In-depth analysis of all 12 personality styles
- Understanding tendencies, preferences, and behaviours shaping work approaches

Promotion of Self-Awareness

- Facilitates self-discovery for enhanced self-awareness
- Further exploration of strengths and potential limiters

Enhanced Collaboration Strategies

- Tailored tips for effective alignment between styles
- Strategies to bridge communication gaps and improve collaboration

Practical Alignment Tips

- Actionable advice tailored to your individual personality tendencies
- Guidance on style awareness, communication nuances, and collaboration techniques

Personal Development Pathways

- Coaching opportunities tailored to each personality style
- Personal intervention tips and areas for growth

Leadership Behaviours Understanding

- Exploration of directive and compassionate leadership styles
- Guidance on maintaining values, setting goals, and ensuring consistency

Communication Styles Deconstruction

- Breakdown of different personality communication styles
- Tips on effective communication, active listening, and creating a harmonious dialogue

Stress Factors and Psychological Safety Awareness

- Identification and management of stress factors
- Strategies to create a psychologically safe environment for collaboration

Alignment Tips and Strategies

- Detailed alignment tips for individuals engaging with counterparts
- Strategies to improve understanding, empathy, and productive collaboration

Versatile Application

- Applicable in both professional and personal contexts
- Suitable for individuals, teams, and organisations seeking better collaboration

Practical Examples and Real-Life Scenarios

- Rich with real-world scenarios for practical application
- Illustrative examples to enhance understanding and implementation

User-Friendly Format

- Presented in clear and accessible language
- Approximately 10 pages, offering a thorough yet concise exploration of styles

See www.shop.equilibria.com/shop for more information.

* * *

ESSENTIAL LEADERSHIP CYCLE

The 8 Essentials of High-Performance Teams

Have you ever been part of a team that you believed didn't realise its full potential? Even though you and your teammates were talented and hardworking, there was still room for improvement. What do you think the issue was? What could the team members have done to address it?

The Essential Leadership Cycle exists to help everyone on a team realise their potential, incorporating the use of E-Colours & Personal Intervention. One of the unique aspects of this model is that each essential has been researched and developed through the lens of personality diversity, as expressed through the E-Colours.

WHAT (Red) is the purpose of the 8 Essentials?

What is the Essential Leadership Cycle (ELC), which contains the 8 Essentials of High-Performance Teams?

The ELC is an organisational performance improvement process for leaders and teams, used as a framework to help you:

- Evaluate the current performance of a team.
- Identify strengths within team performance that should be reinforced and sustained.
- Recognise gaps that can be addressed or closed with the right actions.
- Establish targeted goals to drive progress in each of the 8 Essentials to maximise results.
- Develop strategies to ensure sustainability and long-term growth of team performance.

WHY (Blue) is the ELC worth reviewing?

The ELC and 8 Essentials training, coaching sessions, and workbooks provide tools and guidance to help you put the 8 Essentials into practice and support any team in achieving high performance. A key component of the 8 Essentials is intentional leadership, and understanding the sequential nature of the model is important.

The ELC can also help integrate new members into a functioning team or organisation. A team that consistently applies the ELC can create a common language where leaders and members contribute jointly towards the team's success by ensuring understanding and application of each of the essentials.

There are a variety of books and tools available for improving teamwork, so the concept is not new. What makes the Essential Leadership Cycle unique is that each element is explained, taught, and coached through the lens of Equilibria's personality diversity technology, expressed through the E-Colours.

WHO (Yellow) can benefit from using the Essential Leadership Cycle?

Anyone who works on a team of two or more people towards a common goal can benefit from this content. In fact, the more complex the goal and the greater the challenges faced, the more valuable the 8 Essentials become.

HOW (Green) can you apply the 8 Essentials?

The 8 Essentials workshops are designed to follow the sequence of the Essential Leadership Cycle, with each essential building on the one before. You can start with an online or live assessment, completed either anonymously or by named team members, so leaders can quickly identify which essentials are working well and which require work. There are numerous tools, opportunities for discussion, and reflective questions built into the workbooks to help any team, large or small, enhance their current performance.

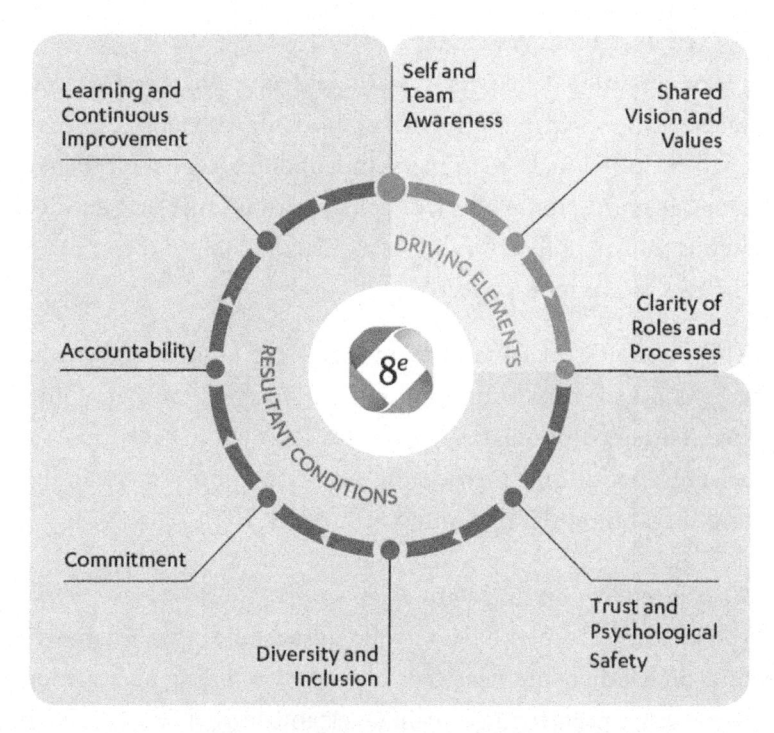

Figure 13 – The Essential Leadership Cycle
Copyright © 2025 Equilibria Services Pte Ltd. All rights reserved.

The sessions, coaching, and workbooks enable leaders and team members to take a deep dive into each aspect of Intentional Leadership to achieve their objectives and continually improve their performance, all through the lens of E-Colours personality diversity.

The sessions also provide guidance, tools, and experiential exercises that can be used to enhance a team's use of each essential and support any team in achieving high performance.

1. Self and Team Awareness

Awareness of self and team is the starting point for success. Developing deeper awareness of both oneself and the team enables individuals to understand and manage their behaviours, fostering more effective collaboration. This foundational step is indispensable, serving as a critical enabler for the rest of the ELC to function effectively.

This awareness of self and team forms the cornerstone of success, acting as both a driving force and essential building block for all other components. E-Colours, Personal Intervention and related applications provide the framework for understanding and integrating the remaining elements.

2. Shared Vision and Values

Once team members have a strong understanding of themselves and each other, the next crucial step in building and sustaining a high-performance team is establishing a shared vision, mission, strategy, and set of values. In Equilibria, we call this a 'Team Compass'.

An organisation-wide Team Compass serves as the foundation for this effort. Clear articulation of vision, mission, values, and strategy at the team level enables members to align with the team's goals, enhancing commitment, effectiveness, and overall cohesion while minimising friction and conflict. Individual teams within the organisation can then develop their own Team Compass, aligned with the overarching vision and values but tailored to their specific function and objectives.

3. Clarity of Roles and Processes

The third essential, as a driving element, emphasises the importance of clearly defined and aligned individual roles, responsibilities, accountabilities, and authority levels. Such clarity enables team members to understand their obligations, areas of accountability, and reporting relationships.

Personality differences, as highlighted by the E-Colours, bring unique strengths and potential challenges that influence how individuals define their roles and follow processes. For team members to work effectively, they must not only have a clear understanding of their own role and associated processes, but also be aware of the roles, strengths, and potential limiters of their teammates. Intentional leaders play a critical role in fostering this clarity and alignment within the team.

4. Trust and Psychological Safety

Trust is a fundamental component of all human interaction, especially within organisations, as it serves as the glue that binds teams together and enables seamless, effective collaboration.

In any organisation, trust acts as a powerful multiplier – enhancing team performance and amplifying the impact of processes such as feedback. When trust is high, team members are more likely to interpret one another's actions and statements positively, reducing friction and encouraging open, constructive communication.

If trust is defined as confidence in the reliability, integrity, and competence of others, psychological safety is the assurance that one can express ideas, take risks, and make mistakes without fear of negative consequences. These two concepts are deeply interconnected.

5. Diversity and Inclusion
Diversity is a fact; inclusion is an act. Diversity is a reality, and inclusion is the deliberate choice to act on it.

Embracing diversity ensures that all team members feel their ideas, thoughts, opinions, and perspectives are valued and respected. Diversity includes a wide range of dimensions – such as personality diversity, diversity of thought as highlighted by the E-Colours, as well as ethnicity, gender, age, nationality, faith, disability, sexual orientation, education, and more.

Diversity represents the range of characteristics that distinguish individuals and groups, while inclusion is the intentional practice of fostering an environment where every person feels valued and accepted.

In an inclusive team, members experience a sense of belonging, and their unique backgrounds, abilities, beliefs, and personalities are appreciated. Bringing together individuals from diverse backgrounds can pose challenges, making trust and psychological safety all the more important. A common obstacle is reluctance to engage in healthy conflict and open discussion, particularly when new members join an established team. Proactively addressing this is key to creating a truly inclusive and high-performing organisation.

6. Commitment
This essential emphasises the link between personal involvement and team commitment, highlighting the importance of

including individuals in the decision-making process to foster collective buy-in.

It recognises that while 100% consensus may be rare, 100% commitment is achievable when each team member feels heard and has the opportunity to contribute their views.

In situations where consensus cannot be reached, it becomes the leader's responsibility to make the final decision, and the team's responsibility to support it. If the decision-making process allows everyone to voice their perspectives, team members are far more likely to commit to the outcome, even if it is not their preferred choice.

7. Accountability

In high-performance teams, accountability is an unspoken standard – it becomes second nature. It is strategically positioned within the Essential Leadership Cycle because it depends on the prior essentials being firmly established and functioning effectively.

Successful teams demonstrate high levels of accountability, both through leaders holding team members accountable and through peers holding each other accountable. This extends beyond outcomes to include the actions and behaviours that lead to those outcomes. For instance, Stop Work Authority is a clear demonstration of peer-to-peer accountability in upholding safety standards.

Personal accountability, such as through Personal Intervention, is equally vital. Team members should actively give and accept permission to hold each other accountable for actions, behaviours, and results, fostering a culture of mutual responsibility and continuous improvement.

8. Learning and Continuous Improvement
Learning and continuous improvement involve evaluating a team's outcomes and processes to identify areas for growth. High-performing teams routinely debrief after meetings, tasks, and projects – reflecting on experiences, learning from them, and sharing ideas within the team and wider organisation.

This process should include all team members and, where appropriate, stakeholders connected to the team's outcomes and deliverables. Teams are encouraged to set aspirational goals for learning and development, and to regularly track their progress, creating a culture of ongoing growth and improvement.

Learn more by contacting info@equilibria.com.

* * *

INTENTIONAL LEADERSHIP

A Purpose-Driven Approach

Intentional leadership is characterised by a clear sense of purpose and direction, with a strong focus on creating and sustaining a positive, productive, and psychologically safe environment within an organisation.

This leadership style is rooted in a commitment to building both self-awareness and team awareness. It involves understanding the unique strengths, potential limiters, communication styles, and interpersonal dynamics that contribute to success – or present challenges – at both the individual and organisational level. Intentional leadership builds trust through open communication and shared expectations, promoting accountability at the personal, individual, and team levels.

By clearly defining roles and responsibilities, intentional leadership ensures alignment towards common goals. It also prioritises the wellbeing and work-life balance of team members, actively supporting these areas to create a lasting, positive impact.

Intentional leaders typically demonstrate these characteristics and behaviours:

- **Clarity of Purpose:** They have a clear understanding of both personal and organisational goals, aligning their actions accordingly to ensure consistency and focus.
- **Conscious Decision-Making:** They make thoughtful decisions, considering the long-term impact on stakeholders, the organisation, and themselves. They carefully weigh alternatives and consequences before acting.
- **Authenticity and Transparency:** They are genuine in their interactions and transparent in their communication – building trust by being open about their intentions and motivations.
- **Empowering Others:** They enable their teams by delegating authority, providing resources, and fostering a culture of accountability. This encourages others to lead with intention as well.
- **Continuous Learning and Adaptation:** They are committed to ongoing personal growth. They also adapt

their leadership style based on feedback and changing circumstances to stay effective.

- **Ethical and Values-Driven:** They adhere to ethical standards and act according to core values. They prioritise integrity, fairness, and respect for others in all decisions.
- **Responding Rather Than Reacting:** They utilise their knowledge of Personal Intervention, invoking PAUSE & PLAY techniques when appropriate – RESPONDING rather than REACTING for intentional outcomes.

Intentional leadership is about setting the tone for a thriving, cohesive team where purpose, wellbeing, and performance are in harmony.

Learn more by contacting info@equilibria.com.

* * *

ADVANCED ERROR REDUCTION IN ORGANISATIONS (AERO)

Advanced Error Reduction in Organisations (AERO) is not a programme, but a transformative approach to thinking, behaving, and applying practical concepts that drive sustainable improvements in Safety, Quality, Effectiveness, Efficiency, and Productivity.

AERO represents the evolution of risk and error reduction, seamlessly combining the principles of Human and Organisational Performance (HOP) with Equilibria's personality diversity technology, embodied in the E-Colours framework.

Extensive research and field experimentation have enabled us to develop a comprehensive data lake analysing every facet of

HOP. This actionable intelligence is further enriched by examining it through the E-Colours perspective, leading to the creation of innovative, practical applications. These range from enhancing understanding and use of the five HOP principles to identifying error traps, assessing Performance Modes, and determining the most effective tools to minimise errors.

We collaborate with clients to embed risk awareness and error mitigation concepts into their organisational practices and programmes. By equipping internal resources with training and certification skills, we enable companies to sustain these capabilities through a proven process that has delivered success across industries worldwide.

Additionally, we offer ongoing support to ensure accurate and effective integration of these concepts into business operations, providing a solid foundation for long-term improvement and success.

The integration and practical application of these technologies enable individuals and organisations to realise their potential in these ways:

- Increasing capacity to recognise and manage risk
- Reducing the probability of errors
- Mitigating the consequences of errors
- Building resilience
- Creating sustainable performance improvements
- Accelerating organisational learning
- Monitoring additional performance improvement metrics

Learn more by contacting info@equilibria.com.

In Step with Emotion: A Tale of Harmony and Detail – Lewis Senior

This story still stands out to me as a powerful reminder of how our individual perspectives – shaped by our E-Colours – can completely transform the way we experience the same moment.

A few years ago, my daughter and I were travelling with a couple of secondees from one of our anchor clients. They were placed with us for a six-month programme, which gave them the opportunity to accompany us as we visited various business units their company was working with around the world. While in Canada, we had the chance to attend a show called *Cavalia*, staged in a massive tent set up in Calgary. The performance was mesmerising – brilliant acrobats and majestic horses moving together in perfect synchrony for more than an hour and a half. At one point, a woman entered the ring with eight horses, and as the music played and the lights cast a magical glow, the audience of 3,000 seemed utterly captivated by the harmony between her and the horses.

My E-Colours are predominantly Yellow/Red, which means I can be quite emotional. That night, my daughter was with me – her E-Colours are Red/Yellow – and honestly, I've only seen her cry a handful of times in her life. With us were the two secondees, whom we called Khun Sa, whose E-Colours are Blue/Red, and Regan Braseth, whose E-Colours are predominantly Green/Red.

When that scene hit its peak, with the woman and the horses moving in what felt like perfect rhythm, I could feel tears running down my face. I glanced at my daughter, and there she was, teary-eyed too – a rare sight. Khun Sa, seated beside her, was also crying openly. I turned to Regan, expecting him to be equally moved, and asked what he thought of it all. He looked at me and said, 'The seventh horse is out of step, and it's really bothering me.'

That response stopped me in my tracks. Most of us had been swept up in the sheer beauty and harmony of the moment. But Regan, true to his Green/Red E-Colours, was focused on the details – and for him, the one horse slightly out of sync had disrupted the entire experience. While the rest of us were caught up in the emotional impact, he simply couldn't look past that one detail.

Reflecting on that night, I realise how powerfully our E-Colours shaped our experience. My daughter, Khun Sa and I were drawn to the unity and beauty, emotionally moved by the connection between the performer and the horses. Regan's detail-oriented viewpoint, however, added a whole new layer to the memory, showing how each person's unique viewpoint brings something valuable. That contrast didn't take away from the magic of the show; in fact, it only made it more memorable. It's a reminder I hold closely: the richness in each moment often comes from seeing it through different lenses.

Guy's Story

Equilibria has taught me not only how to develop, learn and grow as a leader with respect to my E-Colors – leveraging my strengths – but also how to better lead a team or organization by tailoring my leadership style to the E-Colors of the organization. I can't emphasise how important that is.

– *Guy Davis* (Red/Yellow)
– Manager, Technical Innovation & Strategy, USA

Reid's Story

Gaining this invaluable, deeper understanding of oneself and those we interact with daily has been truly transformative.

Throughout my 30-year career in building design, effective communication has been paramount, requiring interaction with numerous team members across a wide range of cultures and nationalities. Cracking the code of communication has consistently led to successful outcomes. Discovering my own personality tendencies, specifically my predominant Red strengths and potential limiters, has proven to be a game changer. Leveraging this awareness and utilising the power of the pause and play button in various situations has significantly enhanced my ability to connect with both family and team members on a deeper level. Furthermore, comprehending the E-Colours and corresponding tendencies of others has equipped me with the knowledge to adapt my communication across a diverse spectrum of personalities. Recognising that we are all unique – but share a common goal of fostering meaningful connections with family, friends and work colleagues – has greatly improved relationships across the board.

– Reid Donovan (Red/Yellow)
– Operations Director, Red Sea Developments, KSA

Scott's Story

Due to recent circumstances, I have been driving a taxi at nights, only to make some additional money, not because I enjoy it, and only for a very short term.

I could have been working 4 weeks on 4 weeks off again in a role somewhere, but I am determined to now make E-Colours and Recruitment my main businesses.

Anyway, being a strong RED, and especially in the old offshore days, I could be aggressive with people and would only fight fire with fire. That's the way it was a lot of times back in the 'bad old days'.

Being involved with Mark, Lewis, Paul, Life Remixed and Equilibria over the past few months has given me a lot to think about in my own behaviours, mainly around topics discussed on their weekly Tuesday Leadership sessions (9-10am UK time), reading through my Premium Report, and definitely around understanding my own 'Strengths and Potential Limiters'.

Driving a taxi in these modern times can be extremely challenging, mixing with all walks of life, and to be honest, some individuals who I wouldn't normally spend time with. I have had a few people in the taxi who have been extremely aggressive towards me, and I found myself slipping back into the 'old Scott'.

At one point I even told myself I would just hand the taxi keys back to the owner and that would be that. I'm 54 years old, why do I need to put up with this? Simply put, I don't!

I then got to thinking about my React vs Respond with these aggressive individuals, instead of grabbing them by the scruff of the neck and throwing them out of the taxi, I referred back to my E-Colours Premium report again and started responding in a completely different manner.

After my pausing, responding calmly, showing them gratitude, and openly showing more of my yellow strengths it amazed me to see how mastering this can flip people's behaviours completely, they went from being aggressive and threatening me, to going quiet, and then when getting out of the taxi, apologising for their initial behaviour!

I really wanted to share this story, as it demonstrates and proves the power of the E-Colours on me, and all of us.

I have also been thinking a lot about adults and youngsters who may have gone down the wrong path, some of which could have found themselves in trouble with the law and locked up.

Do they understand their own personality style in detail? I wonder what impact it could have, letting them see their personality style and allowing them to understand and work on their own strengths and potential limiters.

Something for us all to think about. Thank you all – for turning on the light for me.

— *Scott Qua* (Red/Yellow)
— Recruitment Partner & E-Colours Practitioner, UK

Taylor's Story

One of the best tools I've found from Equilibria is the Planned Engagement Checklist. I used it during a crucial conversation with a rig site supervisor, greatly improving the outcome. This tool has been a game changer in my leadership and communication efforts.

– *Taylor Begnaud* (Yellow/Red)
– Director, Wells Conventional Assets, USA

* * *

Remix Opportunities

By exploring the practical applications, you will have noticed the numerous ways E-Colours can be integrated into various aspects of life. Beyond what is outlined below, how else do you envision incorporating this personality diversity technology into your daily routines?

- Discover the E-Colours Alignment Reports – $49.99 / approx. £42.
- Learn to appreciate others' personality styles and encourage others to interact with the E-Colours.
- Study the Equilibria advanced tools and apply them appropriately.
- Get a tattoo or perhaps wear an E-Colours wristband instead.

CHAPTER 13

E-COLOURS FOR EDUCATION

'Tell me and I forget, teach me and I may remember, involve me and I learn.'

– **Benjamin Franklin**, Founding Father of the United States

If we want to change the world, we must start by helping children understand who they are, and who they have the potential to become.

Every child holds a story waiting to be written, a voice longing to be heard, and a personality bursting with possibility. The question is: what if we gave them the tools to understand themselves before the world tried to tell them who they should be?

Imagine a seven-year-old learning not just their ABCs, but their tendencies – what makes them tick, how they shine, and what might trip them up. Imagine a classroom where a child like Thomas, once labelled as 'difficult', becomes an E-Colours Champion. Where a young girl like Sarah grows into a powerful voice for inclusion – not just in her school, but across her community. These aren't hypothetical stories. They're real, and they're powerful.

Because when we introduce the E-Colours to children, we're not just teaching a tool – we're planting seeds of self-awareness, empathy, and intentional action. We're giving kids a language for emotions they didn't yet know how to express. A framework to understand why their classmate learns differently. A chance to press PLAY when they need to speak up, or PAUSE when they're about to say something they might regret.

And the best part? They get it. Sometimes faster than adults do.

This chapter is a celebration of what's possible when we meet children where they are, speak their language, and honour their natural diversity of personality. From classrooms and playgrounds to dinner tables and sports teams, the E-Colours are helping young people grow into emotionally intelligent, confident, and compassionate leaders of tomorrow.

If we want to build a better future, we need to start with the children. And the journey begins here – with awareness, intention, and a simple, powerful set of coloured wristbands that can change lives.

Let's show them that who they are is exactly who they need to be.

What Does 'Education' Mean for Children?

Do you know where the word 'education' comes from? It's from the Latin *Educo*, which means 'to draw out from within'.

With that in mind, wouldn't it be a good idea to educate children about their own strengths and help them understand their potential limiters?

E-Colours in Schools: A Vision for Transforming Education

From the very beginning, our mission at Equilibria has been to help individuals and teams realise their full potential, whether in the high-stakes world of safety and leadership, in performance-driven workplaces, or in environments where collaboration is essential. Yet if there's one place where the impact of personality diversity technology can be truly life-changing, it's in the classroom.

The desire to bring E-Colours into schools, colleges, and universities is not just an extension of our work – it is a passion every bit as powerful as our commitment to safety and leadership. Imagine a world where students, teachers, and administrators all have the tools to understand themselves and each other better, where miscommunication is reduced, teamwork is strengthened, and young minds are equipped with self-awareness and personal intervention skills from an early age. That vision became a reality thanks to the foresight of one very caring and thoughtful educator.

The very first request to introduce E-Colours into a school came from Sandy Phillips, an English teacher in Texas. Her husband, David, and I had worked closely together in an energy company's Drilling and Completions organisation, where he had seen firsthand the positive impact of E-Colours on safety and teamwork. Inspired by what she observed in her husband's professional environment, Sandy saw the potential for the same transformation in her own world – her school. She asked if we could introduce E-Colours to help build a stronger, more cohesive teaching team. That simple request became the spark that ignited a movement.

Once the teachers and principal saw the benefits, it was clear we had something special. Before long, thanks to the support of Joni Baird and Dave Payne, we were introduced to Dr Rosalinda Mercado, principal of Southwest Schools. What followed was nothing short of extraordinary. The impact we witnessed over the next several years proved beyond any doubt that personality diversity technology belonged in education. It became so evident, in fact, that we launched a nonprofit, E-Colours in Education, dedicated to bringing this work to schools around the world.

For seven years, E-Colours in Education helped teachers, students, and administrators cultivate better communication, trust, and collaboration. Unfortunately, like so many organisations, the nonprofit did not survive the disruptions of COVID-19. Yet the mission never ended. The results we have seen in every instance where E-Colours have been introduced into educational settings continue to inspire us, fuelling our commitment to keep this work alive.

That is why this chapter exists in *Personalities Remixed*. The stories, the evidence, and the transformations we have witnessed are too powerful to leave untold. Our hope is that as you read on, you will not only recognise the extraordinary potential of E-Colours in education, but you will also feel compelled to join us in bringing this life-changing approach to more young minds across the world.

Because the future isn't just shaped by what we teach – it's shaped by how we connect, understand, and inspire the next generation.

Mark Wilkinson: I'd say that would be a lot more useful than remembering historical dates and algebra, wouldn't you agree?

Personally, I wish my school reports had simply told me I was a top E-Colour Yellow, along with all the strengths and potential limiters that go with it. I believe my life story would have been very different if I had been introduced to the E-Colours as a child, especially if the teachers had been aware of both mine and their own personality styles.

Getting to know so much about yourself, your friends, your family, and all those around you is the first step in utilising personality diversity as a child.

Our personality diversity process – the E-Colours – helps to identify different personality styles, enabling you to better understand a lot more about who you are and why you do what you do.

A knowledge of E-Colours leads to a heightened awareness that we do not all think or act the same, and that we all have different communication styles and behavioural tendencies, often largely linked to our personalities.

One of the most amazing things that Equilibria has discovered since 2004 is that when E-Colours are introduced to schoolchildren as young as seven years old, the children engage with the tool with such enthusiasm, sometimes even more easily than the adults. Some amazing discoveries have been made in terms of the use of the E-Colours and the positive impact on schools. These include heightened self-awareness, team-awareness, improved communication, leadership, caring for individuals, better attendance records, improved academic results, and bullying being eliminated – all of which help to produce improved KPI (Key Performance Indicator) results throughout schools.

Thomas's Story – From Zero to Hero – Lewis Senior

Thomas's story is one that has always stayed with me. At one of the schools we partnered with, the principal shared the challenges faced by eight-year-old Thomas, who frequently found himself in trouble. His behaviour had become so disruptive that he was no longer permitted to ride the school bus home. Instead, he had to sit outside the principal's office for up to two hours after school, waiting for his father to collect him.

As mentioned in an earlier anecdote, students had requested to adapt the E-Colours language into terms they could better relate to. Outside the principal's office where Thomas waited, there was a large poster of the E-Colours brain, featuring the students' interpretations of strengths and potential limiters for each primary colour.

After a few weeks of sitting there and studying the poster, Thomas knocked on the principal's door and asked to speak with her. She often recounts this moment with pride and amazement, recalling how Thomas said, 'I now understand why I keep getting into trouble. All the potential limiters for my E-Colours are exactly what I've been doing.'

Thomas was then given his E-Colours wristband, which became a crucial tool for his self-awareness and personal growth. On days when he forgot his wristband, teachers noticed he would draw a PAUSE & PLAY button on his wrist to remind himself of the techniques he had learned. Over time, Thomas transformed from a child frequently in trouble to a role model and E-Colours Champion. His journey has stood him in good stead for many years and remains a testament to the life-changing power of understanding one's E-Colours.

E-Colours as a Cornerstone

E-Colours and the associated tools form a cornerstone of a vibrant, dynamic, and resilient society. They represent the wide array of individual differences in tendencies, behaviours, and temperaments that people exhibit. These variations enrich human interactions and enhance the ability of societies to adapt, innovate, and thrive. While E-Colours are present across all age groups, the development of these diverse tendencies begins in childhood, making children the foundation of personality diversity awareness for the future.

The early years of life are a critical period for personality development. During this time, children begin to form their identities, shaped by a complex interplay of genetic, environmental, social, and cultural influences. As children grow, their personalities are moulded by their experiences, relationships, and the broader societal context in which they live. These formative experiences lay the groundwork for the unique ways in which they will perceive the world, interact with others, and approach challenges.

Children are not merely passive recipients of their environments; they are active participants in shaping their own development. Their curiosity, creativity, and willingness to explore new ideas and perspectives make them key contributors to the diversification of E-Colours. As they engage with the world around them, they learn to navigate different social situations, understand a variety of cultural norms, and develop their own values and beliefs. This process of exploration and learning is crucial for the emergence of diverse personalities.

As the world becomes increasingly interconnected, the importance of personality diversity grows ever more critical. In a globalised society, individuals with diverse personalities bring different perspectives, problem-solving approaches, and emotional responses to the table. Valuing this diversity is essential for fostering innovation, collaboration, and social cohesion. Children, as future leaders, thinkers, and creators, will carry forward the mantle of personality diversity, shaping the societies of tomorrow.

However, the path to nurturing E-Colours in children is not without challenges. Social pressures, cultural expectations, and educational systems can sometimes impose constraints on the expression of diverse personalities. There is a risk of homogenising children's development by promoting conformity and discouraging individuality. To preserve and celebrate personality diversity, it is essential to create environments that support and nurture each child's unique tendencies.

In *Personalities Remixed*, and throughout the following sections, we will highlight the vital role that children play in ensuring a diverse and vibrant future for society – and how the E-Colours can help children leverage personality diversity for their own growth and development.

- Developmental Foundation of Personality Diversity
- The Language of Your Audience
- Social and Cultural Influences
- Learning Styles and the E-Colours
- Benefits of Personality Diversity for Children
- Challenges and Considerations

- Nurturing Personality Diversity
- Why are E-Colours Important for Learning?
- Opportunities for Children

* * *

DEVELOPMENTAL FOUNDATION OF PERSONALITY DIVERSITY

The development of personality diversity – E-Colours – begins in childhood, where the foundations for unique personality tendencies are laid. This period is characterised by rapid cognitive, emotional, and social growth, during which children form the core aspects of their identities. Understanding the developmental foundation of personality diversity involves exploring the various factors that influence this process, including genetic predispositions, family dynamics, early education, and environmental interactions.

Genetic and Biological Influences

Personality development is partly rooted in genetics, with studies suggesting that certain tendencies, such as temperament, are inherited. Temperament refers to the innate aspects of an individual's personality, such as emotional reactivity, energy levels, and adaptability. These temperamental tendencies are observable even in infancy and provide the biological basis upon which later personality characteristics are built.

For instance, a child who is naturally more task-orientated is likely to be drawn towards solitary play and reflective activities, while a more people-orientated child may seek out social interactions and thrive in group settings. These inherent tendencies are not deterministic but interact with environmental factors to shape the child's overall personality. The interplay between genetic predispositions and environmental influences highlights the complexity of personality development, emphasising the importance of supporting diverse temperaments from an early age.

The Role of Family Dynamics

Family is the primary environment in which a child's personality begins to take shape. The dynamics within a family – parenting styles, sibling relationships, and even the emotional climate of the household – play a critical role in shaping a child's development.

Parenting styles, for example, have a profound impact on personality growth. Authoritative parenting, which balances warmth with discipline, is associated with the development of confident, socially competent children. In contrast, authoritarian or overly permissive parenting may lead to conformity or rebellion, affecting a child's ability to express their unique personality tendencies. Moreover, parents who are attuned to their child's individual needs and characteristics are more likely to foster an environment where diverse personalities can flourish.

Sibling relationships also contribute significantly to personality diversity. Siblings often develop distinct personalities, influenced by birth order, gender, and the unique experiences they bring to the family dynamic. These relationships offer children opportunities to build social skills, empathy, and conflict resolution abilities, all of which enrich the development of their personalities. The family unit, therefore, is a crucial environment where personality diversity can either be nurtured or restricted, depending on the nature of interactions and relationships within it.

Hana, Sarah, and Leana Abi Saab – Three Remarkable Sisters – Lewis Senior

One recurring theme in the education sector is how schools have embraced the concept of creating E-Colours Champions, fostering a culture of personality diversity and growth. A standout example of this success is Holmquist Elementary School in the Alief Independent School District, Houston. When the E-Colours were first introduced to the school, key leaders like Principal Kimberly Toney, Diana Cavazos, and Suzie Sanchez became enthusiastic advocates for the initiative.

Diana played a pivotal role by assembling a group of eager champions and regularly bringing them together to deepen their understanding and appreciation of personality diversity. Among these champions, one student, Sarah, quickly became well known for her enthusiasm and willingness to engage. She was often the first to speak up during visits, demonstrating a clear passion for the process. Recognising the potential of these champions, I frequently brought individuals from other organisations to witness firsthand the transformative impact of this initiative in a school setting.

Sarah's leadership extended beyond the classroom. Her engagement with E-Colours influenced her family as well, with her older sister Hana and younger sister Leana becoming involved over time. Their participation highlighted how the programme's benefits extended beyond the school environment, fostering growth and collaboration within their family.

One memorable moment occurred in the months leading up to the Super Bowl in Houston in 2017. For three months, we collaborated with the NFL Experience to offer underprivileged communities a glimpse of the excitement surrounding the event. Sarah and her fellow E-Colours Champions played a vital role, explaining the concept of personality diversity to hundreds of attendees each day. Watching Sarah confidently stand by a large visual representation of the brain, explaining the interplay of strengths and potential limitations, was truly inspiring.

Sarah's dedication didn't stop there. She even appeared on television with Deborah Duncan to explain the E-Colours to a live audience. Later, she was among the first volunteers to help distribute uniforms and E-Colours wristbands to over 10,000 Super Bowl volunteers. Her commitment to promoting the E-Colours was evident in every step she took.

Over the years, I've had the privilege of seeing Sarah, Hana, Leana, and their mother during visits to Houston. Their development into confident, capable young women has been remarkable. As of now, Hana is studying dentistry, and Sarah has been accepted to Rice University on a full scholarship. Their parents firmly believe that their exposure to the E-Colours and associated tools over the years has significantly prepared them for future challenges and opportunities.

You can view various videos of the Abi Saabs' progress on Equilibria's social media sites, including LinkedIn, Facebook, and TikTok.

This story serves as a testament to the profound and lasting impact of empowering young individuals with tools for self-awareness, collaboration, and growth. It's a reminder that fostering champions in any environment – be it schools, families, or communities – can create ripples of positive change for years to come.

Influence of Early Education

Early childhood education plays a pivotal role in shaping personality diversity – E-Colours. During the preschool and early elementary years, children are exposed to new social environments, peer interactions, and structured learning experiences that contribute significantly to their personality development. The approach taken by educators, the curriculum, and the overall educational philosophy can either encourage or stifle the expression of diverse personality tendencies.

For instance, educational settings that promote creativity, critical thinking, and emotional intelligence are far more likely to support the development of well-rounded, diverse personalities. Montessori and Reggio Emilia approaches, which emphasise child-led learning and holistic development, allow children to explore their interests and strengths within a supportive environment. This freedom to explore and express themselves can lead to the growth of unique personality tendencies that might not flourish in more rigid, traditional educational settings.

Moreover, the diversity of the peer group in early education also plays a significant role. Interacting with peers from different cultural, social, and linguistic backgrounds exposes children to a variety of perspectives and ways of thinking, broadening their understanding of the world and their place in it. This exposure to diversity helps children develop tolerance, empathy, and a greater appreciation for differences – all of which contribute to a richer, more diverse personality landscape.

Environmental Interactions and Experiences

Beyond genetics, family, and education, the broader environment in which a child grows up has a profound influence on their personality development. Environmental factors include the socio-economic status of the family, the cultural context, and the community in which the child is raised. These elements shape the experiences that children have and, ultimately, the personality tendencies they develop.

Children raised in environments that encourage exploration and offer a range of experiences – such as exposure to nature, the arts, sports, and diverse social settings – tend to develop more complex and varied personalities. These experiences help children discover their passions, strengths, and preferences, all essential components of personality diversity. Conversely, children growing up in more restrictive or impoverished environments may have fewer opportunities to explore different facets of themselves, potentially leading to a narrower development of personality tendencies.

Furthermore, the cultural context in which a child is raised plays a significant role. Cultures vary in their values, norms, and expectations regarding personality. For example, collectivist cultures may emphasise tendencies such as cooperation, harmony, and conformity, while individualist cultures often value independence, assertiveness, and self-expression. These cultural influences shape the way children develop their personalities, contributing to the diversity of tendencies observed across different societies.

Jazmin and the Case of the Socks and the Stopwatch – Lewis Senior

It was a sunny Friday evening, and Jazmin's parents were getting ready for their big date night – or at least they were trying to. Jazmin, perched on the living room couch, watched the chaos unfold like a live-action sitcom.

Jazmin's mum, Sophia, was a whirlwind of Red/Yellow energy, darting from the bedroom to the kitchen and back, tossing out commands and to-do lists faster than a Formula 1 pit stop.

'George! We're going to be late! Do you really need to check the mirror again? And those socks – are they from 2003? Just grab any pair and let's go!'

Meanwhile, Jazmin's dad, George, the quintessential Green/Blue, was moving at the speed of a cautious turtle. He stood in front of the mirror, one sock on, one sock off, holding two identical navy socks up to the light as if solving a complex riddle.

'Calm down, Sophia,' he said soothingly. 'I just want to make sure these socks match the tone of my trousers. If they're even slightly off, it could throw off the whole outfit!'

Sophia rolled her eyes so hard that Jazmin worried they might get stuck. 'We're not going to a fashion show, George! It's just a dinner at Arturo's. No one's going to notice your socks!'

Jazmin grinned. She'd learned all about the E-Colours in school last week, and she had a sneaking suspicion her parents were living examples of why those perspectives mattered. It was time to put her knowledge to good use.

'Mum, Dad, PAUSE for a second!' she called, hopping off the couch.

'What is it, sweetie?' Sophia asked, mid-stride.

'Yeah, honey, we really need to get going,' George added, now comparing sock heights with a ruler.

'You're not going anywhere if you keep this up,' Jazmin said matter-of-factly. 'Mum, your E-Colours are Red/Yellow, which means you're super action-oriented and hate waiting. Dad, yours are Green/Blue, so you like to take your time and think things through. Right now, you're both stressing each other out because you don't understand what the other needs.'

Sophia and George froze, looking at each other, then at Jazmin.

'Well, aren't you a little therapist,' Sophia said, crossing her arms. 'So, what do we do, Dr Jazmin?'

'Simple!' Jazmin said proudly. 'Mum, why don't you channel your energy into setting a timer for Dad? That way, he has a set amount of time to get ready, and you don't have to stand there getting frustrated. And Dad, instead of worrying about every detail, pick one thing to focus on, like your tie, and just grab the first socks you see.'

Sophia and George exchanged a look.

'That… actually makes sense,' Sophia said. 'I do love a good timer.' She pulled out her phone and set a five-minute countdown.

George sighed but nodded. 'Alright, I'll prioritise. Socks are good enough. Now, which tie, though? Polka dots or stripes?'

'Dad!' Jazmin said, laughing.

Five minutes later, the family stood in the hallway. Sophia tapped her foot but smiled, knowing the timer helped her stay calm. George patted his navy socks – slightly mismatched but invisible under his trousers – and gave Jazmin a thumbs-up.

'You're pretty amazing, kid,' Sophia said, pulling Jazmin into a hug.

'Yeah, thanks for saving date night,' George added. 'Now we'll actually make our reservation.'

'Have fun!' Jazmin called as they headed out the door. 'And don't forget to tip Arturo!'

As the door closed, Jazmin flopped back onto the couch, feeling like a superhero in pyjamas. Maybe this E-Colours thing wasn't just for school after all.

The Importance of Individual Differences

Understanding the developmental foundation of personality diversity also involves recognising the importance of individual differences. No two children, or adults, are the same, and even within similar environments, children will develop distinct personalities based on their unique interactions with the world around them. These individual differences are what make personality diversity so valuable to society.

In this context, it is equally important to acknowledge the role of neurodiversity in contributing to personality diversity. Neurodiverse children, such as those with autism spectrum disorder, ADHD, or other developmental differences, bring unique perspectives and ways of engaging with the world. Supporting these and all children in expressing their personalities and integrating their strengths into broader social settings is crucial for maintaining a rich and diverse human landscape.

Conclusion of Developmental Foundations

The developmental foundations of personality diversity, E-Colours, are laid during childhood through a combination of genetic, environmental, social, and cultural influences. The interplay of these factors creates a complex and dynamic process that shapes the unique personalities of each child. By understanding and supporting these developmental pathways, we can help ensure that personality diversity continues to flourish, enriching society with a vibrant tapestry of individual differences.

In the following sections, we will explore the broader social and cultural influences on personality diversity, the benefits of fostering diverse personalities in children, and strategies for nurturing and supporting this diversity across different settings. Through this exploration, we will see how the seeds of personality diversity, E-Colours, sown in childhood grow into the diverse and dynamic individuals who shape our world.

*   *   *

THE LANGUAGE OF YOUR AUDIENCE

Speak the Language of Your Audience – E-Colours for Students – Lewis Senior

Introducing the E-Colours and associated tools into schools has always been a major milestone in Equilibria's journey. While working with a school in Houston, the principal proposed a remarkable idea: that every educational institution implementing E-Colours should establish a group of 'E-Colours Champions'. This concept became so well developed that each champion signed an agreement committing to uphold specific behaviours, serving as role models and mentors for their peers.

As these champions deepened their knowledge and confidence in understanding and applying the E-Colours, they eventually approached me with a unique request: to translate the E-Colours language into words and examples that would resonate more clearly with students. Recognising the value of collaboration – and inspired by the adage 'No involvement equals no commitment' – we dedicated a weekend to the project. Students, parents, teachers, and leaders from one of our anchor clients came together to co-create an E-Colours language tailored specifically for students and educators.

The impact of those two days was profound, and the results are still felt today through the dedicated student Pocket Books we share around the world. Although this initiative took place years ago, I remain in touch with several of the students involved, many of whom often reflect on the significance of that experience and the positive role it played in their personal and educational journeys.

Here are the strengths and potential limiters the students agreed on.

STRENGTHS

The Strengths of a Yellow (Socialiser)

- Flexible
- Fun-loving
- Playful
- Storyteller
- Hopeful
- Energetic
- Free-spoken
- Creative

The Strengths of a Blue (Relator)

- Peacemaker
- Helpful
- Agreeable
- Happy
- Likeable
- Kind
- Detailed
- Faithful

The Strengths of a Green (Thinker)

- Perfectionist
- Exact
- Persistent
- Serious

- Detailed
- Orderly
- Careful
- Wise

The Strengths of a Red (Doer)

- Keep it simple
- Strong-willed
- Decide quickly
- Work with what you got
- Takes on challenges
- Wants to win
- Independent
- Strong ego

POTENTIAL LIMITERS

The Potential Limiters of a Yellow (Socialiser)

- Lacks boundaries
- Spreading oneself too thin
- Lack of focus
- Blah-blah-blah
- Naïve/Gullible
- No filter
- Emotional
- Dreamer

The Potential Limiters of a Blue (Relator)

- Stubborn
- Unsure
- Awkward
- Possessive
- Insecure
- Resistant to change
- Slow to decide
- Reluctant to speak up

The Potential Limiters of a Green (Thinker)

- Too serious
- Choosy
- Judgemental
- Fears critique
- Fault-finding
- Find fault in oneself
- Delayed
- Not involved

The Potential Limiters of a Red (Doer)

- Bossy
- Pushy
- Impatient
- Distant
- Tough

- Harsh
- Poor listener
- Insensitive

When we have introduced the E-Colours at seven years old and Personal Intervention at nine years old, the results have been incredible. As far as we know, no other personality-based tool can be successfully completed by children. Another great differentiator for Equilibria's E-Colours.

* * *

SOCIAL AND CULTURAL INFLUENCES

Personality diversity is not solely the result of individual development or genetic predispositions; it is also deeply shaped by the social and cultural contexts in which children grow up. Socialisation processes, cultural norms, media exposure, and the evolving dynamics of technology and globalisation all play critical roles in shaping and expanding the spectrum of personality tendencies that emerge in children. These influences contribute to the diversity of personalities seen across different societies and generations.

The Role of Socialisation

Socialisation is the process by which children learn and internalise the values, norms, behaviours, and social skills necessary to function within their society. This process begins at home and extends into schools, peer groups, and the wider community. Socialisation is a key factor in shaping personality because it involves ongoing interactions that help children understand their roles and relationships within society.

From an early age, children are socialised into the cultural and societal expectations of their environment. Family members, educators, and peers all contribute to this process by modelling behaviours, providing feedback, and reinforcing certain tendencies while discouraging others. For instance, a child may be encouraged to develop qualities like empathy, cooperation, and patience in a family that values these tendencies, while a more competitive environment may place greater emphasis on assertiveness and independence.

Moreover, the peer group plays a major role in socialising personality. Children often look to their peers for cues on how to behave and what tendencies are valued or stigmatised within the group. This leads to the development of social skills such as negotiation, compromise, and conflict resolution, all essential for navigating a wide range of social situations. Diversity within peer groups further enriches personality development by exposing children to a variety of perspectives and behaviours.

Cultural Norms and Values

Cultural norms and values are powerful forces in shaping personality diversity. Every culture holds its own beliefs about what constitutes desirable behaviour, and these beliefs heavily influence the development of personality tendencies. For example, in collectivist cultures that prioritise group harmony and interdependence – tendencies often associated with Blue (Relator) tendencies – children may be encouraged to develop qualities like humility, cooperation, and self-restraint. In contrast, individualist cultures that emphasise personal achievement and autonomy – aligned with Red (Doer) tendencies – may foster assertiveness and self-confidence.

These cultural norms are transmitted through family traditions, educational systems, religious practices, and community activities. In many Asian cultures, for instance, the concept of 'face' – the respect or honour one holds within the community – plays a major role in personality development. Children are taught to be mindful of their actions and their impact on the family's reputation, often leading to the cultivation of conscientiousness and social awareness.

However, cultural norms are not static. They evolve over time, influenced by globalisation, migration, and technological advancements. As societies become increasingly interconnected, children are exposed to a mixture of cultural values and practices, leading to an even greater diversity of personality tendencies. This blending of cultures can result in children developing hybrid identities, integrating different cultural influences into their personalities and contributing to the overall richness of society.

Rosalinda's Story

Equilibria, you have been such a wonderful impact in my personal life, and I know that you have done the same for others, whether it was through conversations about E-Colors, handling difficult situations with personal intervention, and being able to grow leaders through your eight essentials.

– Dr. Rosalinda Mercado (Yellow/Green)
– COO, Sunny Glen Children's Home, USA

Jennifer's Story – Lewis Senior

The transformation we have seen since introducing E-Colours into education has been nothing short of extraordinary. When we began working with Southwest Schools in Houston, the principal, Dr Rosalinda Mercado, immediately recognised the potential of E-Colours to benefit her students and staff. Her enthusiasm and advocacy laid the groundwork for a lasting impact.

Soon after we introduced E-Colours to Dr Mercado and her leadership team, she connected us with three exceptional individuals who would become the school's first E-Colours Champions: Jennifer Majano, Diego Masino Rivas, and Ruby Roman. These pioneering students embraced their roles wholeheartedly, establishing a strong foundation for many others to follow.

Each of them has gone on to achieve great success, becoming parents, model citizens, and highly respected professionals in their fields.

Jennifer, whose E-Colours are predominantly Blue/Yellow, stands out as a particularly inspiring example. As a young student, she struggled with uncertainty about her place in the world. Watching her grow into a confident, accomplished individual has been truly remarkable. Her journey serves as a testament to the power of E-Colours in fostering self-awareness, resilience, and personal development.

For any parent concerned about their child's future, we highly recommend connecting with one of the E-Colours Champions. Contact us at info@equilibria.com for more details.

These individuals have experienced the life-changing impact of the programme and can offer valuable awareness into how it might empower your child to thrive.

Media and Technology

In today's digital era, media and technology are ever-present forces that significantly shape personality development. Children are exposed to a constant stream of information, ideas, and role models through television, social media, video games, and other online platforms. These sources influence how children see themselves and others, guide their aspirations, and contribute to the development of their personality tendencies.

Media frequently portrays a wide range of personality styles, from heroes and leaders to rebels and outsiders, providing children with a spectrum of behaviours and tendencies to either emulate or avoid. For example, a child who identifies with a strong, independent character on television may be inspired to develop similar tendencies. Conversely, exposure to negative stereotypes or harmful content can lead to the internalisation of limiting beliefs or undesirable behaviours.

Social media plays a dual role in shaping young personalities. On the positive side, it allows children to explore different aspects of their identity, connect with diverse groups, and express themselves in ways that may not be possible in their immediate environment. This can nurture unique personality tendencies and foster a greater acceptance of diversity. On the negative side, social media can also pressure children to conform to particular ideals, leading to the suppression of individuality and the emergence of more homogenised behaviours.

Technology itself also plays a crucial role. As children engage with technology from a young age, they develop new ways of thinking, problem-solving, and interacting with the world. For instance, time spent on coding platforms or participating in online communities can nurture creativity, analytical thinking, and collaboration. However, overuse of technology can lead to challenges such as reduced attention spans and diminished face-to-face social skills, both of which can affect personality development in different ways.

Globalisation and Cultural Exchange

Globalisation has brought about unprecedented levels of cultural exchange, allowing children to be exposed to a wide variety of cultural practices, languages, and belief systems from around the world. This exposure to global diversity plays a critical role in shaping personality tendencies that are adaptable, open-minded, and culturally aware.

Children growing up in multicultural environments or attending international schools are often more likely to develop a global perspective, reflected in their personalities. They may become more tolerant of differences, more curious about the world, and better equipped to navigate diverse social settings. The blending of cultural influences often leads to the development of hybrid personalities, where children integrate elements from multiple cultures into their own identities.

Moreover, globalisation has facilitated the spread of ideas and movements that challenge traditional norms and encourage the development of diverse personalities. Movements advocating for gender equality, LGBTQ+ rights, and environmental sustainability, for instance, have gained global traction, influencing the values and tendencies that children develop. Exposure to such ideas may inspire tendencies like activism, empathy, and a commitment to social justice, contributing to greater overall diversity within society.

The E-Colours framework offers valuable awareness into how personality tendencies intersect with cultural norms, creating both opportunities and challenges in multicultural environments. A compelling example of this is Equilibria's work in Thailand within the oil and gas industry, where the introduction of Stop Work Authority (SWA) posed significant cultural challenges. SWA is a safety protocol designed to empower individuals to halt any operation if they identify a potential hazard or feel uncertain about a task. While logical in theory, its practical implementation had to navigate deeply rooted Thai cultural values and behaviours.

In Thailand, many individuals in the offshore workforce exhibit Blue as one of their dominant E-Colours. The Blue personality is empathetic, harmonious, and sensitive to others' feelings – qualities closely aligned with the Thai concept of *kreng jai*. This cultural value emphasises respect, politeness, and avoiding actions that might cause discomfort or embarrassment. Additionally, the cultural norm of not challenging elders, seniors, or expatriates complicated the assertiveness SWA required. The fear of causing someone to 'lose face' or disrupting workplace harmony initially made employees reluctant to exercise SWA.

Equilibria's approach focused on helping individuals recognise how their natural tendencies (as identified through their E-Colours) could both hinder and support a safety-first mindset. By encouraging a shift from reticence to speaking up, and framing SWA as an act of collective care rather than confrontation, employees began to appreciate the importance of pressing PAUSE on their cultural instincts and pressing PLAY on voicing concerns. Through ongoing dialogue, structured training, and steady encouragement, a genuine cultural shift emerged. Workers increasingly felt empowered to prioritise safety without feeling that they were violating cultural expectations. This deliberate and thoughtful effort resulted in the creation of a culture of both psychological and physical safety that transcended the initial resistance, ultimately enabling an environment where everyone felt responsible for and comfortable contributing to a safer workplace.

This experience underscores the power of E-Colours in bridging personality tendencies and cultural nuances to achieve transformational outcomes, even in situations where ingrained behaviours initially seem at odds with organisational goals.

The Impact of Socioeconomic Factors

Socioeconomic status (SES) is another critical factor that influences personality development and diversity. SES affects the resources available to children, the environments in which they are raised, and the opportunities they have for personal growth. Children from different socioeconomic backgrounds may experience varying levels of stress, access to education, and exposure to enriching experiences, all of which shape their personalities in distinct ways.

For instance, children from higher socioeconomic backgrounds often have access to a broader range of extracurricular activities – such as music, sports, or travel – which can foster the development of diverse interests and tendencies. They may also benefit from higher-quality education, encouraging tendencies like intellectual curiosity, ambition, and self-discipline. In contrast, children from lower socioeconomic backgrounds may face challenges such as financial instability, limited access to resources, or adverse environments, influencing the development of tendencies like resilience, resourcefulness, and empathy.

However, it is important to recognise that socioeconomic factors do not solely determine personality outcomes. Many children from disadvantaged backgrounds develop strong, diverse personalities despite the obstacles they encounter. In fact, overcoming adversity often leads to the development of unique strengths and perspectives that enrich personality diversity. The key is to acknowledge the impact of socioeconomic factors and create supportive environments that enable all children, regardless of background, to realise their full personality potential.

Conclusion of Social and Cultural Influences

The social and cultural influences on personality diversity are vast and multifaceted. From the processes of socialisation and the shaping power of cultural norms to the roles of media, technology, globalisation, and socioeconomic factors, these influences determine how children develop their personalities and contribute to the richness of tendencies within society. Understanding these forces is essential for creating environments that nurture and encourage personality diversity, allowing children to grow into individuals with unique strengths, perspectives, and identities.

As we continue through this chapter, we will explore the benefits of personality diversity in children and its contributions to society. We will also examine the challenges and considerations involved in fostering diverse personalities, along with strategies for supporting this diversity in educational and community settings. Through this exploration, we will see how social and cultural influences play a crucial role in shaping the future of personality diversity.

*   *   *

LEARNING STYLES AND THE E-COLOURS

Visual Learners

Visual learners benefit from a variety of ocular stimulations. One effective method is the use of colours. Visual learners can often recall what they have seen and prefer written instructions. These students are sight readers who enjoy silent reading. Even better, information presented in video format can greatly enhance their learning. They learn best by observing and enjoy working with tools such as computers, maps, graphs, charts, cartoons, and posters.

Auditory Learners

Students with this learning style recall what they have heard and prefer oral instructions. They learn by listening and speaking, often enjoying activities like talking and interviewing. These students are phonetic readers who enjoy oral reading, choral reading, and listening to recorded books. They thrive when engaging in activities such as interviewing, debating, or participating in panel discussions.

Kinaesthetic Learners

Some people need to engage in continuous movement while studying, such as tapping their fingers, playing with their hair, using a stress ball, or chewing gum. This is natural, but if they are studying with others, care should be taken not to distract them. Kinaesthetic learners also absorb information by touching or manipulating objects. They benefit from involving their whole body in the learning process and remember material best when they act it out. These students learn most effectively through games, hands-on activities, model making, and experiments.

We can now begin to examine learning styles from an E-Colours perspective.

Red (Doer) Learning Styles

Reds can be impulsive, tending to act first and consider the consequences afterwards. They are independent by nature and often prefer to work alone.

Reds tend to:

- Find shortcuts in ways of doing things
- Act quickly if work progress is delayed
- Direct others to act

Reds learn most when they:

- Are involved in new experiences, opportunities, and problem-solving
- Interact with others through business games, team tasks, or role-playing
- Are thrown in at the deep end with a challenging task
- Chair meetings and are allowed to lead discussions

Reds learn least when they are:

- Simply listening to lectures or long explanations
- Reading, writing, or thinking by themselves
- Absorbing and understanding data without action
- Required to precisely follow detailed instructions

A Red Story

As a Red/Green, we operate most comfortably in an environment of order and control, with clear rules that everyone follows. As a youngster, I thrived in such a structured setting and could not understand why some people tried to break the rules or bend them to suit their own needs. I've always seen such individuals as rebels, with a selfish streak, trying to disrupt the harmony of others.

It is only when you begin to introduce the E-Colours concept that you realise people have a different perspective on such environments – seeing them as claustrophobic rather than safe and comfortable. The PAUSE & PLAY techniques are a useful starting point for managing these differences. Different E-Colours thrive in different environments, and it is important to respect these differences – listen to understand, and then seek to be understood.

– *Red/Green*

Yellow (Socialiser) Learning Styles

Yellows are keen to try things out. They prefer concepts that can be applied directly to their work and tend to be impatient with lengthy, abstract discussions containing too much detail. They often enjoy working in environments where they are surrounded by people.

Yellows tend to:

- Have strong communication skills
- Be willing to delegate work
- Have creative problem-solving abilities
- Enjoy working in teams but can tend to hog the limelight

Yellows learn most when they:

- See an obvious link between the topic and their job
- Can try out techniques with feedback, such as role-playing
- Are shown techniques with clear advantages, such as saving time or money
- Are shown a model they can copy, such as a film or a respected leader

Yellows learn least when they:

- Cannot see an obvious or immediate benefit for them
- Do not get a chance to practise, or when there are no guidelines on how to do it
- Cannot see any apparent payback to the learning, such as shorter meetings
- Recognise that the event or learning is 'all theory' with no clear application

A Yellow Story

Being included: *When I wasn't included with friends or a group of adults, I felt bad, jealous, and nervous. I don't think my friends and family realised how important it was for me to be included, even if it was just to listen.*

Being too funny: *I often got into trouble by not thinking about what I was doing or saying. I can still remember one of the two times I was punished in school – in Year 3, when I was joking around in the lunch queue and was shocked when a teacher pulled me out of line and sent me to the head's office. The second was in secondary school, when I went to throw some food and the lunchroom monitor grabbed my hand before I could. I have many other examples from my early life. If I had found a way to channel this energy, I might have accomplished more in school.*

Thinking everything was my fault: *I used to think that everything that went wrong was somehow my fault – and, to this day, I still do. I was a very anxious little kid, and if I had had mentoring to help me see things differently, I wonder if the anxiety I feel today might have been less.*

– Yellow/Blue

Green (Thinker) Learning Styles

Greens like to adapt and integrate observations into complex and logically sound theories, thinking problems through with a precise, step-by-step methodology. They can be perfectionists who prefer to fit things into a rational framework, being objective and analytical rather than subjective or emotional in their thought processes.

Greens are often:
- Resistant to change in work methods
- Very detailed and follow step-by-step guidelines
- Look for history and records to guide future decisions

Greens learn most when they:
- Are placed in complex situations where they must apply skills and knowledge
- Are in structured environments with a clear purpose
- Are offered interesting ideas or concepts, even when not immediately relevant
- Can question and probe the ideas behind things

Greens learn least when they are:
- Forced to participate in situations that emphasise emotion and feelings
- Working on activities that are unstructured, or where the briefing is poorly executed
- Carrying out tasks without understanding the principles or concepts involved
- Feeling they are not on the same wavelength as other group members (people with very different learning styles)

A Green Story

I do not remember what the trigger was or when I actually realised that, in life, I sometimes must switch away from the natural preference I had during the days of my youth. Back then, I would very much enjoy my own time – thinking, planning, designing – whether it was for tasks I set myself or even games I would play, like making Lego spaceships or cars. But first, I would plan and design, actually finding great enjoyment in the design and planning phase itself.

– Green/Blue

Blue (Relator) Learning Styles

Blues prefer to stand back and observe a situation from varying perspectives. They like to gather a wide range of information and views, considering everything thoroughly before reaching any conclusions or making decisions. They enjoy observing others and will listen carefully to different opinions before joining in and offering their own. Blues also prefer working in teams rather than alone.

Blues are often:

- Information-driven
- Work well in a team
- Like to analyse situations from different perspectives in order not to upset anyone or hurt their feelings

Blues learn most when they:

- Are observing individuals or groups at work
- Can review what has happened and reflect on what they have learned
- Are producing reports, analyses, or performing tasks without tight deadlines

Blues learn least when they are:

- Acting as leaders or role-playing in front of others
- Performing tasks with (in their view) no time to prepare
- Thrown in at the deep end
- Being rushed or pressured by tight deadlines

A Blue Story

For me, as a Blue, I would have liked to have learned earlier to:

- *Press PLAY on making sure my thoughts and opinions are heard and included.*
- *Press PLAY on asking for a moment to think through my answer.*
- *Press PAUSE on needing to get my whole thought formed before offering it.'*

— *Blue/Yellow*

* * *

BENEFITS OF PERSONALITY DIVERSITY FOR CHILDREN

Personality diversity among children offers numerous advantages that extend far beyond individual development; it enriches communities, enhances learning environments, and prepares society for a dynamic and interconnected future. Diverse personalities bring unique perspectives, strengths, and approaches to problem-solving, leading to greater innovation, social cohesion, and resilience. In this section, we will explore the key benefits of personality diversity in children and how these benefits contribute to their growth and the wellbeing of society.

Enhanced Creativity and Innovation

One of the most significant benefits of personality diversity in children and young people is the promotion of creativity and innovation. Children with different personality tendencies approach problems and challenges from unique angles, resulting in a wider range of solutions and ideas. For instance, a steadier-paced child may spend more time reflecting and developing well-thought-out ideas, while a faster-paced child might bring energy and enthusiasm to creative sessions. Together, their collaboration can produce innovative outcomes that neither might have achieved alone.

When children are encouraged to express their individuality, they feel more confident in sharing their thoughts and ideas, creating an environment where creativity thrives. Exposure to diverse personalities also broadens children's cognitive flexibility by introducing them to different ways of thinking and interacting with the world. This flexibility is crucial for innovation, allowing children to combine ideas from various domains and come up with novel concepts. In a rapidly changing world, the ability to think creatively and innovate is an invaluable skill – and personality diversity is a key driver of this capability.

Improved Social Skills and Empathy

Personality diversity enhances children's social skills and empathy by exposing them to a wide range of interpersonal dynamics. When children interact with peers who have different personality tendencies, they learn to navigate diverse social situations, communicate effectively, and appreciate various perspectives. This experience is particularly important in developing empathy – the ability to recognise and share the feelings of others.

For example, a naturally assertive child may learn to be more patient and understanding when engaging with a more reserved peer, while a quieter child may develop greater confidence through supportive interactions with more outgoing friends. These experiences help children build strong social bonds and develop the ability to work effectively in diverse teams – a skill that is increasingly important in both personal and professional contexts.

Moreover, exposure to personality diversity helps children develop greater acceptance and appreciation of differences. They learn that there is no 'right' or 'wrong' way to be or behave; rather, individuals are living either in their strengths or their potential limiters. This understanding fosters a sense of inclusivity and respect for both themselves and others. As they grow, these children are more likely to become adults who value diversity and contribute to more harmonious and cooperative communities.

A Yellow/Blue Story

I immediately think of tendencies that are completely explained by my predominant E-Colours. I was more Yellow/Blue as a child. But even then, I can remember being reluctant to speak up to grown-ups I didn't know well. My daddy was always telling me to speak up, say hello, and shake hands. I'm guessing that was simply a child behaviour – a lack of confidence.

I was always getting in trouble at school for talking too much and being the class clown – very Yellow behaviour. I would also speak up too often when the teacher asked questions, to the point where they would have to ask me not to respond so much. I still have this tendency today.

I was also very sensitive – soft-hearted – and got my feelings hurt very easily. Being taller and bigger than everyone else, I got picked on a lot, and my Blue didn't respond well to that, much like when that woman accused me of being a spy in our workshop – it was the same kind of feeling. I can remember a time when a teacher misunderstood something I said and wouldn't listen to my side of the story, and I just shut down, feeling hurt. The thought that someone was mad at me or didn't like me always bothered me a lot.

— Yellow/Blue

Resilience and Adaptability

Another critical benefit of personality diversity in children is the development of resilience and adaptability. Children who are exposed to a variety of personalities and ways of thinking are better equipped to handle challenges and changes in their environment. They learn that there are multiple approaches to solving problems and that setbacks can be overcome by trying different strategies.

For instance, a child who is naturally cautious may learn to take more risks by observing and interacting with peers who are more adventurous, while a more impulsive child may develop better planning and decision-making skills by working alongside peers who are more methodical. This exchange of tendencies and strategies helps children develop a well-rounded approach to life's challenges, making them more resilient when facing adversity.

Adaptability is another essential tendency fostered through personality diversity. Children who interact with a range of personalities learn to adjust their behaviours and communication styles to different situations. This skill is especially important in a globalised world where cultural competence and the ability to work with people from various backgrounds are crucial. By developing adaptability early, children are better prepared to navigate the complexities of the modern world.

Contribution to Academic Success

Personality diversity can also contribute to academic success by creating a rich and dynamic learning environment. When children with different personalities work together, they bring a range of strengths and approaches to the learning process. For example, a detail-oriented child might excel in tasks requiring precision and focus, while a more imaginative child might contribute creative ideas to projects and discussions. This diversity of skills and perspectives enhances collaborative learning and leads to better educational outcomes for all students.

Additionally, personality diversity encourages a broader range of learning styles and problem-solving approaches. Some children may prefer hands-on activities, while others might thrive with structured, analytical tasks. By incorporating diverse approaches into the classroom, educators can create a more inclusive environment that meets the needs of every student.

This not only improves academic performance but also fosters a love of learning and a stronger sense of self-efficacy.

Personality diversity in the classroom also leads to more engaging and meaningful discussions, as students share their unique perspectives. This exchange of ideas promotes critical thinking and helps students develop a deeper understanding of complex concepts. As a result, children are more likely to retain information and apply their knowledge in real-world situations.

Connor's Story

As a result of using the E-Colours in my A-level classrooms, we were able to achieve the highest ALPS score and P8 score for 110 EPQ students across a whole sixth form cohort – hugely accredited to understanding the strengths and potential limiters of students in order to produce high-quality writing, presentations, and project work.

Not only was it valuable to see the E-Colours of students, but knowing my own through using the Premium Report allowed me to hone my teaching abilities to best serve the students.

– *Connor Whiteside* (Red/Yellow)
– RE Teacher, UK

Leadership and Teamwork

Personality diversity is essential for developing leadership and teamwork skills in children. Different personality tendencies lend themselves to various leadership styles and team roles, each of which is valuable in different contexts. For example, a child who is naturally charismatic may excel at motivating and inspiring others, while a more analytical child might take on the role of planner or strategist within a team. By working together, children with diverse personalities can form well-rounded teams that harness the strengths of every member.

Exposure to diverse personalities also teaches children the importance of collaboration and the value of different contributions. They learn that effective teamwork requires a balance of skills and that every team member's input matters. This understanding helps children develop leadership qualities that are inclusive and empathetic, rather than authoritarian or domineering.

Children who grow up exposed to personality diversity are more likely to become leaders who recognise and leverage the strengths of others. They understand that embracing diversity leads to better decision-making and stronger problem-solving, and they are more likely to create inclusive environments where everyone feels valued and empowered to contribute.

One inspiring example comes from a high school football (soccer) team we worked with in Texas. Every player had a clear understanding of their E-Colours, recognising both their strengths and potential limiters. Before the season began, they committed to upholding the principles of the E-Colours, wearing wristbands as reminders and consciously pressing PAUSE or PLAY when necessary.

As the season unfolded, the team became renowned for their exceptional sportsmanship and respectfulness, earning a reputation as the most courteous team in the league. Instead of reacting emotionally when tackled or provoked by opponents, they consistently pressed their PAUSE buttons, maintaining composure and refusing to retaliate. For some players, this self-restraint was incredibly challenging, but they embraced the process and showed remarkable discipline.

As young leaders, the team members embodied the principles they had committed to, setting an outstanding example of using the E-Colours to promote growth and teamwork. Amusingly, their coach – whose E-Colours are predominantly Red/Yellow, known for being passionate and action-oriented – struggled at times to keep his temper when players were fouled. On more than one occasion, after the coach vented frustration at a referee or opponent, the players would cheekily remind him to 'press PAUSE and calm down'.

Their consistent efforts paid off, as for three consecutive years, the team was recognised as the most well-behaved in the league. Their ability to translate leadership tools into action made them not only successful athletes but also outstanding role models.

Long-Term Societal Benefits

The benefits of personality diversity in children extend far beyond individual growth and social interaction; they have long-term implications for society. As children with diverse personalities become adults, they enrich their communities with a broader range of ideas, experiences, and skills. A society that values and nurtures personality diversity is better equipped to innovate, solve complex problems, and adapt to constant change.

For example, in the workplace, teams made up of individuals who live in their strengths and manage their potential limiters are often more creative, productive, and resilient.

In civic life, citizens with a range of personality tendencies are more likely to engage in diverse forms of community involvement, from activism to political leadership. This diversity strengthens democratic processes and fosters social justice and equality.

Personality diversity also helps build social cohesion by encouraging empathy, understanding, and cooperation across different backgrounds. A society that embraces differences as strengths rather than divisions is more inclusive and adaptable. This open-mindedness leads to communities where everyone has the opportunity to thrive.

The Benefits of Personality Diversity for Young People

The benefits of personality diversity in children are extensive, shaping their development, academic achievement, social skills, and long-term contributions to society. By fostering creativity, building resilience, enhancing social skills, and promoting academic success, personality diversity equips young people to navigate an increasingly complex and interconnected world.

The long-term societal advantages – including innovation, cohesion, and inclusive leadership – highlight the importance of nurturing diverse personalities from an early age.

In the next section, we will explore the challenges and considerations in supporting personality diversity in children, along with strategies for nurturing this diversity in different environments. By understanding both the benefits and the challenges, we can create settings that allow every child to reach their full potential and contribute to a vibrant and diverse future.

A Red/Yellow Story

> *Two behaviours that stand out to me from my earliest recollections are my tendencies to 'take action' and my talkative nature.*
>
> *I have always been the one in my peer group to make things happen, rather than getting caught up in an endless list of options. Friends would often ask me to be the one to take the first step on a project or to approach our teachers with an idea.*
>
> *I also remember sitting with my parents and teachers at parent-teacher conferences in grade school and hearing comments that I was bright, but that I 'liked to talk'.*
>
> *As a Red/Yellow, I now recognise that these behaviours align with my natural tendencies. However, I have also learned to press PAUSE on some of these behaviours when needed. For example, I am aware that I tend to dominate conversations, and I consciously limit myself to give others space to share their ideas. I also try to allow people more time to discuss and evaluate ideas before pushing for action to be taken.*
>
> *— Red/Yellow*

A Red/Green Story

> *When I was little, I didn't smile much, and I never really noticed it until I looked back at my childhood pictures. My parents also described me as a 'serious' kid, very laser-focused on my tasks and projects, and I was a perfectionist, especially when it came to colouring inside the lines!*

That obsession with perfection carried over into my secondary school years and continues into my life today. Remember that 'control' issue of wanting to control conversations to control outcomes? I think that stems from being a perfectionist as a child and carrying it into my work life.

Now, I am learning to balance that perfectionism with the idea of 'good enough', and becoming a supervisor has really helped with that.

– Red/Green

E-Colours & Personal Intervention

Personal Intervention is a tool that offers a deeper look into an individual's character. Knowing that our character is shaped by our morals, ethics, and beliefs, we can better understand the decisions we make. As discussed earlier, Personal Intervention introduces the PAUSE and PLAY buttons, which offer awareness into how we choose to respond to various situations.

People identified with Red or Yellow E-Colours often need to use their PAUSE button more frequently, as it is more natural for them to speak openly and act quickly. Meanwhile, those with Green or Blue E-Colours may need to consciously press PLAY to speak up and vocalise their thoughts and feelings.

Figure 14 – PAUSE & PLAY BUTTONS
Copyright © 2025 Equilibria Services Pte Ltd. All rights reserved.

We have found that Personal Intervention significantly aids with social and emotional challenges experienced by students in school settings and through social (and social media) interactions. Consequently, Personal Intervention has helped students become mentors, teachers become coaches, and directors become intentional leaders. Anyone can learn to use the PAUSE and PLAY buttons to improve their communication style. Once introduced to the concept, individuals become more open and transparent about the matters at hand. Empowering individuals within the education system gives them the means to address important challenges, such as bullying and truancy, reconsider how they express themselves, learn from mistakes, and continue supporting one another.

Everyone benefits from having tools and resources to maintain positive social and emotional wellbeing. To promote a more positive outlook on life, Equilibria launched an Anti-Bullying Campaign, sharing compelling stories of current secondary students who described their personal journeys of overcoming bullying.

Our research has shown that this dilemma is global. Nationally, experts have confirmed that 'educating the whole child by including social and emotional skills with academics is critical for success in school and in life'.

Even more powerful, Personal Intervention is suitable for children aged nine and above. This leads to the understanding that the skill set gained, and the process undertaken, can have a lasting, positive impact on many lives.

Through Personal Intervention, individuals can achieve more desirable outcomes by recognising when they sense a trigger and are ready to REACT.

As human beings, we often REACT instinctively to issues, events, or triggers based on our personality.

Typically, these REACTIONS are immediate and do not always produce positive outcomes.

Learning to self-monitor and change our habits in order to RESPOND instead can result in much better outcomes.

Understanding our own personalities and those of the people we interact with, allows us to improve how we RESPOND to both people and tasks.

By practising Personal Intervention, we take a significant step towards realising our potential, at work, at school, and in our social lives.

Hands Up! (from a Blue/Green Perspective) – Lewis Senior

One of the greatest privileges of being part of Equilibria is the opportunity to share our E-Colours technology and its applications in schools. Observing the transformation in young students as they gain a deeper understanding of E-Colours & Personal Intervention is truly remarkable.

Multiple examples come from schools where I have worked with children around the age of seven, many of whom had predominantly Blue/Green E-Colours. A common tendency among them was their reluctance to raise their hands in class. When asked individually why they hesitated, their answers often centred around fears of standing out, concerns about how their teachers or classmates might react, or worries about appearing 'stupid'.

After introducing them to their Blue/Green wristbands and explaining the concept of Personal Intervention, it was heartwarming to see the change. Many students would literally touch their PLAY buttons on their wristbands and muster the confidence to raise their hands. Witnessing this shift in behaviour highlights the profound impact of equipping students with tools to better understand themselves and their interactions with others.

This behaviour has been observed across multiple countries, regardless of gender, culture, or religious beliefs. Yet the Blue/Green perspective remains remarkably consistent. It is incredible to consider that if a seven- or eight-year-old child can develop the confidence to go from never raising their hand to pressing PLAY and speaking up, the potential impact as they grow is immense.

Imagine that same individual entering the workforce, encouraged to 'see something, say something'. Without the empowerment and self-awareness they developed as children, they might have remained silent. However, with the skills cultivated early on, they are far more likely to speak up, contributing to safer, more collaborative, and more effective environments.

Hands Up! (from a Yellow/Green Perspective) – Lewis Senior

Another powerful example of a young student grasping the concept of Personal Intervention came from a 12-year-old whose E-Colours were predominantly Yellow/Green. He attended a workshop designed for parents and teachers and was, by far, the youngest participant.

During the session, as Personal Intervention and the wristband were introduced, it was clear that something clicked for him. At the end of the day, he asked if he could share his thoughts with the group the next morning.

On the second day, as the workshop began, he shared a revelation he believed would change his life. He explained that he often got into trouble at school – not for misbehaviour, but because, as a highly intelligent and quick-thinking individual, he would shout out answers before anyone else had the chance to respond. He realised that this was a natural Yellow/Green tendency, and before learning about Personal Intervention, it had simply been an unconscious reaction.

The boy explained that moving forward, he would press PAUSE on blurting out answers and press PLAY on raising his hand and waiting for his turn to speak. For years after the workshop, I would visit his school, and the principal always proudly shared his progress. His report cards reflected how much his teachers appreciated his improved classroom behaviour and his respect for allowing others the chance to contribute.

Today, that same individual holds a highly respected position in the police force, exemplifying how early self-awareness and intentional action can lead to lifelong success.

* * *

CHALLENGES AND CONSIDERATIONS

While the benefits of personality diversity in children are extensive, fostering and managing this diversity also comes with challenges and important considerations. These challenges arise from balancing individual differences, ensuring equitable opportunities for development, and creating environments that are inclusive and supportive of all personality styles. In this section, we will explore the various challenges associated with promoting personality diversity in children, along with key considerations for parents, educators, and society.

Balancing Individuality with Social Harmony

One of the primary challenges in fostering personality diversity is balancing the encouragement of individuality with the need for social harmony. While it is crucial to support children in developing their unique personalities, it is equally important to teach them how to function within a group and adhere to social norms. This balance can be difficult to achieve, particularly in environments where conformity is highly valued, such as schools or certain cultural contexts.

For example, a child with a highly independent or unconventional personality may struggle in a structured classroom environment that rewards compliance and uniformity. Conversely, children who naturally conform to social expectations may feel pressured to suppress their individuality in order to fit in. Educators and parents must navigate these dynamics carefully, ensuring that each child's personality is respected and nurtured while also promoting cooperative behaviours and social responsibility.

One effective approach is to create flexible environments that allow for a range of behaviours and expressions while maintaining clear expectations for respectful and cooperative interactions. This might involve offering different types of activities that cater to various personality tendencies, such as group projects for those who thrive in collaboration; and independent tasks for those who prefer solitude. By providing options, children can develop their personalities without feeling constrained or forced to conform.

Addressing Bias and Stereotypes

Another significant challenge in promoting personality diversity is addressing the bias and stereotypes that can limit children's development and self-expression. Societal expectations and cultural stereotypes often influence how certain personality tendencies are perceived and valued, reinforcing some behaviours over others. For example, assertiveness and leadership are often encouraged in boys, while girls may be praised more for empathy and cooperation. These biases can restrict children's opportunities to explore and develop a full range of tendencies.

Moreover, stereotypes based on race, ethnicity, socioeconomic status, or disability can further complicate the development of diverse personalities. Children from marginalised groups may face additional pressures to conform to stereotypes or may encounter barriers to expressing their true selves. For instance, a child from a low-income background might be discouraged from pursuing creative interests due to a lack of resources or societal expectations that prioritise practicality over creativity.

Addressing these biases requires a concerted effort from parents, educators, and society to challenge stereotypes and create environments where all tendencies are valued equally. This involves promoting gender-neutral and culturally inclusive practices, providing opportunities for all children to explore a wide range of interests, and actively combating discriminatory attitudes and behaviours.

Ensuring Equity in Development Opportunities

Equity in development opportunities is crucial when utilising personality diversity. Not all children have equal access to the resources, experiences, and support systems that allow them to fully develop their personalities. Factors such as socioeconomic status, geographic location, and family dynamics can create disparities in the opportunities available to children.

For example, children from affluent families may have access to a wide range of extracurricular activities, travel experiences, and educational resources that allow them to explore different facets of their personalities. In contrast, children from lower-income families may have limited opportunities, restricting their ability to discover and nurture their unique tendencies.

To ensure equity, it is important to provide all children with access to a variety of experiences and resources that support personality development. This might include offering free or low-cost extracurricular programmes, ensuring that schools provide diverse and inclusive learning environments, and supporting community initiatives that expose children to different cultures, ideas, and activities. Policies and programmes addressing broader social determinants of wellbeing – such as poverty, housing, education, and life skills – are also essential for creating a level playing field where all children can thrive.

Navigating Parental and Educational Expectations

Parental and educational expectations can significantly influence the development of personality diversity in children. While some parents and educators embrace and support a wide range of tendencies, others may hold specific beliefs about how children should behave and develop. These expectations, shaped by cultural values, personal beliefs, and societal norms, can either support or hinder the expression of diverse personalities.

For example, parents who highly value academic achievement and discipline may encourage diligence and obedience while discouraging creativity or spontaneity. Similarly, educators who focus heavily on standardised testing may inadvertently stifle personality diversity by prioritising conformity over individual expression.

Navigating these expectations requires a sensitive and balanced approach. Parents and educators can be encouraged to recognise the value of diverse personality tendencies and to support children in exploring and expressing their individuality. This might involve creating more flexible educational environments where children are given the freedom to pursue their interests and develop their strengths, even when these do not align with traditional expectations.

Open communication between parents, educators, and children is also essential. In an environment where personality diversity is embraced, children feel empowered to express their needs and preferences, and adults are willing to listen and adapt their expectations accordingly. By promoting a culture of mutual respect and understanding, we can create supportive spaces where personality diversity can flourish.

Managing Conflicts and Misunderstandings

A lack of understanding around personality diversity can sometimes lead to conflicts and misunderstandings, particularly in group settings where different tendencies may clash. For instance, a highly assertive child may come into conflict with a more reserved peer, or a child who prefers structured routines may struggle to collaborate with a more spontaneous classmate. These situations can create challenges in maintaining a harmonious and inclusive environment.

However, conflicts arising from personality differences also present valuable opportunities for learning and growth. By navigating these challenges, children can develop important social and emotional skills such as conflict resolution, empathy, and compromise. The key is to provide guidance and support to help them manage conflicts in ways that respect individual differences.

Educators and parents can play a critical role in this process by teaching children strategies for effective communication, active listening, and collaborative problem-solving. They can also model positive behaviours, such as respecting differences and seeking common ground, helping children learn how to manage disagreements constructively.

Disagreements at any age do not have to escalate into conflict. When managed well, they can become opportunities for personal growth, stronger relationships, and better ideas. By incorporating the E-Colours framework into strategies for navigating difficult conversations, you can tailor your approach to the personality tendencies of those involved, promoting greater understanding and harmony.

Using Strategies for Navigating Difficult Conversations

1. **Approach the exchange with a willingness to learn, not persuade.**

   - **Red (Action-Oriented):** PAUSE your instinct to take charge or push for immediate solutions. Instead, ask open-ended questions to understand the other person's perspective fully.

   - **Yellow (Optimistic):** Use your natural positivity to create a collaborative atmosphere, but avoid downplaying the seriousness of the issue.

   - **Green (Analytical):** Focus on gathering all the facts before drawing conclusions. Stay open to emotional cues, even when they do not align with your usual data-driven approach.

   - **Blue (Empathetic):** Lean into your natural ability to listen and validate others' feelings, but remember to assert your own perspective where necessary.

2. **Be humble and open-minded.**
   - **Red/Yellow:** Your confidence can be an asset, but humility allows space for others to contribute without feeling overshadowed.
   - **Green/Blue:** Balance your natural humility with a willingness to share your ideas clearly and confidently.
3. **Be explicit about your intentions.**
   - State your purpose up front to set a tone of openness.
     - **Example:** 'This is an important topic. I'm curious to hear what people who disagree with me think about this issue.'
   - When closing, affirm inclusivity.
     - **Example:** 'I recognise that not everyone sees this in the same way, and I'd like to understand better where other people are coming from.'
   - Tailor communication to E-Colours.
     - **For Red/Yellow:** Use energetic but non-confrontational language to encourage dialogue.
     - **For Green/Blue:** Lean on clear, structured phrasing to create a safe and inviting conversational space.

Making Requests That Ensure Follow-Through

Making requests of others, especially when it involves tasks outside their usual scope, requires clear and considerate communication. The E-Colours framework helps tailor your approach to the recipient's tendencies.

1. **What do you want, and what would success look like?**
   - **Red:** Clearly define the task with measurable outcomes – they thrive on knowing what 'success' looks like.
   - **Yellow:** Make the task engaging and emphasise how it contributes to the bigger picture.
   - **Green:** Provide detailed instructions and ensure the task aligns with logical objectives.
   - **Blue:** Emphasise the emotional or relational impact of completing the task well.

2. **Who do you want it from?**
   - **Reds and Yellows:** Be specific. Clear delegation taps into their desire to act and shine.
   - **Greens and Blues:** Individual accountability helps avoid misunderstandings or feelings of being overlooked.

3. **When do you need it done by?**
   - **Reds** appreciate urgency but may need reminders to stay focused on timelines.
   - **Greens** prefer reasonable deadlines with no surprises.
   - **Blues** value flexibility and respect for their time management.
   - **Yellows** may need enthusiasm to counter any tendencies to procrastinate.

4. **Why is it important?**
   - **Reds** resonate with a direct explanation of the task's purpose.
   - **Yellows** appreciate how the task supports team or organisational goals.

- **Greens** respond to logical reasoning about why the task matters.
- **Blues** connect with how the task contributes to relationships or team harmony.

By integrating E-Colours perspectives into conflict management and making requests, you will not only navigate misunderstandings more effectively but also create an environment that values individuality while enhancing collaboration and accountability.

Adapting to Technological and Social Changes

The rapid pace of technological and social change presents both opportunities and challenges for encouraging personality diversity in children. On one hand, technology offers children unprecedented access to information, diverse perspectives, and global connections, which can support the development of a wide range of tendencies. On the other hand, the digital age also brings challenges, such as pressure to conform to online trends, the potential for cyberbullying, and the impact of screen time on social and emotional development.

Adapting to these changes requires a proactive approach to managing the influence of technology on personality growth. Parents and educators need to be aware of both the risks and benefits of digital media, guiding children to use technology in ways that support their individuality and wellbeing. This could involve setting boundaries on screen time, encouraging critical thinking about media content, and promoting healthy online behaviours that value diversity and inclusion.

Additionally, as society evolves, there is a need to continually reassess and update the strategies used to understand and appreciate personality diversity. Social changes – such as shifts in cultural norms, economic conditions, and educational practices – can all impact how personality tendencies are valued and developed. Staying informed and adaptable is crucial for ensuring that all children can flourish in supportive and inclusive environments.

Conclusion of Challenges and Considerations

Promoting personality diversity in children is a complex and multifaceted process that requires navigating a range of challenges and considerations. From balancing individuality with social harmony to addressing bias, ensuring equity, managing conflicts, and adapting to technological and social changes, many factors influence the development of diverse personalities. By remaining mindful of these challenges and taking a thoughtful, inclusive approach, parents, educators, and society can create environments that support and nurture the full spectrum of personality diversity.

In the next section, we will explore strategies for nurturing personality diversity in different settings, including the home, school, and community. By implementing these strategies, we can help children develop their unique strengths and contribute to a more diverse, inclusive, and vibrant future.

* * *

NURTURING PERSONALITY DIVERSITY

Nurturing personality diversity in children is a deliberate and ongoing process that involves parents, educators, and the broader community. By creating environments that respect and celebrate individual differences, we help children develop their unique tendencies, leading to more enriched and dynamic societies. In this section, we will explore strategies for nurturing personality diversity across the home, school, and community, while highlighting the importance of a holistic approach.

The E-Colours system presents an opportunity to nurture personality diversity. It's a simple and accessible framework that encourages involvement from everyone. For example, we have received numerous stories from people around the world who have begun to better understand themselves and their families simply by completing the questionnaire, obtaining a Premium Report, and discussing the findings together.

Creating a Supportive Home Environment

The home is the first and most influential environment where personality diversity can be nurtured. Parents and caregivers play a critical role in shaping a child's sense of self and providing the foundation for their personality to flourish. Here are some key strategies for fostering personality diversity at home.

Encourage Self-Expression: Allow children to express themselves freely, be it through art, play, conversation, or other creative outlets. Providing a variety of materials and opportunities for self-expression helps them explore their interests and develop their unique personalities.

Celebrate Individuality: Recognise and celebrate each child's unique tendencies and strengths. Avoid comparing siblings or other children, as this can create feelings of inadequacy or pressure to conform. Focus on each child's strengths, potential limiters, achievements, and qualities.

Provide Choices: Giving children the freedom to make choices fosters independence and self-awareness. Whether choosing their clothes, selecting extracurricular activities, or deciding on hobbies, allowing decision-making empowers children to explore their interests and preferences.

Model Respect for Differences: Children learn by observing adults. Demonstrating respect for different personalities, opinions, and lifestyles teaches them to value diversity. Parents can model inclusive behaviours by being open-minded and showing empathy towards others.

Encourage Open Communication: Create an environment where children feel comfortable sharing their thoughts, feelings, and concerns. Listen actively and validate their experiences, even when they differ from your own. Open communication builds trust and allows children to explore their identities without fear of judgment.

Support Exploration: Encourage children to try new activities and explore different interests. This helps them discover hidden talents and develop a well-rounded personality. Whether joining a sports team, learning a musical instrument, or participating in community service, exposure to diverse experiences can be transformative.

A Red/Yellow Story

> As a Red/Yellow child, I found that I became frustrated very easily and was often caught up in the drive to win. Frustration would trigger a visible emotional outburst, with everyone around me fully aware of my feelings. I would quickly let people know when I didn't want their help or coaching – stand clear, the animal had been released! My celebrations were just as fast and often kept me searching for the next win or 'impossible' opportunity. Celebrations were a major source of motivation for me. I enjoyed receiving the trophy but did not enjoy the group photo – strange, right? I still carry many of those tendencies today.
>
> *– Red/Yellow*

Embedding Personality Diversity in Schools Using E-Colours

Schools are critical environments for nurturing personality diversity using the E-Colours, as they bring together children from a wide range of backgrounds with different tendencies and perspectives. Educators have the unique opportunity to create inclusive and supportive learning environments that truly celebrate diversity. Here are some ideas for embedding personality diversity into schools.

Visibility of E-Colours: Ensuring that E-Colours information is visible and inclusive is a key focus. Highlighting both the predictable and unique nature of every individual helps cast a positive light on personality diversity.

Inclusive Curriculum: Incorporate a range of diverse perspectives, cultures, and voices into the curriculum. This not only enriches the learning experience but also validates the identities of all students. Literature, history, and social studies lessons should reflect a wide variety of experiences and viewpoints.

Differentiated Instruction: Recognise that children have different learning styles, strengths, and needs. Differentiated instruction means tailoring teaching methods to accommodate these differences, allowing each child to engage with the material in a way that resonates with them.

Promote Collaborative Learning: Encourage group work and collaborative projects that bring together students with varying tendencies. This helps children learn to appreciate and leverage one another's strengths, fostering teamwork and mutual respect.

Create Safe Spaces: Establish a classroom environment where all students feel safe to express themselves without fear of ridicule or exclusion. Strong anti-bullying policies, clear behavioural expectations, and an emphasis on empathy and kindness are essential components of a supportive learning space.

Encourage Extracurricular Participation: Offer a wide variety of extracurricular activities that cater to different interests and personality styles. Whether through sports, the arts, clubs, or academic competitions, providing diverse options enables students to explore their passions and develop their identities.

Professional Development for Educators: Provide training for educators on cultural competency, inclusive teaching practices, and the importance of nurturing personality diversity. Conversational competency around personality diversity – and the way information is presented, including the critical Equilibria Ethics – makes a major difference in the understanding, awareness, and ethical use of a modern personality-based tool. Educators who are well-equipped can better recognise and support the unique needs of each student, fostering a more inclusive school environment.

Robert's Story

> *Within our busy school environment, E-Colours has been an excellent learning experience for the entire teaching team. The beauty of E-Colours is that it is insightful, yet simple and easy to use. Tutors found it to be a highly relevant and useful tool when working with one another, and more importantly, it has given invaluable awareness into how they as individuals can be more successful communicators in the classroom, providing a more effective and tailored learning experience for students.*
>
> *– Robert Hunter* (Blue/Green)
> – Head of School, ISCA, UK

Engaging the Community with E-Colours

The broader community also plays a crucial role in nurturing personality diversity and the use of the E-Colours. Community organisations, cultural institutions, and local governments can create opportunities for children to interact with diverse groups and develop their personalities in a supportive environment, using the E-Colours as the fast-track method for doing so.

The sun rose brightly over Maplewood Park as the annual Community Unity Festival kicked off. The event brought together people from all walks of life to celebrate diversity, build connections, and solve common challenges. This year, the organising committee decided to use the E-Colours to better coordinate the event and maximise its success.

The organising team consisted of four key members:

- **Lila (Yellow/Green):** Outgoing and people-oriented, Lila loved brainstorming ideas that would bring smiles to everyone's faces.
- **David (Red/Blue):** A no-nonsense achiever, David thrived on structure, deadlines, and execution.
- **Sanjay (Blue/Red):** A thoughtful mediator, Sanjay prioritised harmony and inclusiveness in every plan.
- **Jennifer (Green/Yellow):** Detail-oriented and analytical, Jennifer was committed to making sure every aspect of the festival ran smoothly.

At their first meeting, each member shared their E-Colours and discussed how their strengths and potential limiters could influence their collaboration. This honest conversation set the tone for a cooperative and respectful planning process.

As the team planned the festival, their E-Colours guided their roles and interactions:

- **Lila's Creativity:** Lila's Yellow side shone as she envisioned engaging activities for the festival – a talent show, a cultural food market, and interactive workshops. Sanjay supported her by ensuring the ideas aligned with the festival's inclusive mission.

- **David's Drive:** David used his Red energy to establish clear timelines and assign responsibilities. He made sure everyone stayed focused and avoided last-minute chaos. Aware that his directness could be overwhelming, he checked in with Sanjay to ensure his feedback remained constructive.
- **Sanjay's Mediation:** Sanjay's Blue E-Colour helped smooth over tensions during heated discussions. When Lila and Jennifer clashed over the feasibility of an ambitious art installation, Sanjay facilitated a compromise that satisfied them both.
- **Jennifer's Precision:** Jennifer leveraged her Green strength to create a detailed event schedule and risk management plan. Her thoroughness ensured that every vendor, performer, and volunteer knew their role and timing.

On the day of the festival, the E-Colours continued to guide the team's interactions:

- **Problem-Solving:** When a food vendor's stall was delayed due to traffic, Jennifer's Green tendencies took charge, quickly reassigning spots to minimise disruption. Lila's Yellow energy reassured the vendor, helping to keep the atmosphere positive.
- **Team Synergy:** David's Red energy kept volunteers motivated as they managed large crowds, while Sanjay's Blue side ensured everyone felt appreciated through small gestures of thanks.

- **Engaging the Community:** Lila's enthusiasm created a warm and inviting atmosphere at the talent show. Her Yellow personality shone as she cheered for performers and connected with attendees.

By the end of the day, the Community Unity Festival was hailed as a resounding success. Feedback from attendees praised the event's inclusivity, organisation, and joyful spirit. The organising team reflected on how understanding their E-Colours had been instrumental:

- **Clearer Communication:** They avoided misunderstandings by adapting their communication styles to suit each other's preferences.
- **Balanced Strengths:** Each member played to their strengths while helping to offset each other's potential limiters.
- **Deeper Empathy:** Knowing each other's E-Colours fostered trust and empathy, turning challenges into opportunities for growth.

Further Ideas for Community Engagement

Cultural and Recreational Programs: Offer community programs that celebrate cultural diversity and provide opportunities for children to engage with different traditions, languages, and art forms. Festivals, workshops, and cultural exchange events can broaden children's horizons and foster a sense of global citizenship. The E-Colours provide an excellent global platform for promoting such interactions and bringing different groups together.

Mentorship and Role Models: Connect children with mentors and role models from diverse backgrounds who can inspire them to pursue their interests and embrace their unique personalities. Mentorship programmes can offer valuable guidance, encouragement, and support – especially for children who may lack positive role models in their immediate environment. Children have shown us how quickly they can mentor others in the community when using E-Colours as the foundation for communication.

Community Service Opportunities: Encourage children to participate in community service activities that help them develop empathy, social responsibility, and leadership skills. Volunteering exposes children to a variety of perspectives and highlights the personal benefits of contributing to the wellbeing of others.

Inclusive Public Spaces: Ensure that public spaces such as parks, libraries, and community centres are accessible and welcoming to all children, regardless of background or ability. These spaces should offer a variety of activities and resources that cater to diverse interests and needs.

Parental and Community Involvement: Create strong partnerships between schools, families, and community organisations to create a cohesive support network for children. Encouraging community involvement in education – through volunteering, attending school events, or serving on advisory boards – helps foster a more inclusive and supportive environment for all students.

Using Media and Technology

In the digital age, media and technology have a profound impact on children's personality development. While these tools offer tremendous opportunities for exploration and self-expression, they also bring challenges related to conformity and social pressure. Here are some ideas for using media and technology to nurture personality diversity.

Promote Positive Media Content: Encourage children to engage with media that celebrates diversity and showcases positive representations of different personalities, cultures, and experiences. Parents and educators can curate such content and discuss the messages conveyed with children. Encouraging everyone to try a 'negativity fast' for 30 days can have a profound impact. Switch off the revolving 24-hour news coverage at least until you can observe it objectionably rather than be emotionally affected by it.

Teach Critical Media Literacy: Help children develop the skills to critically analyse media content. This includes understanding how media shapes perceptions of identity, challenging stereotypes, and recognising the difference between online personas and real-life identities.

Encourage Creative Use of Technology: Provide opportunities for children to use technology creatively, such as through digital storytelling, coding, or online collaborations with peers. These activities promote self-expression, skill development, and exploration of interests.

Monitor and Guide Online Behaviour: Establish clear guidelines for healthy and respectful online behaviour. Teach children about digital citizenship, including how to engage positively with others, respect diverse viewpoints, and protect their privacy online.

Balance Screen Time with Offline Activities: Encourage a healthy balance between digital engagement and offline activities. While technology is a valuable tool for learning and creativity, it is equally important for children to participate in physical, social, and creative activities that support overall wellbeing.

Using Holistic Approaches to Nurturing E-Colours

Nurturing E-Colours requires a holistic approach that supports the whole child – their emotional, social, cognitive, and physical development. Addressing all aspects of a child's wellbeing helps create environments where diverse personalities can truly thrive.

Here are the key elements of a holistic approach.

Emotional Support: Provide emotional support to help children manage challenges associated with developing a unique personality. Teach emotional regulation, resilience, and coping strategies, and always offer a listening ear and validation of feelings.

Physical Wellbeing: Ensure children have access to physical activities and a healthy lifestyle that supports mental, emotional, and physical health. Physical wellbeing is closely linked to mental and emotional health, and a well-rounded approach to development includes attention to physical needs.

Social Connections: Foster strong connections with peers, family, and community members. Positive relationships provide a crucial foundation for exploring and expressing individuality.

Cognitive Development: Encourage curiosity, critical thinking, and problem-solving by providing stimulating learning opportunities. Supporting cognitive growth contributes to the emergence of well-rounded personalities.

Mindfulness and Self-Reflection: Teach children mindfulness and self-reflection practices to develop self-awareness and better decision-making. These skills help children align their actions with their values and manage stress effectively.

Conclusion of Nurturing Personality Diversity

Nurturing E-Colours in children is a multifaceted and ongoing journey that requires collaboration between parents, educators, and the wider community. By creating environments that respect and celebrate individual differences, we empower children to develop their unique tendencies and prepare them to contribute to a more inclusive and dynamic world. Through supportive home settings, inclusive education, active community engagement, and thoughtful use of media and technology, we can inspire children to embrace their individuality and thrive in a diverse society.

Andy's Story – Christchurch School, Singapore

Since 2016, the school has used the E-Colours tool, a Personality Diversity Indicator designed to help students learn about their behaviours to improve communication skills, build stronger relationships, and work more effectively with others. This tool provides a framework for students to reflect on their personality tendencies and behaviours.

Common language is an important factor contributing to a coherent CHR family identity. This includes the level themes, the three CHRian attributes, and E-Colours terminology (such as tendencies, press PAUSE, strengths, and potential limiters). Thus, we design our programmes and events with E-Colours as one of the common languages we use in planning.

At CHR, we introduced Sec 1 workshops to familiarise new students with the E-Colours and conducted refresher lessons for Sec 2 to 5 students.

The E-Colours resources are also printed in the school's student handbook and displayed on posters in the canteen for easy access by all students.

E-Colours is also used as a reflection tool to help students evaluate their behaviour. In CHR, case management goes beyond behaviour correction to consider factors such as unmet needs, family support, and home environment. This approach prioritises personal growth.

– *Andy* (Yellow/Blue)
– Christchurch School, Singapore

* * *

WHY ARE E-COLOURS IMPORTANT FOR LEARNING?

The following case studies illustrate how personality diversity, using the E-Colours, can be nurtured, with positive impacts on attendance, academic achievement, communication, and reductions in bullying incidents.

Case Study 1: Embracing Personality Diversity in a Multicultural Classroom

Background: A public elementary school in a diverse urban area implemented a new curriculum focused on cultural inclusivity and personality diversity, using E-Colours as the foundation. The student population included children from a wide range of ethnic backgrounds, with varied personality tendencies, learning styles, and interests. The school administration recognised the importance of creating an inclusive environment that honoured these differences and worked to develop a comprehensive plan.

Approach: The school introduced the E-Colours platform to allow teachers to tailor lessons to the diverse needs of their students. Teachers received professional development on cultural competency, inclusive teaching practices, and recognising and supporting different personality tendencies. The curriculum was revised to include diverse perspectives, with literature, history, and social studies lessons reflecting a wide range of cultural experiences and values.

The school also created flexible learning environments offering both group and individual work options. Students were encouraged to express themselves through mediums such as art, music, and writing. Regular class discussions explored different perspectives and taught conflict resolution and empathy.

Outcome: The new approach resulted in a more inclusive and harmonious classroom environment. Students reported feeling more valued and respected for their unique contributions, and engagement and participation increased. The school also saw improvements in social cohesion, with fewer bullying incidents and a stronger sense of community among students.

Teachers observed that students were more confident in expressing themselves and developed stronger social and emotional skills. The emphasis on diversity and inclusion supported individual growth and enriched the learning experience for all students.

This initiative took place at Southwest, a charter school in Texas, USA.

Case Study 2: E-Colors & Personal Intervention in Further Education

Among the many schools that have integrated the E-Colors into their education systems, Taft Oil Technology Academy stands out as a powerful example of their transformative impact. In 2013, we were invited to run an E-Colors awareness workshop for the students by an alumnus who had gone on to work for an energy company.

Just a week before the scheduled visit, tragedy struck: a student shot another student and a teacher at the school. In the days that followed, we faced the difficult decision of whether to proceed. After careful consideration, it was decided to move forward, and we are deeply thankful that we did.

The workshop became not only a catalyst for change but also a safe space for students, many of whom were still reeling from the trauma, to express their fears and emotions. It was a privilege to collaborate with the students and Mr. Ted Pendergrass

(Red/Green – Coordinator and Technology Teacher), who helped take the E-Colors to new heights of engagement, leaving a lasting impact on both the students at the time and those who have followed after graduation.

Kristine's Story – EMS and a Successful Interview

Over the past seven years, I've had the privilege of observing Emergency Services students as they begin their careers by participating in an E-Colors Self and Team Awareness session early in their journey. Interestingly, the majority of these students, much like those in school settings, tend to have predominantly Blue/Green or Green/Blue E-Colors. Once they receive their wristbands, they quickly grasp the concept of pressing PLAY and speaking up.

Recently, the head of the EMS department shared a story that reinforced the power of understanding E-Colors and applying the associated tools. Three students who had completed the course were interviewed for positions at one of the top hospital systems in Texas. The delighted department head called me to recount the following.

After the interviews, the leader of the hospital group, who had been on the interview panel, contacted the college to explain why all three students were offered positions. They outperformed other candidates, including those from other colleges and even more experienced EMS practitioners. When each student was asked individually about their strengths and weaknesses, they responded: 'We don't have weaknesses; we have potential limiters, and here is how we're managing them.'

The panel was so impressed with their self-awareness, confidence, and proactive approach, combined with their technical skills, that they unanimously decided to hire all three. This story beautifully highlights the transformative impact of understanding E-Colors and leveraging tools like Personal Intervention.

Personally, my journey, which started back in 2018, has been remarkable. I have learned more about myself, how I respond versus react to people, and how I need to hit my PAUSE button when something's happening and think about what I need to say.

– Kristine Kern (Yellow/Red)
– Professor of EMS, Licensed Paramedic and Professor of Emergency Medical Services, USA

A Yellow/Red Story

From an early age, my mum would always tell me to slow down. Take it easy, be careful, stop rushing. In fact, her words were always… 'take it steady.' So how did this play out? As a kid and young adult working in the oil and gas industry (Schlumberger), I would often go in with the 80% solution, typically not fully baked. I was rushing to action.

I had to make an important presentation in front of Anadrill's VP and flew to Paris to deliver it. This presentation, my General Field Engineer capstone project, determined my promotion. Important? Yes. Did *it change my rush to action? No. I went in not fully prepared, with some incomplete work product that, in my mind, was certainly good enough – but clearly, in hindsight, it wasn't.*

The presentation went badly... extremely badly. I still remember the VP's opening comment: 'You started well with the link to Schlumberger values, and it went downhill from there.' I returned to Aberdeen, and before the wheels had even touched the tarmac, the local manager had prepared paperwork moving me from the engineering path to the field specialist path. My future career was no longer seen in 'Management'. I was destined for domestic market work only. 'Go work on the rigs, young man!'

I have a compelling story of how I eventually moved out of the 'idiot box', which relates to being my authentic self and caring for people – something that, it turns out, was a strength. E-Colours helped me learn something that had been there all along. The desire to rush, to move at a faster pace, got me into so many scrapes – some fun, but many avoidable. I wish I'd had the PAUSE & PLAY tools earlier in my life.

Comfortable in my own skin: *This is a bigger reflection around 'what others think of you' and how you act to realise your potential. Through Equilibria and E-Colours, you come to realise we are all different, learn differently, have different tendencies and strengths, and that no single way is best. However, the view from the primary school floor was that certain ways were seen as better, and that you needed to copy them to develop a good grade, be good at maths and science.*

I wish I had learned this lesson earlier. In my early corporate years, I wasn't being my authentic self. I still remember taking the test and looking around a room of Red/Greens, thinking, 'Please, don't let me be Yellow/Red. Yellow/Reds will never amount to anything in this company.' Giving kids tools that help them realise their differences, and how to adapt their approach, would have been invaluable awareness much earlier in life.

Career planning: *With greater awareness into PAUSE & PLAY and being your authentic self, I would never have become an engineer, met you, or ended up in the oil and gas industry. No regrets – it has been great – but for someone who prefers talking and dealing with people, why would I have chosen work that primarily involved interacting with metal and blowout preventers?*

Reflecting on my career choice, I think I could have had an incredible career in human sciences, psychology, or something similar. Can you imagine how many poor career choices people have made, based on what was expected of them or a lack of understanding about what motivated them? I have several dentist, architect, and doctor friends who all hate their jobs, and it all stems from poorly informed career choices made at 16 when they didn't fully understand who they were or what drove them.

I believe the work you're doing in schools is preventing a lifetime of misery for future accountants who really want to be teachers, cowboys, or innovators.

– Yellow/Red

Dave's Story

The diversity of impact has been enormous – from helping people work more safely, to increasing their potential as leaders, to impacting children in schools and eliminating bullying. It's been an amazing journey, and the legacy that Equilibria has already created in the last 20 years will span generations to come.

– *Dave Payne* (Red/Yellow)
– Former Vice President, Health, Safety & Environment, USA

* * *

OPPORTUNITIES FOR CHILDREN

Personality diversity in children is not merely an enriching aspect of individual development; it is a cornerstone for building a more inclusive and dynamic society. Throughout this exploration, we have examined the pivotal role of childhood in shaping diverse personalities, the influence of social and cultural factors, and the many benefits that personality diversity brings to both individuals and communities. We have also addressed the challenges of fostering personality diversity and offered strategies to overcome these challenges across various settings, including the home, school, and wider community.

The case studies and examples presented show that when children are supported in expressing and developing their unique tendencies, they are far more likely to become confident, creative, and socially responsible adults. These real-world accounts highlight the importance of intentional efforts by parents, educators, and community leaders to create environments that respect and celebrate diversity in all its forms.

The implications of this discussion are profound. Moving forward, it is crucial to recognise that nurturing personality diversity is not just about supporting individual children; it is about laying the foundations for a more empathetic, innovative, and resilient society. By investing in the development of diverse personalities from an early age, we equip the next generation with the skills, perspectives, and values necessary to navigate an increasingly complex and interconnected world.

To achieve this, ongoing research, policy development, and practical application are required. Future studies should continue to explore the subtleties of personality development in children, particularly across different cultural and socioeconomic contexts. Policies should aim to support inclusive education, equitable access to resources, and the integration of personality diversity into all aspects of child development. Practitioners – including parents, educators, and community leaders – must stay committed to fostering environments that honour and nurture the unique potential of every child.

In conclusion, children are indeed the future of personality diversity. By nurturing their individuality and embracing the richness that diversity brings, we pave the way for a world where differences are not merely tolerated but celebrated. This vision of a diverse and inclusive future begins with the deliberate and thoughtful cultivation of personality diversity in the children of today. As we invest in their growth, we are investing in a brighter, more harmonious future for everyone.

* * *

Remix Opportunities

E-Colours offers an incredible opportunity for students as young as seven years old to develop a 'coping tool' that supports them throughout their lives. Reflect on how you can use your sphere of influence to ensure students do not miss out on this transformative and impactful process.

- Introduce the E-Colours to your children and observe the results for yourself.
- Contact us to discuss embedding the E-Colours into your school.
- Create E-Colours champions from as early as ages seven to nine.

CHAPTER 14

REAL TIME LEGACY

'You live, you learn, you love and you leave a legacy – that's life!'

— **Stephen Covey**, author of *7 Habits of Highly Effective People*

Legacy isn't something you leave behind. It's something you live, moment by moment, with every word, every action, every pause.

Too often, we think of legacy as something reserved for the end of a journey, a final chapter, a retrospective moment, a plaque on the wall. But what if legacy isn't what we leave after we're gone… but what we're writing in real time, every single day?

This chapter is about owning that truth.

Whether you're a leader guiding a team, a teacher shaping young minds, a parent nurturing the next generation, or a teammate showing up with integrity, your legacy is already unfolding. The question is: are you crafting it with intention?

Real Time Legacy is not about ego or recognition. It's about impact. It's the ripple you create when you choose to respond instead of react. When you empower someone else to lead. When you invest in developing others, knowing that true influence continues long after the spotlight moves on.

From Dave Payne's reflection on what really matters, to John's simple yet profound desire to leave people with a great experience, to Scott's heartfelt story of transformation – this chapter reminds us that legacy is less about status, and more about service.

Because the truth is: people may forget your title, your targets, even your milestones. But they will never forget how you made them feel, how you helped them grow, and whether your presence brought out the best in them.

So today, right now, in this moment: what are you leaving behind?

Let's explore how to define it, live it, pass it on… and remix legacy into something that starts with your next choice.

Real Time Legacy Process: Steps and Benefits

One of the first questions Jane, the Vice President of a large organisation we work with, asks her newly promoted country managers always stimulates an interesting response. When moving someone into a new area, knowing that their tenure will be three to four years, the challenge comes in the form of: 'What's your legacy going to be when you leave here?' In this context, she paints a picture that she expects her managers to be intentional and conscious of both their actions and inactions while in the role.

When you hear the word 'legacy', what comes to mind?

Our interpretation is that every day we face the decision to react or respond to the various events that occur in our lives. Typically, when we choose to react or respond, we leave someone with an experience. It can be said that the sum of those experiences over time will shape somebody's legacy.

It could be said that the legacy we leave is not entirely within our control – it's the sum of how others perceive us. The only way to gain some control over our legacy is to consciously manage what we do and who we are.

There's an aspect of legacy that's always worth considering, and for whatever reason, we encounter examples of it daily as life unfolds.

The inconvenient truth about legacy is that negative perceptions tend to have a greater impact and travel further and faster than positive ones. Under normal circumstances, positive legacy items may accumulate gradually, but a single negative item can disrupt the flow of those positive perceptions.

A series of negative legacy items can block the accumulation of positive perceptions, and a single significant one can have the same effect.

As natural attrition dissolves previously earned goodwill, a single negative legacy item can prevent the flow of new goodwill – and *that* becomes the legacy we leave behind.

This is why being *intentional* as leaders, parents, friends, and colleagues becomes so crucial.

What are you consciously going to do to leave your legacy?

The perspectives from people of different E-Colours vary when it comes to the subject of real time legacy – important to some, and less so to others.

People with **Green** tendencies told us that, as predominantly independent thinkers, they hadn't really considered that their day-to-day actions and inactions could leave such an impression on others. The common theme was that legacy was something to think about later in life and wasn't high on their agenda.

A frequent comment was, 'I'm just a…' followed by a title or role – many hadn't realised that as leaders, supervisors, or parents, legacy is something that happens continuously.

Those with predominant **Red** tendencies told us that legacy wasn't something they often thought about. From their more task-oriented perspective, the mindset was: 'I'll do what I can while I'm here – and that's it.' Interestingly, the second E-Colour seemed to strongly influence this subject. Those with Red/Green combinations were typically less introspective about the people they had or could influence and more focused on what they had done. In contrast, Red/Yellow and Red/Blue, who are more people focused, had a greater desire to develop others and create a grander future.

People with predominant **Yellow** tendencies told us that legacy was important to them. As socialisers, they felt their desire to help and please others heightened their awareness around intentionally leaving 'something' behind. This group frequently shared personal anecdotes, easily recalling the names of those who had left a positive experience on them at some point in their lives. This translates to 'legacy' for them.

Those with strong **Blue** tendencies told us that legacy is generally part of their thinking. As relaters and supporters, they tend to focus on how others will be affected by their relationships. The way others feel is deeply important to them, and that awareness becomes embedded in their sense of legacy. They often describe themselves as realists, and part of their legacy is to bring order and pragmatism to any situation.

The questions are: How do you want to be viewed, and what kind of legacy do you want to leave?

Steps of the Real Time Legacy Process

1. **Define Your Legacy.**

   - Action: Reflect on the values, beliefs, and impacts you want to be known for. This includes identifying the core principles and contributions that will define your legacy.
   - Purpose: Clarity around your desired legacy helps ensure that your daily behaviour aligns with your long-term vision.

2. **Act Intentionally – Live the Legacy.**

   - Action: Commit to behaviours that reinforce your chosen legacy. Each response and interaction should reflect the values and principles you want to leave behind.
   - Purpose: Consistently embodying your legacy in real time builds trust and strengthens your integrity with those around you.

3. **Shape Future Stewards of Your Legacy.**

    - Action: Identify people who can help carry forward your legacy – whether as mentees, collaborators, or successors.
    - Purpose: This step ensures your legacy is sustainable by creating a support network to uphold and promote your values.

4. **Empower Others – Pass the Baton.**

    - Action: Formally empower others to continue your work and uphold your values. This may involve mentoring, training, or delegating key responsibilities.
    - Purpose: Empowering others ensures the continuity of your legacy beyond your own influence, embedding it within your organisation or community.

5. **Reflect and Adjust Regularly.**

    - Action: Regularly assess whether your actions align with the legacy you want to leave. Reflect on experiences that may have impacted your legacy – positively or negatively – and make adjustments as needed.
    - Purpose: This reflective practice helps reinforce positive legacy elements while minimising the influence of any negative perceptions.

Benefits of the Real Time Legacy Process

- **Enhanced Leadership Integrity**

    Living a Real Time Legacy means aligning intentional actions with your values. This integrity builds trust and respect, positioning you as a leader whose actions match their words.

- **Long-Term Positive Impact**

  Positive actions accumulated over time create a resilient and enduring legacy. The Real Time Legacy process helps ensure your contributions are meaningful and lasting, even as individual negative events may occasionally arise.

- **Sustainable Influence through Empowerment**

  By identifying and empowering others to carry on your legacy, you create a ripple effect that ensures your values and impact extend beyond your personal tenure or role.

- **Focused and Purposeful Leadership**

  Having clarity on your legacy fosters a stronger sense of purpose and direction. This clarity improves decision-making, ensuring actions are aligned with long-term impact rather than short-term reactions.

- **Resilience Against Negative Perceptions**

  The Real Time Legacy process acknowledges the outsized impact of negative perceptions. By cultivating a steady stream of positive experiences and reinforcing your legacy through reflection and intentional adjustments, you reduce the risk of long-lasting negative effects.

The Real Time Legacy process encourages leaders to focus not only on the immediate outcomes of their actions but also on the broader influence they hope to have. This approach empowers leaders to be more intentional, reflective, and proactive, creating a legacy that reflects their values and uplifts future generations.

David's Story – Accomplishment vs Legacy

Anyone who has been around me the past 20 years knows that one of my favourite topics is legacy, or the long-lasting impact you have on others. It's little wonder that one of my favourite books is Legacy: What the All Blacks Can Teach Us About the Business of Life, *by James Kerr.*

In a recent conversation with a longtime friend and mentor, we compared the difference between an accomplished career versus leaving a legacy. I feel we learned something worth sharing for your consideration.

For context, I'll reference my career. I had the privilege of leading one of the highest-performing drilling and completions organisations in the oil and gas industry and served the last 15 years of my career in executive positions with an energy company. By most standards, it could be said that I had an accomplished career. But did these accomplishments ensure the legacy or long-term impact I wanted to leave behind?

My legacy goal was to guide the organisations that I led to a position where they could be more successful ten years after I was gone. Only a year into my retirement, it's much too soon to determine the outcome of this goal, but I believe I made the long-view decisions that were necessary, albeit sometimes at odds with the perceived requirements of maintaining an executive position. An example of one of these actions was the continued investment in leadership development during periods of extreme budget pressure.

Lee Iacocca is my favourite example of someone who was highly accomplished but left behind a flawed legacy. Mr. Iacocca had a highly successful career with Ford Motor Company where he was involved in the development of many iconic products, including the Mustang, Lincoln Mark III, and Pinto. His impact on Ford was considerable. He left Ford to become CEO of Chrysler which was on the brink of going out of business. He famously revived the company, increasing the stock price from $2 per share in 1979 to $48 per share when he retired in 1992. Chrysler introduced the first minivan in 1983, and it led the industry in sales for 25 years. Clearly, Mr Iacocca compiled a career filled with accomplishments. But what about his legacy?

The years following his retirement in 1992 were tumultuous for the company, including an attempted takeover by a corporate raider, multiple partnerships with competing automakers, and bankruptcy in 2009. The ownership of the company went to a partnership that included the United Auto Workers, Fiat, and the US and Canadian governments. In short, Mr Iacocca's storied career is one of tremendous accomplishment, but his legacy is highly questionable. Did he fail to set up Chrysler for success following his retirement?

Career accomplishments are not necessarily equivalent to the impact of one's legacy. Consider the example of a gentleman named Mac Laurie. Mr Laurie's highest position with Unocal was drilling superintendent. Following a well control event on one of Unocal's offshore operations in the 1980s, he developed Unocal's philosophy of well control along with the company's first well control training. Today, the basis of the Company's well control training is directly connected to the approach Mac Laurie developed. Thousands of individuals across the industry have been trained in principles he developed, and quite likely, a significant number of high-consequence events were prevented because of his work. What an impact! That is a legacy. And yet, hardly anyone reading this – or even those who have benefited from the training based on his principles – has ever heard his name.

I'm sure you can think of many other examples of people like Lee Iacocca with careers filled with renowned achievement. Perhaps you have also seen the impact on an industry and the lives of others by someone like Mac Laurie. Great achievement and enduring legacy are not mutually exclusive. However, legacy is borne out of intentional decision-making fuelled by a desire to have a long-term impact that benefits others.

When I had a leader assuming a new role, I would often ask them to consider their exit strategy. By considering the legacy you want to leave at the beginning of an assignment, you will significantly change what you do day to day. It is very easy to get caught up in day-to-day challenges and meeting short-term business goals. By intentionally identifying your legacy and being vocal with your team, you will change how you work and have a much bigger impact.

I encourage you to spend some time contemplating the legacy you desire to achieve with your lifework, and then be intentional in taking the steps necessary to make it happen.

– *Dave Payne* (Red/Yellow)
– Former Vice President, Health, Safety & Environment, USA

Further reflection from Dave on legacy, sent to Lewis Senior a few months after he sent his original thoughts.

I have to say my view of legacy has changed since I retired. I always said I wanted my legacy to be for the D&C organisation to be better ten years after I left than I left it. I've learned a bit about the resilience of organisations. While I'd suggest the Wells organisation is better today, there are areas of real retreat that were important to me. And the changes announced this week will significantly impact that organisation in a negative way. Those changes are beyond anyone's control who leads in Wells.

What I've learned is that the impact we have on people is a much more important legacy than what we do with organisations. Resilient individuals with great leadership skills can survive and thrive regardless of what happens around them. Setting people up to be successful in multiple environments and conditions is more important than trying to steer an organisation after you leave. I think we – and I do mean we – were able to do that. You continue to build your legacy while I am kicking back and enjoying watching the fruits of mine.

– *Dave Payne* (Red/Yellow)
– Former Vice President, Health, Safety & Environment, USA

John's Story

The E-Colors really helped me become a lot more intentional in my actions, my thoughts, and my words, becoming sufficiently self-aware that I can exercise personal intervention, and I just interact better with people and teams. Why wouldn't you intentionally set out to give that person, that team, that group, just an incredible experience?

– *John Johnson* (Yellow/Red)
– CTC Wells Advisor, USA

Scott's Story

It is not an exaggeration to say that E-Colours has completely changed my life for the better.

Being in the Police, we come across high-pressure situations daily. Using the E-Colours tools has allowed me to take a step back, assess the situation, and make calm and rational decisions.

The PAUSE & PLAY tool and concept is the real game-changer for me. Prior to E-Colours, I may have become annoyed very quickly and made a rash – or even stupid – decision, said the wrong thing, and regretted it. The PAUSE & PLAY tool teaches us to RESPOND and not REACT, which makes a huge difference in anyone's results.

Looking at my social media posts from ten years ago, I can only say – I wish I knew about E-Colours back then!

I can only thank Paul, Lewis, David, Laura, Mark, and Emma for teaching us and giving me the opportunity to get involved. The E-Colours community is growing, and I've been introduced to some fantastic people from all over the world just by being part of it.

I feel I can help people with the knowledge I've gained over these last few months. I feel I'm more approachable and can offer advice to those who need it. I'm better at understanding their personality by using the tools. Knowing what phrases and words to use to get the best out of people is a massive win, not only in a work environment but also at home – and it really does work.

It has been a life-changer for me, and I'll be forever grateful to those who introduced E-Colours into my life.

– Scott Mackay (Blue/Yellow)
– Scottish Police Sergeant, UK

Real Time Legacy Checklist – LIFE

L – Legacy: Know the legacy you want to leave.

I – Intention: Live the legacy you want to leave.

F – Future: Choose who will carry on your legacy.

E – Empower: Pass on the baton.

* * *

Remix Opportunities

What's important to you that you want to leave behind?
Describe the legacy you want to leave.

How do you act out or demonstrate the legacy you want to leave?
Describe your behaviours that model the legacy you intend to leave.

Why do you want to leave the legacy you have chosen?
Think about and describe the main reasons why you want to leave your chosen legacy.

Who do you want to involve to carry on your legacy?
Describe who will be involved in carrying out your legacy.

When will you pass on the baton?
Set your goal.

* * *

Authors' Legacies

Paul Grant, Lewis Senior, and Mark Wilkinson, the authors of *Personalities Remixed*, share their thoughts on legacy and the future they see for personality diversity.

Paul Grant's Legacy

Paul Grant's legacy continues to evolve with *Personalities Remixed*, a bold new book that reshapes the way we understand human behaviour. This work strengthens the global reach of E-Colours & Personal Intervention – proven tools that have already empowered thousands to live and lead with greater awareness. Looking ahead, the potential is even greater: integrating E-Colours into education, leadership, families, and every setting where self-awareness and communication matter. We envision a world where individuals recognise their strengths and potential limiters – and consciously choose their responses rather than simply react. This mission goes beyond legacy; it's a lifelong commitment to helping people live intentionally.

Lewis Senior's Legacy

Personalities Remixed is more than a collection of stories; it's a culmination of decades spent walking alongside extraordinary people from every corner of life. Each page carries the voices, lessons, and experiences of those who trusted me with their truths and allowed me to be part of their journeys. For that, I am profoundly grateful.

As the runway shortens, the moments I cherish most are those spent connecting with others - listening, learning, and witnessing the transformative power of self-awareness and intentional leadership. This book is my way of passing forward what I've been so fortunate to receive: the gift of perspective, the courage to pause and play, and the enduring belief that understanding each other can change everything.

While my voice may fade, the impact of this work will echo through the hearts and minds of those who choose to lean in, to lead with purpose, and to honor the humanity in themselves and others. If even one person takes these words to heart and moves through life with greater empathy and intention, then my story - and the stories shared within these pages - will continue to live on.

Mark Wilkinson's Legacy

There was a time in my life when I hit rock bottom – bankrupt, broken, and completely lost, which I've written about in my debut book *Life Remixed*. I didn't know how to move forward, let alone rebuild. That's when I was introduced to the E-Colours & Personal Intervention tool – including the PAUSE & PLAY techniques – and everything started to change.

By understanding my own personality and learning to manage my strengths and potential limiters, I began to rebuild not just my career, but my relationships and self-worth. The E-Colours & Personal Intervention tool helped me reconnect with my mother and brother in ways I never thought possible, healing old wounds and opening deeper communication. They also play a huge role in my relationship with Emma, my wife. Her calm empathy and attention to detail – a beautiful blend of Green (Thinker) and Blue (Relator) E-Colours – are the perfect complement to my Yellow (Socialiser) energy, and together we've created a life filled with love, respect, and balance.

I went from feeling hopeless to achieving a six-figure salary in three years and, more importantly, loving my life. But more than the success, it's the joy I get from coaching others – from seeing the light go on in someone's eyes when they finally understand themselves and others in a deeper way – all of which fuels my purpose. Watching people transform their lives and then go on to become E-Colours Practitioners themselves is one of the greatest rewards I've ever known.

My purpose for writing *Personalities Remixed* – alongside Lewis Senior and Paul Grant – is to empower individuals around the world to understand themselves and others more deeply, to create stronger relationships, and to lead with awareness, empathy, and intention.

This book shares a practical, accessible framework – based on the E-Colours & Personal Intervention tool – including the PAUSE & PLAY techniques – that enables anyone, anywhere, to improve communication, reduce conflict, and realise their full potential. We're not just telling our stories – we're handing you the tools to remix your own life.

And together, we're building a global movement of E-Colours Practitioners – coaches, leaders, and change-makers – who are transforming lives, businesses, and communities for generations to come.

This is my legacy. And it can be yours too.

CHAPTER 15

DEVELOPING YOURSELF

'Repetition is the mother of learning,
the father of action, which makes it the architect of accomplishment.'

– Zig Ziglar (1926–2012), author

You don't become your best self by accident. You become it by design, and it starts with a choice.

By now, you've journeyed through the power of personality diversity, explored the impact of self-awareness, and discovered how the E-Colours & Personal Intervention can transform not only your relationships but also your results. But awareness alone is not the destination – it's the beginning.

Developing yourself is about choosing to show up every day – not just informed, but intentional. It's about deciding that growth isn't something that happens to you. It's something you create. Every conversation, every challenge, every quiet moment is an opportunity to press PAUSE, hit PLAY, and move forward with purpose.

And here's the beauty of it: you don't have to wait for a title, a promotion, or a life event to begin. You can start right here, right now, with what you've learned.

You can lead better meetings. You can parent with more presence. You can connect with more empathy. You can become the kind of person who inspires others to grow simply by continuing to grow yourself.

This chapter reminds us that the true reward of personality diversity isn't just understanding ourselves. It's becoming better versions of ourselves, one intentional moment at a time.

So, as we round out this book, let this chapter be a new beginning. Your E-Colours aren't the final answer. They're your foundation.

And you? You're the architect of what comes next.

We hope you have enjoyed reading *Personalities Remixed* and have discovered how the E-Colours & Personal Intervention system can be applied across all stages of life, from school to the boardroom.

As **Zig Ziglar** said, 'repetition is the mother of learning,' so let's take some time to refresh your knowledge of the E-Colours. Answers to the questions are at the end of the chapter.

Question 1: Which two E-Colours tend to be people-oriented?

Red   Yellow   Green   Blue

Question 2: Which two E-Colours tend to be task-oriented?

Red   Yellow   Green   Blue

Question 3: Which two E-Colours tend to be independent?

Red   Yellow   Green   Blue

Question 4: Which two E-Colours tend to be interdependent?

Red   Yellow   Green   Blue

Question 5: Which two E-Colours tend to be information-oriented?

Red   Yellow   Green   Blue

Question 6: Which two E-Colours tend to be big picture-oriented?

Red   Yellow   Green   Blue

Question 7: Which two E-Colours tend to be faster-paced?

Red   Yellow   Green   Blue

Question 8: Which two E-Colours tend to be steady-paced?

Red   Yellow   Green   Blue

Question 9: The SOCIALISER is associated with which E-Colour? (One answer)

Red   Yellow   Green   Blue

Question 10: The RELATOR is associated with which E-Colour? (One answer)

Red   Yellow   Green   Blue

Question 11: The THINKER is associated with which E-Colour? (One answer)

Red   Yellow   Green   Blue

Question 12: The DOER is associated with which E-Colour? (One answer)

Red   Yellow   Green   Blue

Question 13: What is the strength of a Green? (One answer)

Accurate   Agreeable   Enthusiastic   Decisive

Question 14: What is the strength of a Blue? (One answer)

Accurate   Agreeable   Enthusiastic   Decisive

Question 15: What is the strength of a Yellow? (One answer)

Accurate   Agreeable   Enthusiastic   Decisive

Question 16: What is the strength of a Red? (One answer)

Accurate   Agreeable   Enthusiastic   Decisive

Question 17: What is the potential limiter of a Green? (One answer)

Excitable   Unsure   Critical   Insensitive

Question 18: What is the potential limiter of a Blue? (One answer)

Excitable   Unsure   Critical   Insensitive

Question 19: What is the potential limiter of a Yellow? (One answer)

Excitable   Unsure   Critical   Insensitive

Question 20: What is the potential limiter of a Red? (One answer)

Excitable   Unsure   Critical   Insensitive

Question 21: What is the strength of a Green? (One answer)

Analytical   Calm   Animated   Practical

Question 22: What is the strength of a Blue? (One answer)

Analytical   Calm   Animated   Practical

Question 23: What is the strength of a Yellow? (One answer)

Analytical   Calm   Animated   Practical

Question 24: What is the strength of a Red? (One answer)

Analytical   Calm   Animated   Practical

Question 25: What is the potential limiter of a Green? (One answer)

Emotional   Too serious   Domineering   Slow to decide

Question 26: What is the potential limiter of a Blue? (One answer)

Emotional   Too serious   Domineering   Slow to decide

Question 27: What is the potential limiter of a Yellow? (One answer)

Emotional   Too serious   Domineering   Slow to decide

Question 28: What is the potential limiter of a Red? (One answer)

Emotional   Too serious   Domineering   Slow to decide

Question 29: Which E-Colour is associated with the communication style of 'Likes to explain'?

Red   Yellow   Green   Blue

Question 30: Which E-Colour is associated with the communication style of 'Likes to engage with people'?

Red   Yellow   Green   Blue

Question 31: Which E-Colour is associated with the communication style of 'Likes to tell'?

Red   Yellow   Green   Blue

Question 32: Which E-Colour is associated with the communication style of 'Likes to relate'?

Red   Yellow   Green   Blue

Question 33: Personal Intervention uses two 'triggers' as buttons. What are they? (Two answers)

PAUSE   FORWARD   PLAY   REWIND

Question 34: Personal Intervention allows us to manage which two? (Two answers)

Reflection   Reaction   Response   Release

Question 35: Which E-Colour is associated with the tendency 'Likes harmony at both home and work'?

Red   Yellow   Green   Blue

Question 36: Which E-Colour is associated with the tendency 'Likes results and being goal-oriented'?

Red   Yellow   Green   Blue

Question 37: Which E-Colour is associated with the tendency 'Good at engaging with and influencing people'?

Red   Yellow   Green   Blue

Question 38: Which E-Colour is associated with the tendency 'Likes to be given time to think and plan'?

Red   Yellow   Green   Blue

* * *

> *Just want to say what an honour and a privilege it's been to be able to work with the Equilibria team. It has made me a better person, a better father, a better friend, just holistically a better person all the way around from learning these skills and techniques that I've been afforded.*
>
> — *Fred Brown* (Yellow/Green)
> — Emergency Management Specialist, USA

> *Personally, my journey, which started back in 2018, has just been absolutely remarkable. I have learned more about myself, how I respond versus react to people, and how I need to hit my pause when something's happening and to think about what I need to say.*
>
> — *Kristine Kern* (Yellow/Red)
> — Professor of EMS, USA

* * *

Answers to the Questions

Question 1: Which two E-Colours tend to be people-oriented?

Red   **Yellow**   Green   **Blue**

Question 2: Which two E-Colours tend to be task-oriented?

Red   Yellow   **Green**   Blue

Question 3: Which two E-Colours tend to be independent?

Red   Yellow   **Green**   Blue

Question 4: Which two E-Colours tend to be interdependent?

Red   **Yellow**   Green   **Blue**

Question 5: Which two E-Colours tend to be information-oriented?

Red   Yellow   **Green**   **Blue**

Question 6: Which two E-Colours tend to be big picture-oriented?

Red   **Yellow**   Green   Blue

Question 7: Which two E-Colours tend to be faster-paced?

Red   **Yellow**   Green   Blue

Question 8: Which two E-Colours tend to be steady-paced?

Red   Yellow   **Green**   **Blue**

Question 9: The SOCIALISER is associated with which E-Colour? (One answer)

Red **Yellow** Green Blue

Question 10: The RELATOR is associated with which E-Colour? (One answer)

Red Yellow Green **Blue**

Question 11: The THINKER is associated with which E-Colour? (One answer)

Red Yellow **Green** Blue

Question 12: The DOER is associated with which E-Colour? (One answer)

Red Yellow Green Blue

Question 13: What is the strength of a Green? (One answer)

Accurate Agreeable Enthusiastic Decisive

Question 14: What is the strength of a Blue? (One answer)

Accurate **Agreeable** Enthusiastic Decisive

Question 15: What is the strength of a Yellow? (One answer)

Accurate Agreeable **Enthusiastic** Decisive

Question 16: What is the strength of a Red? (One answer)

Accurate Agreeable Enthusiastic **Decisive**

Question 17: What is the potential limiter of a Green? (One answer)

Excitable   Unsure   **Critical**   Insensitive

Question 18: What is the potential limiter of a Blue? (One answer)

Excitable   **Unsure**   Critical   Insensitive

Question 19: What is the potential limiter of a Yellow? (One answer)

Excitable   Unsure   Critical   Insensitive

Question 20: What is the potential limiter of a Red? (One answer)

Excitable   Unsure   Critical   **Insensitive**

Question 21: What is the strength of a Green? (One answer)

Analytical   Calm   Animated   Practical

Question 22: What is the strength of a Blue? (One answer)

Analytical   **Calm**   Animated   Practical

Question 23: What is the strength of a Yellow? (One answer)

Analytical   Calm   **Animated**   Practical

Question 24: What is the strength of a Red? (One answer)

Analytical   Calm   Animated   **Practical**

Question 25: What is the potential limiter of a Green? (One answer)

Emotional   **Too serious**   Domineering   Slow to decide

Question 26: What is the potential limiter of a Blue? (One answer)

Emotional   Too serious   Domineering   **Slow to decide**

Question 27: What is the potential limiter of a Yellow? (One answer)

Emotional   Too serious   Domineering   Slow to decide

Question 28: What is the potential limiter of a Red? (One answer)

Emotional   Too serious   **Domineering**   Slow to decide

Question 29: Which E-Colour is associated with the communication style of 'Likes to explain'?

Red   Yellow   **Green**   Blue

Question 30: Which E-Colour is associated with the communication style of 'Likes to engage with people'?

Red   **Yellow**   Green   Blue

Question 31: Which E-Colour is associated with the communication style of 'Likes to tell'?

Red   Yellow   Green   Blue

Question 32: Which E-Colour is associated with the communication style of 'Likes to relate'?

Red   Yellow   Green   **Blue**

Question 33: Personal Intervention uses two 'triggers' as buttons. What are they? (Two answers)

PAUSE   FORWARD   **PLAY**   REWIND

Question 34: Personal Intervention allows us to manage which two? (Two answers)

Reflection   **Reaction**   **Response**   Release

Question 35: Which E-Colour is associated with the tendency 'Likes harmony at both home and work'?

Red   Yellow   Green   **Blue**

Question 36: Which E-Colour is associated with the tendency 'Likes results and being goal-oriented'?

Red   Yellow   Green   Blue

Question 37: Which E-Colour is associated with the tendency 'Good at engaging with and influencing people'?

Red   **Yellow**   Green   Blue

Question 38: Which E-Colour is associated with the tendency 'Likes to be given time to think and plan'?

Red   Yellow   **Green**   Blue

ABOUT THE AUTHORS
PAUL GRANT

Paul Grant is a seasoned entrepreneur, having established many successful ventures in the past 20 years, building his net worth to place him within the top 0.15% of the UK's wealthiest individuals. A graduate with First Class Honours in Civil Engineering from Heriot-Watt University in Edinburgh, Paul began his career in the Oil & Gas industry, where he held key positions including Drilling Engineer, Operations Engineer, Rig Manager, Country Manager, Division Manager, Director of Compensation, Human Resources Manager, Vice President of Human Resources, and Director of Marketing. His work has taken him across the globe, from the UK and West Africa to Asia, the Middle East, North and South America.

After transitioning from corporate roles, Paul founded his own companies with various partners, earning a reputation for building wealth, transforming workplace cultures, and driving productivity. He is also a certified E-Colours coach and has contributed to numerous materials on communication, leadership, teamwork, and safety management. Passionate about helping young professionals achieve financial success, Paul dedicates his time to mentoring people on wealth-building strategies.

When he's not working, Paul enjoys spending time with his family in Thailand. *Money Remixed* was his debut book, followed by *Personalities Remixed* and *Business Remixed* on the horizon.

MARK WILKINSON

Mark Wilkinson is a multiple business owner, coach, speaker, and published author. Originally, music was Mark's life as an international house music DJ and record producer. He was resident DJ at the famed Ministry of Sound in London, played music in 65 different countries, and achieved a UK Top 10 hit!

At 33 years of age, Mark collapsed with an incurable disease. It was the start of a hellish experience as his body froze up over the next 18 months resulting in him being unable to walk. He was in constant agony and lived on painkillers. His loss of health and financial setbacks eventually led to bankruptcy, depression, loneliness, and suicidal thoughts.

On a detox in Scotland, Mark was given a DVD of *The Secret*. In it, he learned from Bob Proctor that disease is two words: dis-ease. This brand-new information completely opened Mark's mind to new ways of thinking, feeling, and being. He began to study philosophy and personal development to detoxify and cure his body, eventually completing four marathons.

After hitting rock bottom, Mark took positive action, overcame his health issues, and re-educated himself in a new career in construction Health and Safety. He worked at the London Olympic Stadium for the 2012 Games and then at London Heathrow Airport as HSE Manager overseeing their entire commercial construction portfolio. He next became Head of HSE at a division of a residential home developer having overall HSE responsibility on a 90-acre, £1 billion project.

In 2018, Mark set up his own Health and Safety consultancy, which meant he could also focus on his various property businesses and develop as a coach and speaker.

Mark Wilkinson's debut book *Life Remixed* launched in February 2021. The book tells the story of his roller coaster life as a DJ, how he lost everything, and how he remixed his life.

Mark is now a Fellow of the Institute of Leadership & Management (FInstLM) and a Chartered Member of the institute of Safety and Health (CMIOSH). He holds an NVQ7 Master's in Strategic Management and Leadership (MPhil) and plans to study next for a PhD in Directional Leadership. He is also an E-Colours practitioner and coach

For more information about Mark, please visit:
www.markwilkinsonofficial.com www.liferemixed.co.uk

LEWIS SENIOR

Lewis Senior, a distinguished personality diversity expert and a relentless advocate of Risk Management and Intentional Leadership, stands as an exemplary figure in the realm of transformative coaching and leadership. In 2004, he co-founded Equilibria, an internationally acclaimed coaching organisation that blazed a trail in the worldwide energy business, pioneering revolutionary methodologies, including the E-Colours, Personal Intervention, and the 8 Essentials of High-Performance Teams, all encapsulated within the framework of the Essential Leadership Cycle.

These groundbreaking coaching tools have permeated the global landscape, resonating with individuals, teams, and corporations alike. Their impact is profound: heightened self-awareness, deliberate decision-making, enhanced communication, error reduction, and elevated human performance.

Lewis takes immense pride in Equilibria's monumental achievement, having empowered over 1.4 million PDI questionnaires for individuals to discover their E-Colours. This revelation serves as a compass, guiding individuals towards a deeper understanding of themselves and others. It fuels the harnessing of strengths, the management of potential limiters, the appreciation of diverse perspectives, and ultimately, the elevation of personal, professional, and organisational performance.

As a highly sought-after senior executive performance coach, Lewis possesses an unwavering passion for people. His vision, mirrored by Equilibria, can be distilled into a single, powerful phrase: "Realising Potential". His unwavering commitment is to help every individual understand themselves and those around them more comprehensively, championing the principles of conscious intent in both life and leadership.

Lewis's offshore career began in 1974 in the North Sea. He was there during the Piper Alpha incident which had a significant impact on his journey. He remained offshore until 1996, experiencing a remarkable career progression from roustabout to OIM, leading rigs around the world. In 1996, he assumed the role of HSE Manager for Transocean, solidifying his commitment to the well-being of others.

You can hear many of these experiences on Lewis's THE INTENTIONAL CEO mini-series podcasts: https://linktr.ee/lewisseniortheintentionalceo

As a bonus, he is not just a distinguished expert and advocate but also a passionate and entertaining speaker. His ability to captivate audiences with his enthusiasm and engaging delivery adds an extra layer of impact to his already powerful message.

ALSO BY THE AUTHORS

COMING SOON

Business Remixed - Winter 2025
Love Remixed - Spring 2026

EQUILIBRIA RESOURCES

DISCOVER YOUR E-COLOURS
There are 3 levels of the report – Free, Basic or Premium. For Adults & Teenagers, or 12 years and below.

www.equilibria.com/PDI-home

LEARN MORE ABOUT THE E-COLOURS
Find out about the the history of E-Colours and the coaching services we provide.

www.equilibria.com

VISIT OUR EQUILIBRIA SHOP
Equilibria's online shop offers E-Colours & Personal Intervention books, E-Colours Alignment Reports, coaching tools, and many more resources.

www.shop.equilibria.com

INTERESTED IN INDIVIDUAL OR TEAM COACHING?
Whether you need 1:1 support, leadership coaching, or full organisational training, our team is here to help - get in touch today.

Email: info@equilibria.com

BECOME A CERTIFIED E-COLOURS PRACTITIONER

Be a part of a growing global community of certified practitioners who are transforming lives through the power of personality diversity. Whether you're a coach, facilitator, consultant, educator, business leader, HR or HSE professional, team builder, counsellor, or mentor, becoming an E-Colours Practitioner will elevate your impact and effectiveness.

6 reasons to join our practitioner program today:

1. Enhance your skillset
2. Expand your service offering
3. Stand out with a unique certification
4. Help others reach their full potential
5. Make a lasting impact
6. Join a global community of practitioners

STEP 1 – CERTIFICATION
Get guided by an Equilibria coach through a customisded certification process.

STEP 2 – VALIDATION
Show your skills by leading a workshop or 1:1 coaching session.

STEP 3 – COLLABORATION
Join the E-Colours Practitioner community with ongoing support from us.

For more information visit: www.shop.equilibria.com

BOOK LEWIS SENIOR OR MARK WILKINSON TO SPEAK AT YOUR NEXT EVENT

Lewis Senior and Mark Wilkinson bring decades of global experience in leadership, coaching, and human performance to every stage. Available to book as keynote speakers either in person or virtually, they deliver powerful insights and practical tools tailored to your audience.

For maximum impact, consider adding an E-Colours awareness session before or after the keynote.

Topics include:

- Intentional Leadership for Safety Culture Transformation
- Lessons from 50 Years in the Energy Industry: Enhancing Human Performance and Safety
- Behavioural and Psychological Safety: Preventing Physical and Emotional Harm
- Unlocking Team Potential through Personality Diversity
- Reducing Errors through a New Paradigm: The AERO Approach
- Practical Tools for Creating a Culture of Operational Excellence
- From ill health and bankruptcy to becoming successful and financially free: How you too can remix your life!

To book contact:
lewis.senior@equilibria.com or
mark@markwilkinsonofficial.com

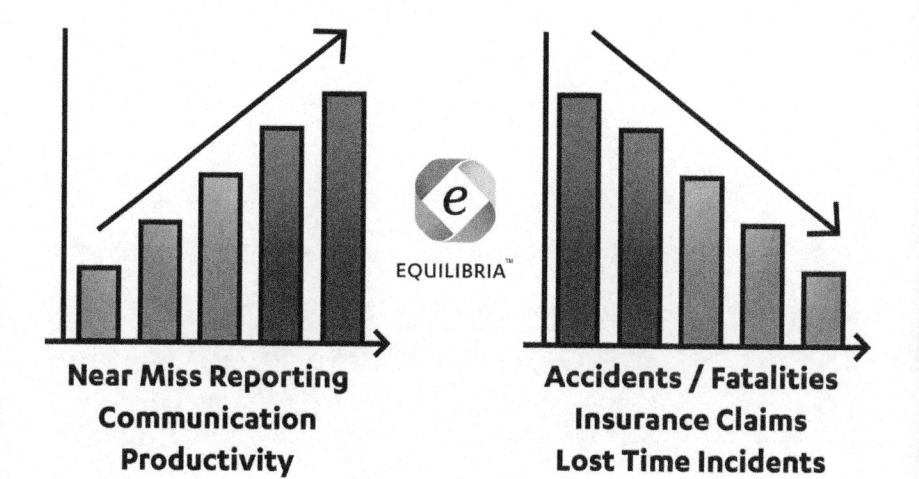

Near Miss Reporting
Communication
Productivity

EQUILIBRIA™

Accidents / Fatalities
Insurance Claims
Lost Time Incidents